God Within

God Within

The Mystical Tradition of Northern Europe

OLIVER DAVIES

Foreword by Rowan Williams

Paulist Press
New York and New Jersey

First published in 1988 in Great Britain by Darton, Longman & Todd Ltd, London. Published in 1988 in the United States of America by Paulist Press, 997 Macarthur Boulevard, Mahwah, New Jersey 07430.

Library of Congress Cataloging-in-Publication Data

Davies, Oliver.
    God within.

        Bibliography: p.
        Includes index.
        1. Mysticism—Europe, Northern—History.
    2. Mysticism—History—Middle Ages, 600–1500.
    I. Title.
    BV5077.E853D37   1988   248.2′2′094   88-31401
    ISBN 0-8091-3041-6 (pbk.)

Printed and bound in the United States of America

To the memory of Cheslyn
as a token of my warm affection and respect

Contents

Foreword

Interest in the history of Christian spirituality continues to grow, to an extent it would have been difficult to imagine even ten or fifteen years ago. Translations of patristic and medieval texts have proliferated, to everyone's great advantage, and an increasing number of surveys of the field as a whole is appearing – *Dictionary of Christian Spirituality* (SCM 1983) and *The Study of Spirituality* (SPCK 1986) are two of the best-known recent examples. Various authors long regarded as too recondite for the general Christian reader have been reclaimed and presented in new and attractive dress.

Prominent among such is Meister Eckhart, probably the greatest mystical writer of medieval Germany. Difficult and teasing, his works have provided ample material for some very odd interpretations, though recent years have seen the publication of a number of reliable introductions to his life and work. What we have not yet seen, however, is an accessible attempt to set him in the context both of his precursors and of his followers, and it is this task that Dr Davies so admirably carries out in this volume. It is no disrespect to the other authors he expounds to say that Eckhart is in an important sense the dominating figure of the book. Dr Davies shows how Eckhart's extraordinary vision grows out of the religious and intellectual milieu of the day, and, in the course of this, provides an exceptionally helpful guide to both the basic principles of the philosophical systems presupposed in the Middle Ages and the educational methods of the period. Equally importantly, he points out some of the eccentricities or imbalances in the great teacher's thought, so that the giants of the next generation – Tauler and Ruusbroec especially – can be read as seeking to hold on to Eckhart's master themes, such as the birth of the Word in the empty, denuded soul, while also doing justice to the affective and relational dimension of biblical and traditional spirituality, and to the centrality of the public life of the sacramental community.

As Dr Davies's first chapter makes clear, the whole book is a sustained examination of the strengths and weaknesses of what he calls the 'mysticism of being' – that aspect of Christian spirituality that is concerned with the transformation of what it is to be human in a 'direct' sharing in the life of God, rather than a primarily personally-oriented or community-oriented style of prayer and Christian life. It is not that these styles are in flat contradiction or that they are mutually exclusive, but that they show distinctive priorities within the family of Christian practices and languages; Eckhart's successors show how bridges can be built between them. And in a thoughtful and original epilogue, Dr Davies sets out the lessons we may draw today from the fourteenth century: the need is no less great for a sense of direct contact with God, and for the hope of a comprehensive transfiguration of human nature; but we are perhaps even more aware, in a savagely individualistic age, of the risks of concentrating on the priority of the 'interior', let alone the 'private', dimensions of spirituality. The fourteenth-century writers, English as much as continental European, are indispensable witness to the experiential depth of Christian living; but they are so because they are themselves part of a larger world – not isolated religious geniuses. As so often, it is Julian of Norwich who is brought in, briefly but tellingly, to sound a more accessibly personal note after the searching complexities of so many of her contemporaries. The life of the church nourishes both Julian's exploratory and affective sensibility and the passionate negations of the 'mysticism of being'. This is a book that succeeds in doing justice to both, and encouraging us to learn from both, rather than dogmatizing about a normative or essential form of Christian mystical utterance.

Dr Davies writes out of a great store of learning, and a ready familiarity with his texts in their original tongues; he is entirely at home with the often baffling ins and outs of critical historical scholarship in this field – the establishing of dating and authenticity, the difficulties of deciding on the primary forms of texts that have a long history of revision and reworking. But the learning is lightly worn, and this book is a thoroughly readable invitation into what has often seemed not only uncharted but positively menacing territory. It has a great deal to offer both the specialist and the general reader, and deserves to be warmly welcomed by all those seeking to 'enlarge their hearts' by encountering the experiences of the great friends of God in the Christian past.

ROWAN WILLIAMS

Preface

My purpose in undertaking the writing of this book was threefold. In the first place I felt that the fourteenth-century mystical writers of northern Europe as a distinctive spiritual movement had been largely ignored. I wished therefore to show the extent to which they form a specific school, which differs, for instance, from that of sixteenth-century Spain or seventeenth-century France, a school moreover which could be said to be, as North Europeans, our own cultural possession. The second purpose followed from the first and was to examine the place of that school within the context of the universal inheritance of the Christian church. It was the third purpose however which was my primary aim, and this was to allow a number of first-rate mystical writers, who are all too easily banished to the academic sidelines, to find a broader audience; to let them be heard, in the hope that their special and precious voice will nourish the spirits of many.

My heartfelt thanks are due to a number of friends who have all made a contribution to this book in some way. I owe special thanks however to Dr Huw Pryce and Dr Joseph Canning of University College of North Wales, Bangor for their many helpful remarks; and to Professor Rowan Williams of Christ Church, Oxford for much kind criticism and support.

OLIVER DAVIES

1

The Medieval Background

THE MYSTICISM OF BEING AND ITS ORIGINS

A distinguished scholar of spirituality, W. R. Inge, once wrote that of all kinds of human thought 'mysticism is almost always and everywhere the same'.[1] There is truth in this statement. But at the same time we can see, in the development of spirituality within the Christian tradition, that there exist distinct forms and schools of mysticism which sometimes occur at different places and times, and which sometimes coexist. Mysticism of course is a difficult word to define, but we will not go far wrong if we take it as meaning an *experience* of God.[2] That is, mysticism means the divine not as an idea or the basis of a theological system nor as a mere image self-created or received by tradition, but a sense within the human person that a transcendent and divine being or power is *immediately present* to him or her. As such it seems fair to understand the response of many people to liturgy, and to the sacraments as being in essence mystical. It is the common experience of the faithful that attendance at a church service mediates something of the divine to them, and that the individual Christian is able to *commune*, with God, not in an unmediated way, but certainly in a very real and meaningful one. This may be identified as the first and by far the most common form of mysticism.

The second school of mysticism is rarer, although it is contained to a degree in every authentic Christian conversion. Those who follow the Christian path generally do so because they find something in the person of Jesus which speaks to them directly. The relationship with Christ, as mediated through scripture and the church becomes alive: something of personal value and meaning. Indeed all Christians are asked to draw themselves and their lives into the centre of this *address*, this *dialogue* with Christ. Now there have been times when the sense of a personal encounter with Christ has become so profound for certain individuals that it has found expression in a visionary and particularly intense form of Christocentric spirituality. In its visionary forms this is, generally, a medieval phenomenon, and it owes much in its origins to the secular poetry of Courtly Love which was such a powerful influence around the twelfth century. Certainly it reflects this secular tradition in its intensely romantic, even at times erotic, imagery and language. Likewise in its visionary character it may well owe something to the medieval custom of practising quite severe forms of mortification, which led to a general weakening of the body and susceptibility to visionary experience. The very serviceable German name for this kind of mysticism is *Brautmystik* (which we may translate as 'bride mysticism' or 'nuptial mysticism'). This name derives from the preference among such visionaries and mystics for speaking of Christ as a Bridegroom and the human soul as his bride. One of its principal practitioners was St Bernard of Clairvaux who, in the twelfth century, wrote a commentary on the Song of Songs, a fertile influence upon the *Brautmystik*, in which, following the example of earlier commentators, he spoke of Christ in these terms. Many other writers followed suit, particularly women religious in the newly formed convents of Flanders, northern France, Holland and the Rhineland (including parts of Austria and Switzerland as well as Germany and the Netherlands), who displayed great visionary gifts centring on Christ as the Bridegroom of the soul.

Both these mystical forms are linked to a specific time and milieu. The former is based upon the external forms of religion and, as such, reflects the prevailing ecclesiastical attitudes and practices. It is unthinkable outside the catholic Christian tradition of sacrament and ceremony. The second is steeped in the style at least of the Christian Middle Ages, and few people today would devour the works of St Elisabeth von Schönau, St Mechthild von Magdeburg or St Gertrude the Great (although they wrote passages of great brilliance), in which the soul engages in a lengthy dialogue with Love, or the apostles speak in a vision to the fervent mystic.

The fourteenth-century North European mystics who we shall be discussing in this book belong, in general, to a third kind of mysticism which is less bound to a specific milieu or to a particular time. Further, although it exists firmly and deeply within the Christian tradition, it may also be discovered in the literature of non-Christian religions. It was in fact to this type of spirituality that W. R. Inge was referring in the quotation given above, and it is no coincidence that the book from which the quotation is taken is his work on Plotinus, the Greek Neoplatonist philosopher. This is a school of mysticism which describes a direct and unmediated experience of God in which the soul rises or is raised beyond the material world to share, briefly, in the glory of the Godhead. It is a process which may be summed up in Plotinus's own words: 'the flight of the alone to the Alone' (*Enneads*, VI, 9, 11). Dom François Vandenbroucke describes it thus:

> The journey by which the soul returns to God, by which it will recover its lost likeness to Him, is a dialectic. It is described in terms which are clearly intellectual and speculative, but side by side with them go a total stripping of self, a faith which becomes clear vision, a love which flowers into undivided possession, and a Unity into which disappear, as Ruysbroeck says, all 'persons, modes and names' in the simplicity of God's essence.[3]

German scholars have a way of creating apt names for things and they call this kind of mysticism *Wesensmystik*. The word *mystik* means 'mysticism' and *Wesen* really means 'essence' or 'inner nature', and it refers here both to what is most essential within man and most essential within God. I have translated it as 'mysticism of being' as a title in this chapter in the belief that 'mysticism of essence' would sound slightly scholastic, or dry, the very opposite of its true significance. Precisely this school of spirituality is most universal, and most relevant to us today. We are less inclined to think in terms of 'essences' than our medieval forebears, and the translation of 'Wesen' as 'being', a vital concept in modern philosophy and theology, is intended to underline the contemporary significance of this, the purest and most timeless form of Christian mysticism.

We find therefore three kinds of mystical experience within the Christian church. The first of these is a form which we may call the mysticism of the sacraments and of the liturgy. The second is a Christocentric spirituality which is based upon imagery that is sometimes biblical and sometimes secular, and upon revelation. This can in certain circumstances lead in its more intense form to visions in which a supernatural dimension entirely effaces everyday reality. The third kind, on the other hand, aims specifically to transcend images and to enter the 'darkness' and the 'nothingness' of the Godhead itself in a journey which leads the soul to the shedding of all that is superfluous, contrary or unequal to God as he is in his most essential Being. The technical word for this kind of spirituality is 'apophatic' (from the Greek word meaning 'to deny'). It is also known in Latin as the *via negativa* or the 'negative way'.

This third category of the 'mysticism of being' contains however a further and important division. Certain mystics have stressed that we enter into the Godhead by a process akin to cognition, to knowledge. We achieve union with God as one who *knows* is in union with that which is *known* (for example Meister Eckhart). This is essentially an *intellective* way (the word 'intellective', being altogether vaguer than 'rational' or 'intellectual', is ideal for this kind of 'spiritual intuition or intelligence'). Other mystics however have said that we enter into union with God through *love*, and the unity we possess with him is the union of the lover with the beloved (for example Ruusbroec and the author of The Cloud of Unknowing). It seems then that with regard to the mysticism of being we may speak of a way of love and a way of knowledge.

It is primarily the origins of the way of knowledge that we find in the work of the Greek philosopher Plato. The distinctive tone of a love-mysticism does not really appear until the work of the Jew, Philo of Alexandria, some five centuries later who combined Plato's vision with the warmth of the Jewish devotional tradition. Although the thought-world of Plato was very different from that of the Christian mystics of the Middle

Ages, we find in his work the clear outlines of what is most essential in their spirituality: a process of ascent. For Plato reality was to be found only in a transcendent sphere, in the domain of what he called the Forms, or Ideas of things, which we may think of as being archetypes or the blueprints of all that is. According to Plato the human soul has the power to perceive the forms directly through *understanding* (*nous*) and with which, in fact, it enjoys a certain affinity (*syngeneia*). Indeed so fundamental was the relationship between the soul and the Forms for Plato that he believed that we had had knowledge of them prior to our birth on earth and that it was only on account of this knowledge, imperfectly recalled, that we had knowledge of things on earth. Similarly, regaining knowledge of the Forms in contemplation (*theoria, noesis*) through our intellectual and moral purification becomes the goal and meaning of our lives. Not only is the 'intellective' element in Plato important from the point of view of what is to follow, but also the way in which we may arrive at knowledge of the Forms which Plato outlines. This includes a strong element of detachment from the coarser impulses in our own nature, and from involvement of the spirit in the concrete forms of the physical universe. Plato's world is essentially a hierarchical one, and our ascent to reality involves a continuous tuning of the self to the higher principles and a weaning of our nature away from the coarser impulses which bind us to the earth.

Plato's message was certainly not lost on the Christians.[4] It did not come down to them directly from him however, but in the form which Platonism took in the hands of teachers of the later classical period who drew on him for their inspiration. Plotinus was one such thinker, whose writings exercised a great influence on St Augustine prior to his conversion to Christianity. In Plotinus we find Plato's thought in a more synthesized and coherent form, although what is most distinctive in him is his emphasis on the *unity* of the Godhead. For Plotinus the whole purpose of human life was a return to the transcendent unity of the Godhead, through the principle of *Nous*, Mind or Intelligence. The ultimate Godhead is the One, beyond the Forms and beyond being itself. It is to this that the human soul returns, through a process of moral purification but, most particularly, through an inward journey deep within itself where it discovers the principle of *Nous*, of Intelligence. That is the place or principle of intellectual truth and reality where the advancing soul comes closest to the sublimity of the One. Once again, therefore, there is a purgation and an ascent through the powers of the mind which culminates in the freely given ecstasy of divine union, although this time that ascent has an inward aspect to it of deepening introspection. We find something similar in the thought of Origen, who, like Plotinus himself, studied under the philosopher Ammonius Saccas in Alexandria. For Origen, spiritual ascent is through the contemplation of God by *nous* in a transforming vision. His mysticism is similarly one of light, of a purified intellectual understanding in which the soul leaves the darkness of ignorance behind and advances into ever increasing divine revelation. Origen was particularly influential among the Desert Fathers. His thought was transmitted to the eastern church though Evagrius, and his influence can be felt also in the *Conferences* of John Cassian, which came in time to be an important text for the western church.

The 'apophatic' love mysticism apparent in Philo entered the Christian fold through the work of the fourth-century Cappadocian Father St Gregory of Nyssa. For Gregory union with God is the miraculous gift of the Creator God, and it comes about through love. The ascent of the soul is from light into darkness, and contemplation is only a stage of the journey whose culmination is the embrace of God, who can only be known through love in the darkness of his incomprehensibility. This same tradition is apparent also in the late fifth-century Syrian monk known as pseudo-Dionysius. This key figure was mistaken for the Athenian convert of St Paul, and hence the work, which is a highly Platonic one, enjoyed a particularly high status among the Fathers of the medieval church. It established an alternative to the 'light mysticism' of Plotinus and Origen in that knowledge of God came to be something that was understood to be an entry into darkness. The soul follows a path of systematic negation of all which is not God, which eventually leads to a place in which it encounters God in an unknowable manner, in ecstasy and in love. Most importantly, it was pseudo-Dionysius who, through his commentators, was a major transmitter of the mysticism of love to the Middle Ages where, together with the way of knowledge, it was to be a potent force indeed.

THE MEDIEVAL CHURCH

Although the school of spirituality which our mystics of the fourteenth century represent was one which has its origins in early Christianity and before, and is arguably the type of mysticism which can most claim universality, the individuals whose life and thought we are to consider in this book were very much men and women of their age. In order to understand something of their medieval context, it would be wise to cast an eye first at the developments and the process of reform which had taken place over the preceding centuries and which gave the church of which they were a part certain characteristics quite different from those of the modern churches of today. In fact, accustomed as we are to an ecclesiastical world of defined positions, sophisticated theological discourse and heightened self-awareness, we will be surprised, perhaps even shocked, at the colourful pluralism of the church in the early medieval period. In contrast to the earnest self-definition which has exercised Catholic and Protestant minds since the Reformation, the early medieval church, in the form of 'Christendom', was a ubiquitous phenomenon which happily absorbed all manner of alien practice and thought, and which straddled the land and permeated men's minds so thoroughly as to appear to them almost invisible.

And yet to all appearances the church in the early centuries of the medieval period provided the peasant peoples of Europe with little more than a sceletal form of Christianity. Uneducated priests worked in the service of a secular lord or were attached to a church that was in the private possession of a secular ruler. The monastic sphere fared little better; the monasteries became very much the 'family business' of the temporal ruler who founded them, and they were treated as such. Entire communities might change hands as if they were livestock, and the lay abbot, while exercising control over the community, might have no sympathy whatsoever for their religious life. Such communities were founded primarily in order to pray for their founder and his family in expiation of their sins and to serve the social convenience of the feudal system of which they were a part. Among the scattered monasteries of Europe there was little uniformity of religious practice, most houses using a mixed rule, differently applied. The need for reform was evident, and it first emerged in the monastic life in the work of St Benedict of Aniane who was summoned to Aachen by the Carolingian Emperor Louis in order to establish a stricter monastic norm, based upon the ancient Rule of his namesake, St Benedict of Nursia. This Rule, celebrated for its wisdom, moderation and spiritual purity, advocated a religious life based on 'conversion of morals' and an exact balance of choral prayer, study and physical labour. St Benedict of Aniane did not stress the third element, nor did his Aachen Decrees as they were called (816 and 817) win acceptance everywhere, but his reform served the vital function of establishing the Benedictine rule as the monastic ideal and norm.

The death of St Benedict of Aniane in 821, the fragmentation of the Carolingian Empire and the savage Viking invasions across Europe in the ninth and tenth centuries shattered the incipient reforms of the religious life and threatened its very foundations. It was with great difficulty that Odo, a young man from Tours who had been inspired by a reading of the Benedictine Rule, was able to find a community with whom to live the full monastic life. The abbot of the monastery which he eventually found in a remote area of the Jura was still familiar with the Anianic reforms, and it was this noble-spirited and uncompromising man, Berno of Beaume, whom William of Aquitaine asked in c. 909 to found a community of monks in Cluny in France. This movement quickly spread through a system of daughter houses, each being subordinate to the next and so on, and all subject to the jurisdiction of the abbot of Cluny, who was thus required to travel a great deal, and beyond him, the jurisdiction of the Pope himself. Berno insisted also that the election of the abbot should be in the hands of the monks themselves and not at the discretion of the local ruler. The influence of secular rulers was therefore circumvented, allowing a monastic reform movement to gain ground which led to a revitalization of liturgical life and to a more cohesive and authentic monastic spirituality.

The influence of the Cluniac movement upon the church at large was immense, as monks from their ranks became priests, bishops and eventually popes who sought to counter the extensive influence of secular values and practices in the contemporary church. Such practices included that of simony (the purchase of ecclesiastical office), so shocking to modern sensibilities, neglect of clerical celibacy and the dominance of the secular powers in the affairs of the church to the extent that the local temporal ruler had the final say in the appointment to important ecclesiastical posts which he could and did manipulate to his own political ends.

Reform began at the top, and the first major victory for the reformers came in 1059 with a decree which gave the decisive voice in papal elections to the cardinal bishops. During the primacy of the monk Hildebrand as Gregory VII (1073–85), the papacy began to flex its muscles and sought above all to tear ecclesiastical appointments out of the grip of the secular powers. This vital contest, known as the Investiture Struggle, which arose between Gregory VII and the Emperor Henry IV, culminated in 1122 in the Concordat of Worms. This left the advantage decisively with the papacy. Lessons were learned during this period which would serve the papal cause well, although the increased ambition of the papacy in the secular realm led to problems of a different kind. The fourteenth century, which saw a nadir in papal prestige and fortune, began with the Bull *Unam sanctam* (1302) in which Pope Boniface VIII was able to define his office in terms close to those of absolute monarchy.

The very success of the Cluniac houses as monastic establishments quickly led to difficulties. They became progressively bigger and more numerous until finally they constituted a lame and unwieldy empire. In addition the ever-increasing emphasis on the chanting of the extended Divine Office seriously reduced the private, reflective and scholarly dimension of the monk's vocation, as originally portrayed by St Benedict, as well as reducing the period of manual labour to a bare minimum. The monks would spend the greater part of their day in elaborate liturgical celebration, which was matched by the rich and extravagant architecture of the Cluniac houses. These monasteries became so large and powerful that a substantial number of the monks were involved in the extensive administrative duties of running the establishment as well as servicing the numerous points of dependency on the feudal order outside the cloister of which they were a fully integrated part. What had been a movement for reform became itself in need of reform.

The late eleventh century witnessed the foundation of the Cistercian and the Carthusian Orders, both of which represented a return to the principles of primitive monasticism. The latter was an eremetical order, founded by St Bruno of Cologne at Grande Chartreuse, laying great stress on the hermit life, but it was the Cistercians who spread most rapidly, becoming the dominant monastic force of the day. Their principal founder, St Bernard abbot of Clairvaux (d. 1153), became perhaps the foremost church figure of his time as the highly gifted and articulate advocate of the new, more rigorous monastic principles. In particular, the Cistercian use of lay brothers, called *conversi*, served to free the monks from the feudal round of rents, dues and administration, which choked the life of the older Benedictine foundations. The Cistercian rediscovery of the value of manual labour, as enshrined in the original Rule of St Benedict, also served the important function of enabling the uneducated peasant class of Europe to share in a path of monastic sanctification, a path which had long been the preserve of the aristocracy alone. Similarly, the Cistercian return to the primitive Rule with its fewer hours of public devotion allowed the monks themselves to integrate more spiritual reading and physical labour into their 'work of God'. This same monastic ideal coloured the foundation of the Premonstratensian order, named after Prémontré, the place of their foundation, which also became influential in working towards a return to the ancient system of communal life among parish clergy, deemed to be a vital underpinning of clerical celibacy, and the fostering of spiritual values. The Premonstratensians espoused in particular the flexible Augustinian Rule (which in a later century was to be the formal basis of the small community which gathered around Jan van Ruusbroec). This was the ancient code of monastic practice which derived from an adapted form of Letter 211, written by St Augustine to his sister, in which he advised her on the essentials of the religious and communal life. This quickly became widely influential across the European continent through the formation of the Canons Regular or Augustinian Canons who, as part of the Gregorian Reform and among other of their achievements, had succeeded in implanting the apostolic values of celibacy and communal prayer in an area of vital ecclesiastical interest: the chapters of the European cathedrals.

The reform of the church in the Middle Ages proceeded largely from the monastic world in which the dominant ideal was one of personal sanctification through asceticism, prayer and monastic obedience within the context of community life. The popular or lay church knew little of this experience, and the people of God were served by a largely illiterate and generally uninspiring rural clergy. The change, when it came, was rapid and widespread and followed upon the formation of the two Orders of Friars, who were to exercise unparalleled influence during the thirteenth and fourteenth centuries. The first of these was created, almost against his will, by St Francis of Assisi, and the other was the work of St Dominic. The Friars had a number of things in common. Both orders espoused the principle of radical poverty, and both came to value and to excel in the new learning that followed from the translations of Aristotle's works. Most importantly both the Franciscans and the Dominicans were inspired by an evangelical zeal, which had been largely dormant for hundreds of years, and which led them to go out to the masses to preach and to teach the word of God. And yet they still remained a monastic force. They both lived in celibacy and under obedience and both took a monastic rule, although this was adapted in such a way as not to stifle but rather to support their prime evangelical vocation.

Finally, the reform of the church must also be seen in the light of the first four crusades which took place between 1095 and 1204 and in which some of the great monastic figures of the age were involved. St Bernard of Clairvaux had himself called for the Second Crusade of 1147, and it was during the

'internal crusade' against the Albigensian or Cathar heresy
that St Dominic, the founder of Meister Eckhart's own Order,
discovered his vocation as friar and preacher. The crusades,
although of mixed fortune and consequence, increased the
sense of European unity and cohesion, both in terms of organization and common heritage. They stimulated a greater
awareness of Christendom and provided an incentive, through
contact with other world religions, for a deeper self-understanding and keener self-definition.

MEDIEVAL THEOLOGY

If the general organization of the church and of the clergy
was particularly vulnerable to secular influence and values
during the early Middle Ages, then it is no less true to say
that theology was at a low ebb. There is much truth in the
frequently heard view that there was not a single major
western theologian between Gregory the Great in the seventh
century and St Anselm in the eleventh. The ninth-century
Carolingian renaissance did however see some important
theological activity in the work of the erudite Alcuin from
York and Theodulf, while Paschasius Radbertus, Hrabanus
Maurus and Ratramnus initiated a debate on the nature of the
Eucharist and on predestination which foreshadowed some of
the great debates of the Reformation. But a major change of
method and a greater depth of critical understanding are
evident in St Anselm's *Cur Deus Homo*, which was written in
c. 1097 and which bears comparison with the works of the
great scholastic thinkers to come. The new spirit of Anselm's
thought is summed up in his own phrase from the *Proslogion*
'Fides quaerens intellectum' ('Faith seeking to understand').
Anselm's proof in the *Proslogion* for the existence of God as
'that no greater than which can be thought' enjoyed a
distinguished career and interested minds as diverse as Kant,
who dubbed it the 'ontological proof', Leibniz, Hegel and
Karl Barth. The ebullient and contentious Abelard was a
very different personality from the saintly Anselm, but his
work *Sic et Non* was similarly influential, largely on account of
its method, according to which Abelard juxtaposed conflicting

statements on the faith from the Fathers as a stimulus to the student's powers of critical synthesis. This challenging new spirit was expressed in the words from the Prologue to *Sic et Non:* 'By doubting we come to questioning, and by questioning we perceive the truth.' Abelard's work had a considerable influence on Gratian's *Decretum* of 1140, which standardized canon law for centuries to come, and on Peter Lombard's *Sentences*, which became the standard theological textbook in the following years. Abelard's achievement was not original in that it developed a technique used by lawyers before him, but it showed a much greater awareness of the power that resided in the current medieval canon of classical logic, comprising Boethius's translations of Aristotle's *Categories*, *On Interpretation*, and Porphyry's *Isagoge* (an introduction to the *Categories*).

Anselm and Abelard's contributions can be seen to be part of a greater process of change as the limited cathedral and monastic schools of the Dark Ages began to give way to educational institutions which were the forerunners of the modern universities. The eleventh century was a time of expansion in all manner of ways as cities burgeoned north of the Alps on the pattern of those which already flourished in northern Italy. The increase in population and wealth led to greater specialization of labour, and to the establishment of a scholarly class which functioned outside the monasteries and which owed less allegiance to clerical principles. It was principally these men, intent on new discoveries and representative of the new exploratory spirit of the age, who searched the libraries of Europe for the remaining and, as they were to discover, far more important works of the Aristotelian corpus. By the end of the twelfth century virtually every single work by Aristotle had been translated (largely from Greek, as the literal character of medieval translation often made the Arabic versions, themselves translations of Syriac texts, rather bizarre). Their dissemination was slow but complete, and by the mid thirteenth century they constituted the texts for study in the *trivium* and revived *quadrivium* of the schools and determined the logical methods current there.

THE MEDIEVAL UNIVERSITY

Although itself deriving more from personal experience, the mysticism of any period necessarily draws upon the concepts and intellectual tendencies of its own age. The intellectual life of the European Middle Ages centred upon the universities which evolved from the places of learning known as *studia generalia* (sing. *studium generale*) that developed in the late eleventh and early twelfth centuries. In the north, in Paris, there were many foreigners among the masters, whereas in the southern city of Bologna it was the students who were the foreign element. Medieval law afforded little protection to exiles, and the non-natives quickly perceived that their interests would be best served by forming scholarly guilds for mutual assistance and protection. Thus the *universitas* was born, and the two archetypal universities, Bologna with its *universitas* of students and Paris with its *universitas* of masters, became the alternative models to be followed in the foundation of every other European university.

The medieval university system could be rigorous in the extreme, and the medieval student began his studies at a much younger age than his modern counterpart. If he took a higher degree, he would remain a student for some sixteen to twenty years. The Arts Faculty courses took pupils from the age of fifteen and thus provided an education which was roughly equivalent to that of the modern secondary school. Their purpose was to perfect the students' knowledge of Latin and to give them a grounding in secular thought which, by the mid-thirteenth century, meant a knowledge of a number of Aristotelian texts dealing with logical method, ethics, metaphysics and with the natural sciences. The length of study was normally six years (which however by the mid-fourteenth century, the period with which we are largely concerned, had dropped to four and a half years), and included the requirement of four years attendance at lectures, both those given by masters ('ordinary' lectures) and by graduates of the faculty, known as bachelors ('cursory' lectures). In the *ordinarie* the masters tackled major problems of analysis and central contemporary themes whereas the bachelors in their *cursorie* were asked only to provide a running commentary on the text. A student would finally qualify from the Arts Faculty after taking part in a number of disputations over a period of two years (called 'sophismata') and himself delivering a course of 'cursory' lectures.

The situation in the Faculty of Theology was generally rather different, one reason being that along with law and medicine, theology was a higher faculty and did not admit students until their initial studies were complete. Students of theology were therefore a good deal more mature than those in the Faculty of Arts, and may also have had some additional experience as clerics in the world. Relatively few men opted to follow the theology course in comparison with law, for instance, which offered dramatic career prospects inside and outside the church. Theology attracted the pure thinkers and in consequence, despite the low number of students, it enjoyed high esteem. The course was long and thorough in which the student was required to attend lectures for four years on the Bible and for two years on the theological compendium of Peter Lombard's *Sentences* before becoming, if he was at least twenty-five years old, a Bachelor of Divinity. The candidate, known at this point as a *cursor*, would then embark upon his own series of lectures on the Bible, followed by one or two years on Lombard's *Sentences*. He was also required to take part, in a subordinate role, in the disputations which were the heart of intellectual life in the medieval schools and which took several forms. Generally a theme was proposed by a master in the form of a question (for example 'Whether the act of willing presupposes the act of understanding').[5] An unfortunate known as the *respondens* would reply to the question and would answer objections then raised against his own position. The master who framed the question would finally sum up the arguments in his *determinatio*. These regular disputations in the presence of many masters and their pupils were important occasions but it was at the *quodlibet* disputations (literally 'whatever' – so named because the topics considered could be of any kind and raised by anyone), held at Advent and Lent, that the most exciting encounters took place. The education which a student in the Theology Faculty received was in essence a lengthy training in the skills of the *disputatio*, for which he required a thorough knowledge of scripture and of the major commentators, profound familiarity with the major extant works of secular and Christian philosophy and, above all, an instinctive grasp of the logical techniques of oral disputation. Thus, when the *cursor* bachelor had finished his three or four year period of lecturing on the Bible and the *Sentences*, he would enter a four year period of participation in the faculty's disputations, under the guidance of his master, and it was on the grounds of his performance at the *inceptio*, an 'examination disputation', that he was accepted as a Master of Theology, thus acquiring the right to teach. The minimum age requirement for the Master was thirty-five.

PLATO AND ARISTOTLE

There would be little point in considering the flesh and bones of the education system of the Middle Ages if we did not also have some idea of the spirit which inhabited it. It is easy enough to make use of terms such as Platonism and Aristotelianism without ever touching upon the salient points which distinguish them. A brief overview of the beliefs of Plato and of his distinguished pupil may serve the aim of clarifying a little the issues which confronted thinkers in the Middle Ages.

As we have already seen in our consideration of the origins of the mysticism of being, the very core of Plato's system of thought was his belief in a realm of transcendent reality. When Plato asked himself how it is possible that we know things in the world, how we identify, for instance, an individual table with the species table, an individual tree with the species tree and so on, he decided that the answer was that there exists in some transcendent sphere the ideal form of such things and that we, prior to our birth in a human body, had knowledge of these ideal forms and thus, through memory, are able to recognize their physical counterparts here on earth. This idea proved to be of profound consequence not only for the evolution of philosophy but also for that of theology. Its importance for the latter was, above all, that it postulated the existence of a realm that was both transcendent and of a higher order of reality, the domain of the Good and the True. This reality was moreover, for Plato, one with which the soul of man had a natural affinity and with which, through contemplation and self-purification, it could commune. Whether or not Plato conceived of a God in any remotely Christian sense, the purity of his idealism and the archetypal character of his thinking inspired generations after him to assimilate and to develop along theistic lines specific aspects of his thought. Plato himself, not least on account of the dialogue form which he preferred, never constructed a philosophical system as such. His work is characterized rather by a dynamic exploration of the same themes from different starting points, leading to some obscurity and apparent inconsistency. It was largely the thinkers of so-called Middle Platonism who absorbed his thought and turned it into a system. The form of the Good, of which Plato had but briefly spoken in *The Republic* as being among the eternal Ideas the *primus inter pares*, was fused with the Aristotelian Prime Mover, the Primary Cause of all things, and became in their hands the ultimate principle, the Supreme Mind, at the top of the hierarchy of being. This in turn generated a tension which led to the notion of a Second Mind, or Logos, created from the first, which mediated between this high point of being and the material world (an idea that was highly influential upon the Fourth Gospel). The second, and perhaps most important synthesis of Platonic thought, was that of Plotinus, who stressed the supreme principle of absolute unity and simplicity. The Manifold, he argued, proceeded from the One to which, through purification and contemplation, it shall return in a cosmic rhythm. The One moreover is entirely removed from the hierarchy of being in the Plotinian system, and stands above it, utterly transcendent and remote. The third impulse of the Platonic spirit in this early period is the work of Proclus, who taught at Athens during the fifth century after Christ. Proclus streamlined the tradition yet further, laying more emphasis however on the intermediate beings and powers located between the Neoplatonist God and the material world, the angels, spirits and gods, thus opening the door to theurgy and magic.

It seems an extraordinary fact to us now but it was not through the actual works of Plato, so familiar to us today, that Platonic thought was disseminated. These were relatively

unknown during the critical early centuries of the Christian
period, so that St Jerome, writing in the introduction to his
commentary on the Letter to the Galatians, states: 'How
many nowadays know the works or even the name of Plato?
A handful of idle old men.'[6] The massively influential Platonic
concepts were transmitted through the interpreters of Plato,
such as Plotinus and Proclus, through charismatic teachers,
such as Ammonius Saccas, and were eagerly taken up by
the Church Fathers who sought philosophical categories with
which to elucidate the Christian revelation. Thus the idea of
hierarchy appealed to the early Greek Fathers, the Apologists,
with their incipient notions of the Trinity, and led, more often
than not, to a form of Subordinationism (whereby the Son is
seen as being inferior to the Father, who was himself never a
problem to the Greeks). Neoplatonic influence could also be
felt in its stronghold of Alexandria in the resistance to the
belief in the full *physical* incarnation of Christ that marked the
Alexandrian position during the great Christological debate of
the third and fourth centuries. Plotinus, with his belief in the
ecstatic ascent of the soul to a remote impersonal Godhead
through the taming of the physical appetites and the pursuit
of contemplation, represented a Platonic tradition which exercised a powerful influence on Origen and the Fathers of the
Egyptian deserts, and on St Augustine, who was certainly one
of the principal Latin transmitters of elements of Neoplatonic
thought to subsequent ages. Proclus was no less influential
through Dionysius the pseudo-Areopagite, whose mystical
works contained Proclean notions of a 'superessential'
Godhead and of a mystical hierarchy of beings suspended
between the unknowable divinity and our material world.
Pseudo-Dionysius was translated into Latin in the ninth
century by the Irishman John Scotus Eriugena, who himself
wrote works under his influence, and, supported by the
erroneous belief that the author was St Paul's Athenian
convert, his work exercised a profound influence throughout
the medieval period (being positively identified as the work
of a later writer, probably a fifth-century Syrian monk, only
within the last century). Proclus's own work, *The Elements of
Theology*, was also of great importance because, in the form of
extracts under the title *The Book of Causes* (*Liber de Causis*), it

was long believed to belong to the corpus of Aristotle's works and hence enjoyed special esteem.

Platonic ideas, in their Christian frame, could be summed up as a strong statement of the transcendence of God, coupled with a belief in the participation of the creation in him. This has often led to an intense mysticism, expressed in a theory of the soul's intuitive, mystical ascent to God and contemplative union with him. Neoplatonism has set up various tensions among those Christian thinkers most influenced by it, including a certain disdain for the material realm and the human body, leading to a reluctance to accept the full physical incarnation of the Word, among other things. A further danger has been the temptation to obscure the distinction between the Creator and the created, the error of pantheism, and it was on these grounds that the work of John Scotus Eriugena, for instance, suffered condemnation in the thirteenth century. A similar charge was to be levelled at Meister Eckhart and certain of his followers. Such was the influence of Neoplatonism in its various forms on the development of Christian theology that the first Christian centuries may in fact be seen as a struggle to define a position of orthodoxy both in the light of Neoplatonism, and in the face of it.

If the patristic age can legitimately be named the age of Plato, then the theology of the medieval schools from the twelfth century onwards reflects the influence of Aristotle. The rediscovery of Aristotle revolutionized theological method, as we have seen, and his natural philosophy both flooded the faculties of Arts and demanded inclusion in the *Summae*, the great syntheses of the thirteenth and fourteenth centuries. Aristotle had differed from his master Plato on a number of accounts. He had dispensed with a belief in the objective existence of the ideal forms, for instance, and preferred to understand the objects of the world as being composite, consisting of undifferentiated material and specific form. According to Aristotle we have knowledge of things in the world by virtue of such universalizing forms, but those, rather than being something existent in themselves, are an abstraction we make with our own mental processes from the objects we perceive in the world, and he believed that all knowledge originates in our perceptions of material things. The transcendent element therefore, the dominant characteristic of Plato's thought, has yielded place in Aristotle to a more concrete, scientific or empiricist frame of mind. Aristotle's thought contained two precepts however that were hostile to the Christian revelation, first a belief in the eternal existence of the universe (which therefore precluded the Christian doctrine of the creation), and secondly an understanding of human identity as an indivisible union of soul and body that was irrevocably dissolved at the moment of death. Just as certain of the Platonic formulations had caused much disturbance in the Christian camp during the early centuries, so too the assimilation of Aristotle was neither quick nor easy. Indeed there was a deep suspicion, particularly among the monks, even of the rational methods of the 'New Logic' and a fear of where they would lead to in questions of faith. Thus Lanfranc opposed Berengarius, St Bernard pursued Abelard, and the Pope, in 1210, 1270 and 1277, moved against the new learning by banning the study of a number of books in the Faculty of Arts at the all-important University of Paris. Opposition came from the Arts faculties too, this time of a different kind. The theologians worked upon the revelations of scripture and the authoritative pronouncements of the Church Councils, to which was now added the seemingly untouchable status of 'the Philosopher', and their at times immensely subtle reasoning was used to create a reasonable synthesis of what were regarded as a priori truths. The proto-philosophers of the Arts faculties however (known as 'Averroists' after the important Arabian commentator on Aristotle, Averroes, who believed in the primacy of reason over faith) wished to apply scrupulous logic to all things, even to canons of time-honoured belief. As may be imagined, this movement quickly encountered ecclesiastical opposition and condemnation.

One scholar has spoken of the 'great new intellectual fact of the later Middle Ages' as being 'the divorce between faith and knowledge based on natural experience'.[7] Certainly this is the process which we can see reflected in the thought of the major figures of the scholastic period. The Franciscan St Bonaventure held the new secular philosophy in grave suspicion and preferred the Christianized philosophical system of St Augustine to that of Aristotle. The 'seraphic doctor', as he was later called on account of the impressively devout, sublime quality of his thought, constructed a philosophical system which owed far more to the spirit of St Francis, who saw the full presence of the Christian revelation in the least part of creation, than to the insights of the New Logic. His is a system which puts union with God as the goal of all, and the pursuit of philosophy is held strictly subordinate to the ascent of the mind to union with God through a devout and sanctified life. The characteristic Franciscan philosophical position is therefore to give far greater emphasis to the operation of the will, which in the faithful is the agent of love, than to the processes of reasoning. This is the key distinction, and point of debate, which divided the Franciscan from the Dominican masters (and in which Eckhart was himself to play a public role). It was left to St Thomas Aquinas, the most distinguished of Dominican thinkers, to absorb and integrate Aristotelian thinking with the articles of the Christian faith, which he achieved largely by excising what was inimical to Christianity and harnessing what was theologically positive, or at least neutral, to the philosophical service of Revelation. In so doing, St Thomas reconciled philosophy and theology by ascribing to each its proper sphere of competence. Thus the existence of God and his divine attributes could be proved, along Aristotelian lines, by natural reason, whereas creation in time and the Divine Trinity could not. These were the property of revelation and could only be known through faith. In particular, Aquinas adapted the influential Aristotelian notion of things being *in act* and things being *potential* in his own theory of the distinction between the *essence* of a thing and its *existence*. This enabled him to portray the radical difference between the Creator and his creation by stating that in the case of God essence and existence are one. This idea similarly fused the remote First Cause God of Aristotle with the living and personal Judaeo-Christian God of Exodus who states 'I am that I am'. Direct knowledge of God, for Aquinas, was not given to man in this life and, according to his system, we are able to know of his existence and his nature only through the processes of reason and by analogy with the material universe, although the knowledge of God which this yields is certain. Aquinas thus closely reflects the spirit of his Greek master, whose conception of the Godhead was explicitly intellectualist (as Mind in perpetual self-reflection). It is worth noting however that even in Aquinas the influence of Plato can be felt, particularly in his doctrine of the Divine Ideas, perfect patterns of all that is, preserved eternally in the mind of God, which is an adaptation via Plotinus and St Augustine of the original Platonic Forms or Ideas. Within the terms of his age, St Thomas Aquinas's achievement represents the highest point of harmonization and accord between natural reason and revealed religion. The major thinkers who followed him however were less convinced of the powers of reason and hence less able to use philosophy to justify the precepts of faith. Thus the Franciscan thinker from the lowlands of Scotland, Duns Scotus, found that only the infinity of God was provable through reason; the other divine attributes were not. He denied the Thomist distinction between existence and essence, stating that they were logically the same, and saw the difference between God and his creatures as consisting in the fact that to God belonged Infinite Being, whereas his creatures possess only finite being. A Franciscan contemporary of Meister Eckhart, William of Ockham, who probably hailed from Surrey, went a step further. When he applied his 'razor', or the 'principle of economy', he discovered that only individual objects in the world are truly knowable; all the precepts of the Christian faith were thus the product of revelation, and could be known fully only through faith. For obvious reasons William of Ockham with his scepticism is often seen as standing at the end of the scholastic period as a pointer to what was to come: the radical division of the methods and conclusions of natural, secular philosophy, developing along empiricist lines, from the traditional province of revelation and the articles of faith.

THE DOMINICAN ORDER

Our brief overview of the medieval world of which our fourteenth-century mystics were a part would not be complete without some comment on the profoundly influential Order of which Meister Eckhart, Johannes Tauler and Henry Suso were members. Dominic de Guzman, a nobleman from Castile and a canon of Osma Cathedral, was travelling with his bishop and friend Diego of Azevedo in the south of France when they came upon Cistercian legates, appointed by the Pope to counter the Albigensian heresy which was widespread in the region. The Cistercian abbot of Cîteaux and his companions had met with little success in the two years of their campaign. They asked advice of Diego, who saw that the failure of the monks to convert the heretics to orthodoxy was the result of their substantial retinues which placed them in a poor light in the face of the severe asceticism and poverty espoused by the Albigensian leaders. Diego and Dominic therefore urged that they too should embrace a lifestyle of poverty and, when the Cistercians had sent away their retinues, the small group embarked upon a highly successful evangelical crusade among the people of Languedoc. In course of time Dominic emerged as leader of the crusade, travelling and preaching the catholic faith and relying upon alms for his livelihood. In 1215 he was offered a house in Toulouse, and there formed around him the beginnings of a community which espoused the same apostolic, evangelical principles. Pope Honorius III gave official recognition to the Order in 1216, but decrees of the current Fourth Lateran Council obliged the new Order to adopt a rule which was already in existence. Dominic chose the Augustinian Rule with which, as a canon regular, he had long been familiar. In the following year Dominic sent his small band of friars out to found new communities, dispatching the greater part to the key university towns of Paris and Bologna. There was, from the very beginning, a particular enthusiasm for learning in the new Order, which well supported the original calling to the ministry of preaching the gospel.

Dominic's small band of some sixteen friars in Toulouse, of which he sent seven to Paris, bore a swift and rich harvest. Within some six years there were around 120 members of the Order in Paris alone, where they founded the Convent of St Jacques (which was later to house Eckhart and possibly Tauler), and by 1234 it is likely that nine of the fifteen doctors of divinity at Paris were Dominicans. The age was one of lay involvement and reform. Mass movements were seeking new spiritual values in a radical return to the life of the gospel. Some of these movements, such as the Poor Catholics, remained within the church, but others, such as the Waldensians and Cathars (Albigensians), did not. The increase in population of the new towns, and the far greater influence of the urban populace, contributed to the popularization of the evangelical spirit. It was primarily the espousal of religious poverty, and of a genuine personal piety, that marked the young Dominican Order, coupled with an avid interest in the new intellectual discoveries and the new learning. Above all, unlike the monastic orders of previous centuries, their *raison d'être* was the salvation of others' souls, not of their own.

The same spirit of 'modernism' and revival is evident also in the structures which the Order adopted. St Dominic possessed a genius for organization and bequeathed the Order a hierarchical structure which, while delegating considerable powers to individual superiors, guaranteed that they would use them moderately, through election and scrutiny. The Dominicans also set about organizing their own colleges which were, in effect, universities. The first tier of their educational institutions was the *studium particolare* at which gifted local boys would study. Those who excelled would then advance to a Dominican *studium generale*, such as those at Paris, Oxford or Cologne, where they would receive a high quality theological education. Indeed the *studia* of the Dominicans, and later of the Franciscans, were the greatest centres of learning in Europe, and, through their socially egalitarian system of education, the Mendicant Orders were able to train as well as attract the finest minds of the time. Indeed their outstanding academic success, their papal privileges, coupled with their sovereign indifference to the interests of the secular universities of which they were a part, led on more than one occasion to violent clashes between the mendicant and the secular scholars.[8]

THE FOURTEENTH CENTURY

The fourteenth century is best understood against the background of the 'Golden Age' of the century which preceded it. The thirteenth century is commonly regarded as a period of growth, unification and vast cultural and intellectual achievement. In the field of theology it was the age of the great syntheses, when Aquinas and Bonaventure held the stage with their cohesive and all-embracing theological systems. The threat of secularization implicit in the rediscovery of the Aristotelian corpus had been successfully countered while the strength and vitality of the new learning had, it seemed, been successfully blended with the precepts of traditional Christianity.

In the field of church organization, it was a time of great development and expansion. The powerful personality of Innocent III dominates the early decades of the century, and in the Fourth Lateran Council of 1215, this gifted Pope, who officially adopted the term 'Vicar of Christ', is able to give expression to his vision of a reformed, cohesive and centralized church. The thirteenth-century church was more streamlined than it had been for a millenium. Many of the bishops had received an advanced education at the universities, and they exercised a more effective pastoral control from their chapters in the major centres of European population. Canon law had also developed into a pliant instrument of rationalization and standardization which secured the papacy increasing centrality and influence within the universal church, while guaranteeing bishops fuller authority within their local area. The church reflected in the influential Fourth Lateran Council possessed a high degree of self-confidence and an enhanced sense of its own organic unity within the world.

The papacy also appeared to be gaining the upper hand in the long struggle with the German emperors. Around the turn of the century Sicily, which had long been a papal fief and an important counterbalance to the hegemony of the emperor in the North Italian territories, came into the hands of Henry VI. The papacy responded, and there ensued a long struggle for political supremacy, which ended towards the middle of the thirteenth century. Under Innocent IV, Rome won the independence of the German bishops from secular interference, forcing the emperor to relinquish all control over the operation of ecclesiastical office.

If the thirteenth century saw the advent of the friars, who were to be an enormously important force in the life of the church, it also saw the continuing rise of serious heresies. The heresies, new and old, of southern France and northern Italy constituted a radical new danger to the church in that they had spread and taken root at all levels of society. It was in order to counter the Catharist heresy, which was particularly widespread in southern France, that the papal Inquisition was born. The existence of the Inquisition in this period testifies again to the self-confidence, cohesion and centralization of the thirteenth-century church as well, of course, to the manifold sins to which the abuse of these qualities will lead.

If in general the tenor of the thirteenth century was one of positive construction, of synthesis and achievement which found artistic expression in the building of the splendid cathedrals of Chartres (after the fire of 1194), Reims and Amiens in the High Gothic style, then it is fair to say that the fourteenth century was marked by a process of disintegration and division. A key factor in this was the fortunes of the papacy itself, which had significantly increased its influence and prestige inside and outside the church during the course of the thirteenth century, guided by a sequence of powerful and diplomatically adroit popes. This trend reached its culmination in Boniface VIII's Bull *Unam sanctam* (1302) which stated the temporal and spiritual claims of the papacy in the clearest and most extravagant terms. The object of his criticism was Phillip IV of France, who was in hot dispute with the Pope on the matter of who possessed the right to tax French clergy and on the king's right to pursue a bishop for treason. Despite the *gravitas* of the papal utterance against the French king, which called him to complete submission and pointed to the universal authority of the Roman pontiff even in the secular realm, the Pope himself was seized by a band of ruffians acting on behalf of the French king. Although he was recaptured, Boniface VIII died of shock soon afterwards.

The fourteenth century therefore began with an explosive disjunction between the claims of the papacy to universal authority and its actual fragility in the face of French royal power. Within a few years of the *Unam sanctam* débâcle, a French pope had moved the papal residence to Avignon in southern France, where it was to remain in its 'Babylonian Exile' until the last quarter of the century. Worse things, however, were in store. In 1377 Clement XI was persuaded, by St Catherine of Sienna among others, to move back to Rome. After his death and the election of Urban VI to succeed him, a schism was formed within the church as a rival Pope, Clement VII, was set up in Avignon with the backing of the French king. This parlous state of affairs was to endure for decades, as two (and eventually three) papal lines were created, and it precipitated an unprecedented constitutional crisis within the church whose effects were to last until well into the fifteenth century.

Partially as a result of this weakness within the institutions, and partly, no doubt, as a result of the perceived avarice of the papacy and curia, who employed more sophisticated and effective schemes for raising revenue to fund the building of the palace at Avignon and the Pope's Italian wars, the fourteenth century witnessed the first serious challenges to the unity of catholic Christendom. The protests particularly of John Wyclif in England and, in lesser degree, those of Jan Hus in Bohemia seemed to go beyond mere cavilling at the taxation and the politics of the church and to be a critique of its very essence.

Historians are accustomed to use dramatic language when speaking of the fourteenth century. It has been described as 'the age of adversity', 'an age of unrest' and 'not a happy time for humanity'.[9] It is certainly true that the century was marked by the unusually virulent activity of heretical groups, in particular the spiritual Franciscans, whose campaign taxed Pope John XXII's powers in the first decades of the century. They were inspired in part by Joachim of Fiore, whose millenarian vision of a third age, the 'Age of the Holy Spirit' was a rallying point for many of the disaffected elements that existed in the church of the day. A second important heretical group was that of the 'Free Spirit'. They were most influential in the northern European cities, and they appear to have advocated a perpetual state of union with the Godhead which releases the individual from all moral constraint. We shall return to this movement particularly in our discussion of Eckhart and Ruusbroec. The 'Brethren of the Free Spirit', as they were called, gained a good deal of influence among the Beguine communities of Germany and the Low Countries. The latter were an interesting phenomenon, and they, too, were an important factor in the mystical life of northern Europe. Essentially, the Beguines were a women's movement which existed on the margins of church institutional life. Its origins can be traced to the area of Liège, in eastern Belgium, and to the late twelfth century when a considerable number of women, denied entrance to the Premonstratensian and Cistercian Orders, sought to found their own form of the religious life by living in celibacy and in community, although without formal vows. Their desire to earn their own living by gainful employment or mendicancy within the world brought them into direct conflict with the church authorities. Certain of the Beguines (and their male counterparts the Beghards) appear also to have fallen victim in some degree to the pernicious heresy of the 'Free Spirit', probably on account of neglect by their pastors. It was principally against these women that the Council of Vienne pronounced in 1312, seeking to distinguish the devout Beguines from those who followed the Free Spirit heresy. There existed among the Beguines from the earliest days a particularly lively and distinctive spirituality which was frequently, although not always, of a visionary and ecstatic nature. The *béguinages*, or Beguine communities, flourished in the expanding towns of Germany and, above all, in the Low Countries where, in cities such as Ghent and Brussels, they are still to be seen today.[10]

The fourteenth century was also a difficult age of transition in the field of theology. It was a time when 'the search for understanding moved from metaphysics to evidence, and speculation from an independent world of abstractions to concrete meanings in the real world'.[11] Thus the great syntheses of the thirteenth century, the *Summae* of St Bonaventure or St Thomas Aquinas, were replaced by the more sceptical

and austere spirit of the Nominalists. It was a time of controversy when the major positions had been laid out, Realist and
Nominalist, Thomist and Scotist, Dominican and Franciscan,
and free theological debate was often reduced to narrow-
minded, party-political bickering.

There was much therefore in the debilitated state of the
institutional church as a whole which was likely to foster a
more internal and individual spirituality, which mysticism
represents. There had always been problems, of course, and
the fourteenth century was no exception with the long war
between England and France and its agonized experience of
the Black Death, which was at its height around 1348 and
1349. The Great Plague sent tremors throughout all levels of
society, and had catastrophic effects in many parts of Europe.
It created the Flagellant groups whose turbulent passage
could be witnessed in the fields and cities of Europe. What
was distinctive during this period, however, particularly in
its later stages, was the conspicuous failure of the religious
orders to foster and give institutional form to the deeper
stirrings of men's souls. The only religious Order to expand
significantly during the course of the fourteenth century were
the Carthusians. As one scholar has observed, although
'simony, pluralism, immorality, greed, injustice' all existed,
what was exceptional in the fourteenth-century church was
the 'absence of a countervailing spirituality'.[12]

2

Meister Eckhart

Mystical writers, especially medieval ones, are notorious for leaving scant, if any, information to posterity regarding the circumstances of their lives. We are therefore fortunate in being comparatively well-informed on the salient details of Eckhart's life. The bare fact that such information is recoverable is in itself significant, and is an indication of Eckhart's standing within the society of his day, and the degree to which he influenced it. Nevertheless a good deal of what is generally written about Eckhart rests as much on guesswork as evidence.[1] We do not know for instance when Eckhart was born, although the year 1260 would make sense in the light of his later career. One manuscript refers to him as 'Eckhart of Hochheim', and indeed two villages of that name existed in the central German province of Thuringia (now in East Germany), one near Erfurt and the other near Gotha. It is not known which Hochheim is meant, nor whether Eckhart really belonged to the local nobility, as has been claimed. But it is likely that Eckhart entered the distinguished local Dominican priory of Erfurt in or around his fifteenth year and that it was at the *studium particolare* there that he received his initial education in the *artes*. Alternatively, it has been suggested that he went to Paris for his early education, and that he studied under the controversial Siger of Brabant. This is not impossible as two students from each province were permitted to do their early training in Paris, but it must be said that there is no evidence at all that this was the case. It is likely, although not certain, that Eckhart received the first stage of his higher education at the Dominican *studium generale* in Cologne. Established in 1248, this centre had become famous under the leadership of St Albert the Great, who had been St Thomas Aquinas's teacher and had made an outstanding contribution to the early reception of Aristotelian texts. Albert died in 1280 at the age of eighty, in the same year in which Eckhart, following a five year study of the arts, would have arrived there.

A manuscript from 1294 contains evidence that Eckhart was in Paris in that year as a reader of Peter Lombard's *Sentences*.[2] He would have been part of the convent of St Jacques which housed the Dominican students at the university. Ecclesiastical offices soon followed, and Eckhart was made Vicar of Thuringia and Prior of Erfurt, his home community. It is to this period that his *Commentary on the Lord's Prayer* (*Super Oratione Dominica*) belongs, and the splendid *Talks of Instruction* (*Rede der underscheidunge*), in which he provided spiritual nourishment for his brethren during their communal meals. Towards 1300 he was in Paris again for more advanced studies and, in 1302, he received the title of Master of Theology. The fact that it was granted him by papal decree indicates that he must have been involved in the controversy surrounding the allegiance of the friars to the University of Paris around the year 1303, as was the distinguished Franciscan thinker from Roxboroughshire, Duns Scotus. His departure from Paris at this time may also have been the result of the general expulsion of religious who refused to side with the French King, Philip the Fair, in his conflict with the Pope.

At the beginning of the fourteenth century the success and growth of the Dominican Order led to the division of provinces. Teutonia, the massive German province, was subdivided and a new province of Saxony created, of which Meister Eckhart in 1304 was given overall charge. In 1307 he was also made Vicar General of the province of Bohemia. It should be noted that the peculiarly democratic system of election to office in the Dominican Order meant that not only Eckhart's superiors wished him to take responsibility, but also those he was to govern. The status of his position is also important for an evaluation of his character. Saxony stretched from the Netherlands to Prague, and it contained some forty-seven monasteries and some nine large convents for women. The pastoral and organizational responsibilities were immense. Eckhart appears to have accomplished his duties successfully, for the appointment to Bohemia in 1307 was primarily in order to undertake the difficult reforms required in the area. In 1310 the Province of Teutonia attempted to poach Eckhart from Saxony but was overruled by the General Chapter who, in the following year, sent their leading theologian back to the Dominican chair in Paris, a distinction Eckhart shared only with St Thomas Aquinas. During his previous period at the university he had acquitted himself well in a debate with Gonsalvus of Valvoa, who was to become General of the Franciscan Order, defending the Thomist, Dominican position of the primacy of intellect over will, and his return to Paris suggests that the Dominican authorities wished to use him as a key part of their campaign against the increasing influence of Duns Scotus and his Franciscan school. During this final sojourn at Paris, of no more than some two years, it is likely that Eckhart began his commentary on the Bible which he was to continue later in Strasbourg and Cologne. From Paris he went to Strasbourg, possibly to serve as Vicar General there with pastoral responsibility for the many women's convents of southern Germany. He finally returned to Cologne, in 1324, where he must have taken over direction of its Dominican *studium generale*, continuing the practice of spiritual direction among convent communities. It was also in Cologne that he wrote the greater part of his works.

The successive posts, spiritual and administrative, which Eckhart was given during his lifetime, and which represent a high degree of responsibility, suggest that he was well-integrated into his Order and that he held a position of considerable respect within it. This is an important point to bear in mind as we consider the accusations of heresy which were made against him by the Franciscan Henry of Virneburg, Archbishop of Cologne, who was currently involved in an active inquisitorial campaign against the Beghards of that city. The first sign of trouble was a successful defence Eckhart made in 1326 of propositions removed from his early work, the *Liber Benedictus*, in a document which has not survived. His accuser on this occasion was Nicholas of Strasbourg, who was a Dominican appointed by Pope John XXII to remedy abuses in the German Province. Nicholas was the *lector* in the *studium generale* at the time, and was therefore Eckhart's immediate subordinate. One scholar has percipiently suggested that this may have been a strategic manoeuvre with the purpose of preempting a more serious move against Eckhart by the Archbishop, who throughout the whole affair displayed an unfailing and ruthless animosity towards him. Nicholas of Strasbourg found Eckhart's works to be thoroughly orthodox.[3] But if this was indeed such a manoeuvre, then it failed in its aim. In the summer of 1326, Henry of Virneburg instigated inquisitorial proceedings against Eckhart and appointed two commissioners to investigate his case: Reinerius Frisco, a cathedral canon, and Petrus de Estate, a member of the Franciscan Order. The Archbishop's lack of objectivity and determination to inflict the maximum possible damage upon the distinguished Dominican teacher can be judged from his recourse to the machinery of the Inquisition, very different from the scrutiny applied to the work of theologians such as St Thomas Aquinas and Siger of Brabant (or even William of Ockham, who was a determined opponent of Pope John XXII), and from the fact that the interests of the Franciscan Order, keenly opposed in the prevailing atmosphere of controversy to those of the Dominicans, were well represented on the investigating commission. With good reason, Eckhart was to retort that no Dominican, whether learned or not, had ever been accused of heresy before. The injustice was compounded by the commission's acceptance of the testimony of two fugitive Dominicans, Hermann de Summo and Wilhelm von Nidecken. Both of these men were notorious trouble-makers and perjurers. Nicholas of Strasbourg instigated proceedings against Hermann of Summo, who fled to Avignon where he was arrested. Wilhelm, similarly, intended flight to Avignon but was arrested before he could leave Cologne. The Archbishop, in response, initiated proceedings against Nicholas of Strasbourg himself, the papal representative in the German Province, on account of 'obstructing the enquiries of the Inquisition'.

The first list of forty-nine suspect propositions was drawn

up in September 1326, including 15 from the *Liber Benedictus*, 6 from Eckhart's lost defence of it, 12 from the commentaries on Genesis and Exodus, and 16 from the sermons. This list was quickly followed by another which consisted of fifty-nine propositions, all taken from the German sermons. In the same year, in his *Defence*, Eckhart convincingly contested the compilation of the list, defending certain of the propositions, stating that others were reproduced inaccurately, and protesting his complete adherence to the teachings of the church. He also contested his detractors' competence, pointing out that he was, as a Dominican, outside their juris-diction. On 13 February 1327 a second defence was read out in Latin in Cologne by his fellow Dominican, Konrad von Halberstadt, with Eckhart himself simultaneously giving a vernacular translation. His defence stressed that heresy was a matter of the will and that he refuted anything in his teaching which could be shown to be wrong or 'heretical'. Three weeks earlier, on 24 January, Eckhart had finally appealed to the Holy See, submitting to its decision in advance.

Eckhart accordingly journeyed to Avignon himself in order to defend his case before a papal commission. This commission, which included the distinguished Cistercian Cardinal Jacques Fournier, who was to become Pope Benedict XII, reduced the number of questionable propositions to twenty-eight, and distinguished between those which showed 'error or the mark of heresy' and those which were neverthe-less capable of orthodox interpretation. The propositions were repeated in Pope John XXII's Bull *In agro dominico* of 27 March 1329. Meister Eckhart himself died, sometime between 1327 and 1329 and presumably at Avignon, before this bull was issued.

The condemnation of Eckhart's work and ban on their transmission sent by Pope John XXII to the Archbishop of Cologne in 1329 appears to have had a much greater effect upon the Latin works of Eckhart than upon his German treatises and sermons. The Latin works have survived in only some four major manuscripts, which indicates that they were never widely read and that they cannot be regarded as having been influential.[4] The German works on the other hand have survived in numerous and widespread manuscripts, at least in the areas in which Eckhart himself taught, pointing to their far greater popularity. For the modern reader an acquaintance with the substantial volumes of the Latin works of Meister Eckhart requires a good deal of application, as brief passages of soaring metaphysics alternate with long sections of extremely tedious repetitive argument and fanciful biblical exegesis. In this, of course, Eckhart is merely reflecting the traditions of the medieval schools, with their emphasis on extended argument and the continual quotation of accepted authorities. The subjectivity of his biblical exegesis is no less characteristic of the age; the Christian tradition of understanding scripture as allegory is first fully formulated by Origen in the fourth century and does not yield to a more critical and objective manner of reading, in which there is an attempt to understand biblical texts in the terms of those who wrote them, until the modern period.

The Latin works of Meister Eckhart include an early interpretation of the Lord's Prayer (which draws heavily on St Thomas Aquinas), an opening lecture on Lombard's *Sentences*, a series of five disputations called the *Quaestiones Parisienses*, including a dispute on the primacy of knowledge over the will with the Franciscan Gonsalvus of Valvoa, and a commentary on Lombard's *Sentences*. Some doubt has surrounded the attribution of the latter composition, but it is now generally regarded to be the work of Meister Eckhart during his last visit to Paris. The greater part of Eckhart's Latin works, however, is the 'Tripartite Work', or the *Opus Tripartitum*. As the name suggests, it was conceived in three parts, the first of which, the 'Book of Propositions' (*Opus Propositionum*), was to contain one thousand theses in fourteen sections. The method in the little that Eckhart wrote of this part of his work is that of dialectic, familiar to us from earlier Neoplatonist works, such as the *Elements of Theology* by Proclus, which had been translated from the Greek by William of Moerbecke in 1268. The second section, the 'Book of Questions' (*Opus Quaestionum*), was to contain all the academic disputes which Eckhart wished to preserve, and their order was to follow that employed by St Thomas Aquinas in his *Summa Theologica*. The third part, the 'Book of

Expositions' (*Opus Expositionum*) was to be in two sections, the first containing scriptural commentaries and the second presenting sermons on scripture. We possess only the Prologues from the first two parts of the 'Tripartite Work', and it is from this third part that we possess most material, including commentaries on Genesis, Exodus, Ecclesiasticus, the Book of Wisdom and the Gospel of St John. Of the sermons, some sixty were written or have survived, many of which are drafts of the German sermons and some of which are academic sermons delivered to clerics on days of particular ecclesiastical significance. Eckhart's intention, as stated in the important General Prologue to the 'Tripartite Work' was to mesh the three parts together so that they would form one commanding whole. Thus the first exegesis of the account of creation at the beginning of Genesis would be matched by the first dispute on 'Whether God exists' and the first proposition: 'Being and God are one.'

More uncertainty prevails regarding the authenticity of some of the surviving vernacular pieces in view of the fact in particular that Eckhart himself seems never to have edited them. The *Talks of Instruction* (*Rede der underscheidunge*), however, can be regarded as authentic and is placed between 1294 and 1298, at the beginning of Eckhart's career. It is a singularly powerful work of practical spirituality that was written when Eckhart was head of the Dominican Priory in Erfurt. The great Eckhart editor and scholar Joseph Quint shows a special admiration for it, describing it, despite the early date, as 'the most important and most mature' of Eckhart's German works.[5] We certainly find in it all the uplifting power, balanced rhythms and beauty of language which is characteristic of some of the later works, combined with a certain down-to-earth humility which the later works sometimes lack. The *Liber Benedictus* can be dated to around 1308. It includes two short pieces, the first of which, *The Book of Divine Consolation* (*Daz buoch der goetlichen troestunge*), was written for Queen Agnes of Hungary who was known person- ally to Eckhart and whose father, King Albert I of Habsburg, was murdered in that year. The second piece is *On the Noble Man* (*Von dem edeln menschen*) and it may originally have been a sermon delivered in the presence of Queen Agnes of

Hungary. Here Eckhart shows his philosophical as well as his pastoral side as he explores the many grounds of hope that exist for the Christian faced by suffering. Some doubt has surrounded the authenticity of the treatise *On Detachment* (*Von abgescheidenheit*), which has a rather more programmatic feel to it than Eckhart's other works, but it is now generally regarded as authentic.[6] A considerable number of sermons exist, in over two hundred manuscript sources, and they have survived in the form of *reportationes*, which means that they were copied down by those who heard the sermons, with a greater or lesser degree of accuracy. Around a hundred sermons are believed to be genuine, although not all of these are yet available.

We shall not go far wrong in considering the teaching of Meister Eckhart if we remember at all times that he is that rarest of beasts: a theological mystic, a mystical theologian. Every system of thought, be it theological or secular, is in essence the attempt of one individual to come to terms with their own life-experience. This is true of a St Thomas, a Karl Marx or a Sigmund Freud, although institutional approbation has lent their particular systems the hard sheen of objectivity. We may identify in the nature of their work emphases and points of originality which are an expression of their own personalities and experience. This truth takes on a particular acuity in the case of Eckhart who, it may be safely assumed, enjoyed the experience of mystical union with God and was guided by that experience at every point in the elucidation of his speculative system.[7] Such an experience of the contemplative heights is inevitably challenging, elusive and beyond definition, and it is not surprising therefore that Eckhart's theological system, in comparison with those of his great contemporaries, is shot through with what are apparent contradictions and paradoxes. Most such formulations can be broken down, paraphrased and satisfactorily understood within the terms of his system as a whole, but the fact that a man of Eckhart's scholarly training and stature should appear to contradict himself so frequently must serve as a warning to his reader that the vision which we sense at every turn of his thought, the heart of his work, is not a static but a dynamic one.

One way of coming to an understanding of that vision is by comparing it briefly with that which sustains the work of Eckhart's great *confrère*, St Thomas Aquinas. Inspired by the spirit of Aristotle, Aquinas's world is one supported through divine creation and causality in which the aspects of the real world reflect analogically the existence and the nature of the Divinity. It is a profound, magisterial and unwavering vision of a creation which leads the reflecting mind of man to worship, to reverence and to the serene knowledge of God. Eckhart too is concerned with knowledge of God, and with the processes of intellection. But in his case, such knowledge is primarily possible because God has implanted within his creature something that is *of his essence*, a facility to progress beyond the creature through understanding, a capacity to penetrate the veil of the created world, of God himself as Creator and apex of being, and to reach the very heart of the Godhead: the divine 'ground' or 'waste', beyond name and conception. Eckhart's vision is clearly anything other than the serene understanding of Aquinas; it is a thrusting, dynamic force which seeks to peel away dimensions of illusion or phenomenal knowledge in order to grasp deeper truths. It is a soaring vision which seeks to draw the listeners in its train, bringing them through paradox to sudden points of spiritual understanding. Eckhart's vision is essentially a Platonic one in that it does not rest content with recognizing the presence of God and his laws in the created universe but seeks to transcend that universe through a faculty within the soul itself and to penetrate to levels of greater, more profound reality.

It is scarcely surprising that Eckhart's work has almost always been associated with controversy and that he has himself been surrounded by an aura of legend and mystery. So varied are the approaches to Eckhart, in fact, that they have themselves become the subject of a scholarly study.[8] It was the German works which were rediscovered first, in the middle of the nineteenth century by the Viennese scholar Franz Pfeiffer (1857), a Protestant liberal who published a ground-breaking though incomplete and, by modern standards, inadequate edition of the sermons and treatises. It is true to say that the Protestant response to Eckhart was one of great interest, although he had intially been seen as a purveyor of a crude pantheism (Schmidt, 1839). Protestant commentators have in general stressed his speculative and Germanic character, although his piety and emphasis on purity of intention rather than works has led to a view of him as precursor of the Reformation. J. Bach (1864), writing in an intellectual climate dominated by Hegelian Idealism, saw Eckhart as the 'father of German speculation', and C. Ullmann (1866; also F. Daab, 1935; P. Meinhold, 1935 and H. Bornkamm, 1936) presented him as a precursor of Luther. During these years of the Third Reich, this tendency took an extreme form as Eckhart was proclaimed to be the founder of a pure, 'Aryan' theological tradition, free of Jewish, international and Roman influence.[9]

Catholic scholars, on the other hand, have been more concerned with the doctrinal character of Eckhart's thought, with the relationship between his system and other medieval systems, and finally with the question of his orthodoxy. Catholic interest in him began with the work of the distinguished Dominican scholar H. S. Denifle, who published an edition of selections of the Latin works in 1886. Denifle countered the Protestant view of Eckhart as challenger of the *status quo* and precursor of the Reformation by showing the extent to which he reflects contemporary scholastic positions. His view of Eckhart was coloured by his own neo-Thomist convictions, and he initially judged him to be a weak and inconsistent thinker where he deviated from scholastic orthodoxy, although this was a view that evolved and changed.[10] The discovery in the 1920s of the documents relating to the trial of Eckhart quickened interest in the question of Eckhart's catholic orthodoxy and prompted a series of studies which addressed themselves to this issue (Daniels, 1923; Thery, 1926). Some catholic scholars did not seek to scrutinize the papal condemnation but viewed him as an outright heretic (Della Volpe, 1930), whereas others, following Denifle, argued for an understanding of Eckhart's thought as a variant on the orthodox system of St Thomas Aquinas (Karrer, 1926; Koch, 1959). Modern scholarship has been greatly aided by the definitive edition of his Latin and German works, under the oversight of J. Koch (Latin) and J. Quint (German), which began to appear in 1936. The general view of Eckhart today is one that stresses the Platonic aspects of his thought, which distance him from Aquinas, while at the same time arguing for a more orthodox interpretation of the disputed propositions in the light of his complete thought.[11] It is felt that the Avignon commission which found him unorthodox failed to take adequate account of the significance of the twenty-eight condemned propositions within the context of Eckhart's work as a whole, and there is a large measure of agreement among scholars today that, despite some unwise formulations, the theology of Meister Eckhart is fundamentally consonant with the teaching of the Catholic Church.

THE METAPHYSICS

The writers we are viewing in this book cannot really be said to have been philosophers or academic theologians in any strict sense, although their work is full of the sort of philosophical presuppositions which people made in the fourteenth century. The sole exception is Meister Eckhart, with whom we begin, who received a complete academic training and who held professorial office. If we are to tackle his spiritual teaching, which has seized the minds of many since his rediscovery and never more than in the present day, then we must look also at his 'technical' work in which he discusses such issues as confronted his fellow inquirers. Furthermore, if we are to come to an understanding of the pattern of relationship which Eckhart envisaged between man and God, then we must see this within the context of his teaching on the creation and on the relationship between God and his world as a whole.

Creation

Medieval teaching on the creation was a contentious issue, fraught with difficulty and condemnation. Pointing to the eternal existence of God and the necessary dependence of all that is upon God as First Cause, Aristotle had taught that the world, too, exists from eternity. This was a position counter to the Judaeo-Christian tradition that creation was absolute and from nothing: *creatio ex nihilo*. The problem for the Christian philosophers was how to reconcile Aristotle with traditional teaching while preserving his compelling ideas on the logic of causality. Siger of Brabant came extensively under the influence of Aristotle, including his teaching on the existence of the world from eternity, and suffered condemnation for his Aristotelian views in 1277. The belief that the world exists from eternity was therefore taboo, and it is quite typical of Meister Eckhart that he should leap feet first into what was an extremely delicate and sensitive issue.

The first three propositions from the work of Eckhart which were condemned in *In agro dominico* concern his doctrine of the creation. It was stated that Eckhart indeed taught the Aristotelian heresy that the world had existed from all eternity. Modern research however is adamant that in the condemned propositions Eckhart is doing no more than restating in his characteristically provocative way what is in essence the orthodox Christian view of the creation.[12] Eckhart's point is that we cannot speak of a creation in time. We cannot do so for that would imply that time existed before the creation. Time, Eckhart argues, belongs not to God, who dwells in all eternity, but is part and parcel of the created world. It is therefore absurd to speak of creation in time, as if time were something which could preexist the creation (LW, I, 190f). Rather, creation is something which happens from eternity, for God the Creator dwells in eternity, the Son is begotten from eternity by the Father, and in the Son there is contained in blueprint all that is to be. In this latter point Eckhart is following St Augustine, who taught that all things exist conceptually, as 'seminal ideas' (*rationes seminales*), in the Son, and only later are they fully realized. The eternity moreover in which God dwells and in which he creates is, according to Eckhart, a perpetual *now*, in which neither past nor future exists, and it is from this *now* that God creates the world, in an eternal act of creation (ibid.).

Creation therefore for Eckhart is eternal and is from eternity, for God, who is eternal, cannot act in any other way. This does not mean to say that Eckhart believed that the object of creation, the world, had existed from all eternity (which would be contrary to the orthodox Chrisitian teaching, and which view he specifically denied in his *Defence*); rather he sees the whole matter from God's point of view. As such Eckhart is closely following St Augustine and St Albert the Great, both of whom taught that God's creation was outside time.

We immediately encounter something in Eckhart's teaching therefore, even in his view of the creation, which is characteristic of his thinking throughout. Theologians generally speak of the relationship between God and his creation from the point of view of the created; Eckhart however chooses to view the matter from the point of view of the Creator. In so doing he is following a trend which is more typical of the Christian mystical tradition than the Christian philosophical one, and it is this which leads to what German scholars have called the *Perspektivenwechsel*, or constant fluctuation of perspective, which we find in his work.

Eckhart strikes a more orthodox and uncontentious note when, speaking of the dependence of the creature upon God for its existence, he says that we receive our being 'not only from God, but directly from him, without any mediation' (LW, I, 173). Further, it is the presence of God, as being, which maintains his creation in existence; without him we are 'nothing' (DW, I, 70). Here Eckhart is standing squarely in the tradition of God as Fount or First Cause of being, as we find in the school of Chartres, for instance, or in adapted form in St Thomas Aquinas. It is God, finally, who calls us from nothingness into being:

> Therefore God created all things not in such a way that they existed outside him or beside him or beyond him in the manner of artifacts, but he called them from nothingness, that is from non-being, into being which they find and receive and possess in him. For he is being. (LW, I, 162)

Eckhart shows a strong sense of the creative power of God and he speaks in a strikingly beautiful passage from his commentary on the Book of Exodus of the creative life engendered within the Trinity itself through a process of self-reflection:

> The repetition of 'I am who I am' shows the purity of the affirmation of God to the exclusion of all negation. It shows also a kind of self-reflexion of being upon itself, a dwelling or settling within itself; it shows even a rising up, or self-generation – being seething within itself, flooding and simmering in and upon itself; it is light which shines in and upon itself, which penetrates itself entirely and which floods and radiates back into itself from all sides . . . for life means a kind of overflowing, in which something swells within itself, first pervading itself utterly, every particle, before spilling out, overflowing. That is why the emanation of the Persons in the Godhead is the basis of the creation, and precedes it. (LW, II, 21ff)

Being

We live in a world of perceptible objects and, following the practice of the Middle Ages, Eckhart ascribed to every specific entity the quality of being. Each entity possesses being 'from and in its wholeness', and it is this quality of being which permits us to distinguish between one thing and another; it is 'the principle of distinction' (LW, I, 177). Now we possess being in a twofold form, which is to say that we have being 'in our own form' (LW, I, 238), our specific individuality, and secondly we possess being through the *idea* of ourselves as it exists in God the Son, 'through whom all things were created' and who is 'the model and ideal pattern of all things' (LW, I, 188f). Here Eckhart is again alluding to the 'seminal ideas' of St Augustine. Eckhart defines such an 'idea' as 'the what of a thing and the why of all its properties' (LW, I, 187). In our individual, concrete being we are vulnerable and subject to impermanence and cessation, whereas the being we possess from the 'idea' of ourselves in God is unchanging and eternal.

The idea that we possess a kind of being which is beyond that of our everyday existence and that this being is lodged within the Deity itself is to be of great importance in Eckhart's spiritual teaching. Just as the inner life of the Trinity which he describes in the passage quoted above is a dynamic one, so too is the creation itself dynamic. The world flows back into the Godhead through an act of what the Neoplatonist Plotinus called *epistrophe*, or 'return'. For Eckhart the possibility exists for us to transcend our own temporal natures and to return to our eternal being within God himself. The temporal being that we possess is for Eckhart a fragile thing. It is something we 'have' or 'possess': it is a gift to us, and like all gifts it may at any stage be taken away again. We have being, but we do not possess it 'a se ipso', which is to say 'on our own account', but as we have seen above, it comes to us 'from God and from Him alone' (LW, I, 132).

In many ways Meister Eckhart's own point of departure is being itself, and he pronounces on it with great clarity. At the same time however it is in this area that we must be most on our guard for that 'shift in perspective' mentioned above. Despite the lucidity of some of the statements we have quoted, there are other occasions when Eckhart appears to say things which are clean contrary to the view outlined above. For instance, at first it seems that we *possess* being whereas God *is* being, but then we encounter the formulation that 'God alone truly exists' ('solus deus proprie est', LW, I, 132). And then, in the German works, we find the view repeated many times that we, God's creatures, are 'pure nothingness' (DW, I, 69f; DW, I, 185), and that we have no existence of our own at all. Rather than dismissing Eckhart as someone who did not know what he really thought (as was done at one stage in the past), it is important at this point to recall what was said about the *dynamic* character of Eckhart's system. These apparent contradictions on the concept of being reveal the movement which is the heart of Eckhart's method. In essence he has progressed from what is an orthodox statement of scholastic theology, namely that we receive our being from God as his creatures, to a statement which belongs specifically within the Christian mystical tradition. That we have no existence in ourselves is a commonplace of mystical language, and it results from the immediacy of the encounter with the Godhead, who is experienced as the source or place of being. Of course Eckhart is able to find quotations from theologians such as St Jerome and St Anselm in order to support his view, for both state that in a particular sense it can be said that we have no being when compared with the being of God, but Eckhart is alone among theologians when, framing the 'poetry' of the mystic in the language of the scholar, he consistently and emphatically denies being to the creature: 'All creatures are a pure nothingness. I do not say that they are only worth little, or that they are anything at all. They are absolutely *nothing*. Whatever has no being is nothing' (DW, I, 69f).

God and Godhead

We find this same dynamic principle at work when Eckhart speaks of what he understands to be the nature of God. Initially, as we have seen, God is equated with being; Eckhart's 'Book of Propositions', the first section of the 'Tripartite Work', begins with the principle 'God and being are one'. Elsewhere he says that 'being is the essence of God' ('Esse est deus per essentiam', LW, I, 164), that God is 'naked, unveiled being' (LW, IV, 108), and that God's 'truest nature is being' (DW, I, 131). A point of progression arrives when Eckhart, in a disputation entitled 'In God being and understanding are one' from his second period in Paris, argues that if God is the 'cause of being', then he cannot be being itself, and he speaks of the nature of God at this point as 'puritas essendi' (LW, V, 45), which we may translate as the 'purity or essence of being'. In the same piece Eckhart goes on to define the essential nature of God as 'intelligere', which generally means 'to think', 'to know' or 'to understand'. Its meaning here however is more that of 'awareness' or 'consciousness'. In the passage on the Trinity quoted above, we have already seen how Eckhart conceived the dynamic nature of God to result from the fact that he is Being itself in self-reflection. When he declares that the essence of God is *intelligere*, he is systematizing this idea and stressing that God is entirely *in act* in the perpetual activity of self-knowing, self-reflection. His Being is in fact identical with this eternal act of self-knowing; in his exposition of the Book of Genesis Eckhart says that 'the nature of God is intellect, and for him

to be is to understand' ('sibi esse est intelligere', LW, I, 194f).
We find it again in the more dramatic language of the German
sermons, where the sense of intellect as 'self-reflection', 'self-
possession through knowledge', is forcefully underlined:

> Foolish teachers say that God is pure being, but he is as
> far above being as the highest angel is above a gnat. If I
> spoke of God as being, I would be saying something which
> is as untrue as if I said that the sun is pale or black . . .
> When we receive God in being, then we receive him in the
> forecourt in which he dwells. But where is he then in his
> temple, where he appears in holiness? *Intellect* is the temple
> of God. Nowhere does God dwell more truly than in his
> temple. In the words of another master: God is intellect
> which lives in knowledge of itself alone, which remains
> within itself, where nothing has ever touched it, for there
> it is alone in its stillness. In his knowledge of himself, God
> perceives himself in himself. (DW, I, 145f)

The progression then in Eckhart's discussion of the nature of
God is from the idea of God as being, as absolute being, to
an understanding of God as the transcendent cause of being,
and finally as the principle of self-knowing, self-possessing
intellect infinitely above being. This same progression is
expressed in Eckhart's arresting concept of divine nature as
'Godhead' (*gotheit*). He begins by stressing the absolute
distinction between 'God' and 'Godhead': 'God and Godhead
are as far apart from each other as heaven and earth' (Q,
272). 'God' on the one hand is active, for it is he who created
us and who holds us in being, whereas the 'Godhead', on the
other, is beyond all action and is unknowable; it is God as
he is in himself:

> So all creatures speak of 'God'. And why do they not speak
> of the Godhead? All that is in the Godhead is *one*, and we
> cannot speak of it. God is active and does things, while the
> Godhead does nothing, for there is no activity in it, nor
> has it ever sought any activity. (Q, 273)

Eckhart goes further: 'in the ground, the earth, the river, the spring of the Godhead' it may be said of 'God' that he has 'ceased to become' or that he 'unbecomes' ('entwird', ibid.), and elsewhere he speaks of 'God' as something which we, in our ascent into the divine nature, must overcome. Although Eckhart will often use the word 'God' where he might have used 'Godhead' (but not vice versa), it must be said that this is again unwise language which is easily misunderstood. We might think that Eckhart is here speaking, at best, of a distinction within God himself and, at worst, of two Gods, whereas his real intention is to speak of God on the one hand from the point of view of his creatures and, on the other, to speak of God as he is in himself.[13] Indeed Eckhart stresses that unity is the very essence of the divine when he says: 'God alone has unity. Unity is the special characteristic of God; it is on account of his unity that God understands that he is God, and without it God would not be' (DW, I, 368). We would be wrong to think of a *distinction* therefore, but more a *progression* within our own understanding of the Divine. No other single complex of ideas exemplifies so well the character of Eckhart's thought as a journey, a pilgrimage, through an ever changing conceptual landscape into a deepening awareness of the utter transcendence and unknowability of God.

THE HUMAN SOUL

The spark of the soul

The view that the human intellect is a portion of divine life is central to the Neoplatonic tradition. In the *Timaeus* Plato speaks of the 'divine principle' which the Demiurge implanted in man. For Plotinus similarly, *nous* or 'mind' is of divine origin and enjoys a kinship with the nature of the One itself. For St Augustine too it is by virtue of our rationality that we are made in the image of God, and on one occasion he refers to the 'spark of reason' by which man is made 'in the image of God' (*The City of God*, XXII, 24, 2). Generally however the use of the image of the spark to signify something within man which enjoys a special affinity with the Godhead is traced to St Jerome who, in his commentary on Exodus,

spoke of *synderesis*, or the 'spark of conscience' as an innate
orientation within man towards the good. Peter Lombard
took up this term, as did St Thomas Aquinas, and it was the
latter who gave it its classic definition. The concept of a spark
within the soul enjoyed favour also in the Franciscan tradition
where, at the hands of St Bonaventure in particular, it came
to signify the principle of love which is the 'summit of the
soul'.

We find in Eckhart a considerable number of references to
this divine element in the soul, which he calls sometimes the
'fortress' (*bürgelîn*), the 'ground' (*grunt*) or the 'spark' (*fünkelîn*)
of the soul. Sometimes he refers to it in terms very much like
those of St Thomas Aquinas, as an innate and inextinguish-
able inclination to the good, and sometimes he goes beyond
them in stressing the affinity with God which this part of the
human soul possesses:

> . . . the spark of the soul, which is created by God and is
> a light imprinted from above, and is an image of the divine
> nature, which always opposes what is not divine. It is not
> a power or faculty of the soul, as certain teachers suggest,
> and is always inclined to the good; even in hell it is inclined
> to the good. (DW, I, 332f)

> The soul receives its being directly from God. Therefore
> God is close to the soul, closer than it is to itself. Therefore
> God is present in the ground of the soul in the whole of his
> divinity. (DW, I, 162)

> See, as he (the Godhead) is unified and One, he enters into
> this Oneness which I call a fortress of the soul . . . The soul
> is like God in that part and in no other. (DW, I, 44)

At other times he wishes to deny it all names, and to suggest
even that it is beyond the created order:

> I have occasionally said that there is a power within the
> soul which can alone be said to be free. Sometimes I have
> called it a refuge of the spirit, sometimes I have said that
> it is a light of the spirit, sometimes I have said that it is a
> spark. But now I say that it is neither this nor that, and

yet still it is a Something which is as high above this and
that as Heaven is above Earth. That is why I now speak
of it in a nobler manner than I have ever done before,
although it mocks all my reverence and the manner of my
speaking of it, and is above such things. It is free of all
names and has no form; it is completely free and solitary,
as God is free and solitary in himself. It is entirely unified
and one, as God is unified and one, so that no one can
enter it. (DW, I, 39ff)

So close to the divine nature does this 'Something' in the soul
become that Eckhart says of it in another sermon that it has
not been created nor ever could be: 'I have occasionally
spoken of a light in the soul, which is uncreated and uncreatable' (Q, 315). Here Eckhart is striking a distinctly pantheistic note, by effacing the distinction between Creator and
created, and indeed this statement was included among the
condemned propositions. Elsewhere he appears to be
amending the boldness of this particular formulation, in terms
which recall the conciliatory language of his *Defence:*

There is a faculty or power within the soul of which I have
frequently spoken. Were the soul composed entirely of this,
then it would be uncreated and uncreatable. But this is not
the case. For the rest of the soul is dependent upon time,
and thus is touched by createdness and is itself created.
(DW, I, 220)

Whether Eckhart speaks of this divine spark in terms of likeness, analogical affinity or indeed identity with God, he
stresses that it is only by virtue of its presence within us that
we are able to know God:

When God is at work in the soul, everything in the soul
which is contrary to his nature is purified and cast out in
the heat of the flame. Truly! The soul enters God more
truly than any food enters into us. We can go even further
and say that the soul is transformed into God. There is a
power within the soul which cuts away whatever is coarse,
and becomes united with God. That is the spark of the

soul. My soul becomes even more closely united with God than the food that I eat does with my body. (DW, I, 331)

This 'spark' or 'something in the soul' Eckhart defines in one sermon as intellect or reason (*vernunft*). In doing so, and in stressing its likeness to God, he is recalling his central theological idea of God as *intelligere*, as 'thought', 'awareness' or 'understanding': 'The spark of reason, which is the head of the soul, which is to say the "man" of the soul, is something like a spark of divine nature and a divine light, a ray and an imprinted image of divine nature' (DW, II, 211). Indeed this element within us has further characteristics which liken it to the Godhead: 'God, who has no name – who is beyond names – is inexpressible, and the soul in its ground is also inexpressible, as he is inexpressible' (Q, 229f). Most importantly it possesses the quality of divine unity and transcends the dimension of created images and things:

> There is no truth where the soul possesses only its natural and created being. I say that there is something which stands above the created nature of the soul. But some clerics cannot understand that there is something which is so akin to God and so unified. It has nothing in common with anything at all. Everything created is a nothingness, but for this thing all that has been and all that could be created is alien and remote. It is One in itself, and receives nothing from anything beyond itself. (DW, II, 88)

> There is something which is above the created being of the soul and which is untouched by any createdness, which is to say *nothingness*. It is something which even the angels do not have, although theirs is a pure being, undiluted and deep. Even that does not touch it. It is akin to the divine nature, it is united in itself, it has nothing in common with anything at all. This is where some clerics stumble. It is a strange land and a desert, and it is more without name than nameable, more unknown than knowable. (DW, II, 66)

By entering into this special place within himself, the individual can ascend into the Godhead, passing all created images and things:

> I have spoken of a power in the soul. In its first outreach it doesn't grasp God in so far as he is good, nor does it grasp God in so far as he is truth. It penetrates further, to the ground of God and then further still until it grasps God in his unity and in his desert. It grasps God in his wilderness and in his own ground. Therefore it does not rest content with anything but seeks further for what God is in his divinity and in his own nature. (DW, I, 171f)

> Whenever this power sees something which is an image, be it the image of an angel or the image of itself, then it does not yet see perfectly. Even if it sees God or how he is an image or a trinity, then it does not see perfectly. But when all images have departed from the soul and it sees single Unity, then the pure being of the soul, passive and resting within itself, encounters the pure formless being of Divine Unity, which is being beyond being. O wonder of wonders! What noble passivity it is when the being of the soul perceives nothing but the pure Unity of God. (DW, III, 437f)

Moreover part of this journey involves a point of 'breakthrough', which leads to a transcendence even of the God of the creatures:

> The teachers say that two powers flow from the highest point of the soul. The one is called the will and the other reason. The highest perfection of these two lies in the highest power, which is called reason. Reason can never rest. It does not seek God in so far as he is the Holy Spirit, nor in so far as he is the Son: it flees the Son. Nor does it desire God in so far as he is God. Why? Because there he still has a name. And even if there were a thousand Gods, it would break through continuously, for it desires him where he has no name. It desires something better, something nobler than God, in so far as he has a name. What does it desire then? It does not know: it desires him as

Father. Therefore St Philip says: 'Lord, show us the Father, then we will be satisfied!' (John 14:8). It desires him where he is a place from which goodness springs; it desires him where he is a seed from which goodness flows; it desires him where he is a root, a vein, in which goodness springs forth. And only there is he Father. (DW, II, 31f)

Now see! So unified and simple is this 'fortress' in the soul, which I have in mind and of which I am speaking, beyond all manner, that that noble power of which I have spoken is not worthy to penetrate this fortress even once for a single moment, and also that other power of which I have spoken, in which God glimmers and burns with all his wealth and with all his bliss, that too does not dare enter the fortress. So simple and unified is the fortress and so beyond all manner and all powers that no power or manner, not even God, can ever find its way into it. In truth: God himself cannot enter there even for a moment, and never has entered, in so far as he exists in the manner and nature of his Persons. This is easy to understand for this Oneness has no manner and no nature. And therefore, if God is to enter there, then it will cost him all his divine names and the nature of his Persons; he must leave them outside its walls, if he wishes to enter inside. Rather, as he is in himself One, beyond all manner and nature, he is neither Father nor Son nor Holy Spirit in this sense, and yet he is Something, which is neither this nor that.

See, he can enter this Oneness, which I have called the fortress of the soul, as he is himself One and Unified, and in no other way. (DW, I, 42ff)

In passages such as this, we cannot fail to gain the impression that Eckhart has all but divinized the human intellect. He applies to the human mind, in its highest and most inward nature, the apophatic vocabulary that is normally reserved for the Godhead. A central idea underlying this point is Eckhart's belief, to which we have already referred above, that all things in their essential being are contained *in principio* in the Godhead. This is the Augustinian theory of the 'seminal ideas', the blueprints for all things, created with the Son in the

Trinity. In the case of mankind, however, this correspondence with the divine nature enjoys a special intimacy because the nature of God as *intelligere* accords with the cognitive character of our own spiritual essence. Although Eckhart devotes little time to actually developing this idea, it seems nevertheless to provide a context for his theory of the Divine Spark in the soul.

A further, and possibly more important, element in this theory is the influence of a fellow-Dominican, Dietrich von Freiberg. Dietrich developed a complex and sophisticated theory of knowledge which portrays the human intellect as a reflex of the divine mind. He was born around 1250, and as a Paris professor and Provincial of the German Dominican Province of Teutonia, held some of the highest offices of his day.[14] Essentially Dietrich von Freiberg fused the Augustinian *abditum mentis* or 'innermost part of the soul' with the 'active intellect' of the Aristotelian theory of knowledge. This means that Dietrich believed that we are in our most essential nature cognitive beings and that the principle of cognition within us is *wholly active*. It cannot be acted upon in any way by the external world. Echoing in some ways St Augustine, Dietrich believed that in perceiving objects of knowledge the human intellect is essentially *perceiving itself*. All that *is* is contained *in nuce* within the intellect and can be drawn out to form the apparent object of knowledge which, in reality, is the human intellect in encounter with itself. The human mind, therefore, is wholly self-contained, and exists beyond the created dimension of time and space. The human mind, moreover, only *knows* because it participates itself directly in the divine intellect, with which it forms a virtual unity. Here once again Dietrich is speaking from within the Augustinian tradition of illuminationism, whereby the light of human knowledge has its source within the divine Light, but Dietrich has taken this idea much further, pushing it, it must be said, to its furthest limits.

There are of course distinctions to be made between Eckhart's understanding of the intellect and that of Dietrich von Freiberg. And yet, clearly, there is much that they have in common. The peak, or essence, of the human intellect, being wholly *actual* and wholly self-contained, inhabits a dimension beyond time and space, where it enjoys a profound kinship with the mind of God (or, for Eckhart, God in his essence). Dietrich was no mystic however (although his German sermons, much acclaimed by his contemporaries, may have argued otherwise, had they survived), and the works which have come down to us are carefully argued, systematic treatises which shun the rhetorical flourishes so beloved of Eckhart. In comparison with Dietrich, Eckhart appears to be concerned not with abstract theory (which is probably why he gives us so little of it), but solely with a cognitive union with God *as an experience*, one moreover which entirely fills the horizons of our being. Eckhart's concern is specifically with our knowledge of God, and in this he betrays a further Dominican influence, that of St Thomas Aquinas.

In our introduction we touched upon one of the major issues which divided the Dominican and Franciscan Orders during the medieval period: the question of the primacy of love or knowledge. The answer we adopt to this matter will have a considerable influence upon our understanding of the Beatific Vision, our final union with God in heaven. Thomas Aquinas's view on the Beatific Vision was that we possess God in the Beatific Vision not by love and the will but by knowledge, for only in this way, he argued, can we possess him wholly. For Eckhart too our deepest possession of God is by cognition, but, unlike Thomas, he did not reserve this blessed state for the afterlife but believed it to be possible now, and for all people. This is very much the thrust of many of his finest German sermons, and it is one of their features which lends them an undeniable sublimity. This particular understanding of our union with God however throws up certain difficulties. The dominant theories of knowledge throughout the Middle Ages were all influenced by the prin- ciple of *assimilation*, which derives from Aristotle. According to the Greek philosopher, we must in a sense become that which we know; we must be its equal. If we are to know God, then we must become God, or at least be drawn up to his level by grace. Thomas Aquinas's answer to this problem was the concept of the *lumen gloriae*, the 'light of glory', which he believed God would shed upon us in the final vision in order to divinize us and to make himself fully accessible to our

knowledge. Meister Eckhart had no such theory of light, and
needed to find something within us in this life which enjoys
an actual affinity with the Godhead and thus enables us,
along the lines laid down by Thomas, to know God. Dietrich
von Freiberg's theory of the intellect was a powerful force in
the Dominican schools of the late thirteenth and early fourteenth centuries, and it was to this, it appears, that Meister
Eckhart turned.

The birth of god in the soul

If the thoeretical base of Meister Eckhart's teaching is that
of a late medieval, Dominican, Augustinianism conditioned
at certain points by the teaching of St Thomas Aquinas on
the Beatific Vision, then the idiom, flavour and power of
his spirituality is entirely his own. Nothing exemplifies that
spirituality better than Eckhart's teaching on the birth of God
in the soul.

Eckhart uses two distinct images when he speaks of our
union with God. He speaks sometimes of an ascent of the
soul, by reason, beyond the God of the creatures into the
hidden nature of the Godhead itself, and sometimes of a
descent of the Godhead into a hidden place within the human
soul. In each case he is attempting to convey the same sense
of the unity of human kind with God, experienced at a most
profound level. Now the nature of God is to give birth to his
Son:

> The Father gives birth to his Son, and thereby feels such
> delight and peace that it consumes his whole nature. For
> whatever is in God drives him to give birth; indeed, God
> is compelled to give birth by his Ground, his Essence and
> his Being. (DW, II, 263)

> God gives birth to his only begotten Son in you, whether
> you want him to or not, whether you are awake or asleep;
> he fulfils his own nature. (DW, I, 387)

> The Father has no choice but to give birth, the Son has no
> choice but to be born. The Father gives birth to everything
> which he possesses and which he is, the abyss of divine

Being and the divine Nature, in the birth of his Son. (DW,
II, 84)

It is this, the *gotesgeburt* or birth of God in the soul, which
becomes for Eckhart the central image of our union with God,
and it is in the divine 'Something' of the soul that this birth
takes place:

> That power of the soul of which I have spoken and in
> which God is present, blooming and verdant, in the entirety
> of his divinity, and the Spirit in God; in this same power
> the Father gives birth to his only begotten Son as truly as
> he does in himself, for he has true life in this faculty of the
> soul, and the Spirit gives birth with the Father to the same
> only begotten Son and to itself as the same Son and is the
> same Son in this light, and is truth. (Q, 163)

> God is present, active and powerful in all things. But in
> the soul alone is he fruitful, for all creatures are only the
> footprint of God, whereas the soul is by its nature modelled
> in God's image. This image must be ennobled and
> completed by this birth. No creature is responsive to this
> action of God and to this birth but the soul alone. Truly,
> whatever perfection enters the soul, whether it be divine,
> simple light or grace or blessedness, it can only enter the
> soul through this birth and in no other way. If you wait
> for this birth in you, then you will find all goodness and
> all consolation, all bliss, all being and all truth. But if
> you don't, then you will miss also all goodness and all
> blessedness. For it brings you pure being and steadfastness.
> And as for what you seek beyond this, the things that
> perish, seek them how and where you will, for they will
> indeed all perish. Only this gives being, all else passes
> away. And in this birth you will share in the divine infusion
> and in all God's gifts. The creatures, who do not possess
> the image of God, are not responsive to it, for the image of
> the soul belongs especially to this eternal birth, which
> happens specifically in the soul and is completed by the
> Father in the innermost part of the soul beyond all created
> images and faculties. (Q, 425f)

The consequence of this birth of God in the soul is to transform us into the Son. In the Latin works Eckhart speaks of our absorption into the nature of the son *by adoption* ('per adoptionem', LW, III, 101) and says: 'God became man for us in Christ and adopts us as his sons and dwells in us as a father in his sons' (LW, III, 102). In the German sermons however he speaks of our union with the Son in bolder terms, stressing that it is a union *without distinction:*

> The Father gives birth eternally to his Son in his own likeness. 'The Word was with God, and the Word was God': It was the same in the same nature. And I say further: he gave birth to the Word from my soul. Not only is my soul with him and he with it in his likeness, but he is in it; and the Father gives birth to his Son in the soul entirely in the same way as he gives birth to him in eternity. He must do so, whether he wishes to or not. The Father gives birth to his Son without ceasing, and I can say more: he gives birth to me as his Son and as his same Son. Further: Not only does he give birth to me as his Son, but he gives birth to me as himself and himself as me and myself as him and as his nature. In the innermost spring, I spring forth in the Holy Spirit; in that place there is one life, one being and one act. All God's action is one; that is why he gives birth to me as his Son, without distinction. (DW, I, 109f)

So far we have been looking at the speculative aspect of Meister Eckhart's thought, the encounter of the soul with God in its innermost place, and the birth there of the Son. The speculative mysticism of Eckhart is however far from being other-worldly in the negative sense of being dissociated from our everyday lives in the world. On the contrary such a metaphysical process as the 'birth of God in the soul' is one which has the deepest consequences for our daily living. In one passage from the German sermons, Eckhart suggests that there are three things which we require if this birth of God in us is to come to fulfilment and we ourselves are to become the Son:

But that person is truly the Son who does all things from love. The second thing which well serves to turn us into the Son is detachment – that when we are ill, it pleases us just as well as when we are in health. If our friend dies – God's will be done! If we lose an eye – God's will be done! The third thing which a son must have is that he can never rest his head upon anyone but his father. (DW, II, 33f)

He speaks elsewhere of the absence of suffering as a sign that our own will is so absorbed into that of the Father that we have gained true sonship in him:

There are two kinds of birth for human kind: one into the world and one out of it, which means to say a spiritual birth into God. Do you wish to know whether your child is being born in you and whether it is present, that is whether you have been changed into God's Son? As long as you have pain in your heart about something, even concerning sin, your child is not yet born. If you grieve, then you are not yet a mother, but rather you are in labour and close to giving birth. Do not therefore despair, if you grieve on account of yourself or your friend: if the birth has not yet taken place, then it is near at hand. But it is completed when we experience no grief, for then we have the being, the nature, the substance, the wisdom and the joy which are God's possession. Then the same being as that of the Son is ours and is in us, and we enter the same being as God. (DW, III, 325)

In a wonderful passage from another sermon Eckhart gives a further example of the way in which our life is radically changed by the experience of the *gotesgeburt*, the 'birth of God':

When this birth has really happened, then no creature can hinder you any more on your way; rather they all point you to God and to this birth. We can represent this with the image of a flash of lightning. Whatever lightning strikes, be it a tree, an animal or a man, it turns that object immediately towards it. If a man has his back towards the lightning, he turns around in that moment to face it. If a tree has a thousand leaves, they all turn instantly towards the flash. See, it is the same for those who know this birth: they are instantly turned towards it by whatever is present to them, however coarse. Indeed, what was previously an obstacle for you, now comes to your aid. Your face is completely turned towards the birth, in everything which you see or you hear, whatever it may be. You can perceive nothing but this birth in all things so that everything speaks to you of God for you have God alone in your mind's eye. It is like when we look directly into the sun so that wherever we look, we will see the image of the sun. When it is not the case that you seek God in all things and hold him before your mind's eye, then you do not yet know this birth. (Q, 437)

THE SPIRITUAL LIFE

The link between Eckhart's spiritual teaching and his metaphysics is to be found in the concept of 'detachment' (*abgescheidenheit*). This may be summed up as an ego-less form of being in which our normal self-centred concerns are released in a state of profound equanimity and detachment. The full thrust of this concept goes deeper however, and it embraces the sense of non-being which results from our containment in the Godhead, who is beyond being. Thus it is important to understand that when he speaks of detachment, Eckhart has in mind a *state of consciousness beyond the created ego*, and not the ego's struggle to purify itself from selfish attachment to the world. Detachment is the state that comes about in the soul when the powers of the soul are gathered into its own highest point, where it transcends all creatureliness. As such, it is aimed at undercutting the entire principle of the ego and hence, secondarily, all that flows from it.[15]

In the short treatise *On Detachment*, now generally regarded to be by the hand of Eckhart, he states that detachment excels all other virtues for 'all the virtues are in some way connected with creatureliness, whereas detachment is free of all creatures' (DW, V, 401). It transcends even the key Christian virtue of humility, for 'Detachment comes so close to nothingness that there is nothing that can stand between nothingness and it. Therefore perfect detachment cannot exist without humility' (ibid. 405). Indeed detachment is an authentic expression of the creature's own true nature as nothingness:

> Perfect detachment is free of any concern to be below or above any creature. It wants to exist for itself, independent of anyone's wishes, and seeks neither to be like nor unlike any creature, neither to be this nor that. It does not wish to be either this or that because to do so would mean that it wished to be *something*. But detachment wishes to be *nothing*. That is why all things are untouched by it. (ibid. 406)

Eckhart stresses that the nothingness which the creature experiences in detachment is a highly creative state, and is an invitation to God to enter the soul:

> If therefore the heart is to be in a state of preparedness to receive the All Highest, then it must rest in nothingness, and that offers the greatest of all possibilities. Since the *detached* heart is at the highest point, then it must rest in nothingness, for that is where the greatest receptivity exists. Let me draw an analogy from nature: If I wish to write on a wax tablet, then whatever has already been written on it, however noble it might be, prevents me from writing on it, and if I wish to do so then I must first erase whatever is on it. The tablet is never better for writing on than when it is clean. It's exactly the same with God who, if he wishes to write in the highest way on my heart, must first remove everything from my heart, whatever can be called this or that, so that he is left with a *detached* heart. Then God can work within it in the highest way and according to his highest will. (ibid. 425f)

Meister Eckhart was the first Middle High German writer to use the word *abgescheidenheit*, and it is likely that he developed this specific idea of *detachment* as a keynote of his spirituality over a period of time. Such statements as we find above would then represent his maturity, after a lifetime of reflection. But we find a wealth of references to a form of spirituality which is based on the absence of self and on detachment from the phenomenal world in the early *Talks of Instruction*, and in later works where the actual word *abgescheidenheit* is lacking. Towards the beginning of the *Talks of Instruction* he defines the 'free mind' for instance, in these terms:

> A free mind is one which is not deceived by anything and is not bound to anything, it is one which has not bound its best part to any specific manner of devotion and which does not seek itself in anything, living rather in God's will and stripped of itself. (ibid. 190)

Eckhart typically stresses that it is God's intrinsic nature to enter into us when we 'leave ourselves' or practise what he likes to call 'poverty' (*armuot*) or 'poverty of spirit':

> He wants to be entirely our possession. This is what he wills and seeks, and that is why he is as he is. This is the cause of his greatest bliss and joy. And the more he can be our possession, the greater is his bliss and joy, for the more we are in possession of other things, the less we possess him, and the less love we have for all things, the more we receive him, with all that he offers us. Therefore when our Lord wished to speak of the beatitudes, he placed poverty of spirit at their head, and it was the first among them in order to show that all blessedness and perfection has its origin in poverty of spirit. (ibid. 296f)

> I say by the eternal truth that God must pour himself in his whole essence into that person who has emptied himself even to the ground of his own being; he must hold nothing back from his ife, his being, his nature nor from his divinity in its entirety. He must pour all this in a fructifying way into that person who has left themselves for God . . . (Q, 314)

> As far as you depart from all things, thus far, no less and no more, does God enter into you, with all that is his . . . (DW, V, 197)

This self-stripping or denuding of ourselves before God is the very heart of Eckhart's practical spirituality. And it is a process which is very much involved with the will, as can be seen from this quotation, also from the *Talks of Instruction*, which speaks of religious obedience:

> When a person takes leave of their ego in obedience, and strips themselves of themselves, then God must needs enter into them, for when someone does not want anything for themselves, then God must will for them what he wills for himself. When I have placed my own will in the hands of my superior and will nothing for myself, then God must will on my behalf, and if he neglects something for me, then he neglects it also for himself. It is like that in all things: When I do not will anything for myself, then God wills on my behalf. (ibid. 187)

Eckhart stresses that this process is not merely the attuning of the human will to the divine, but a virtual extinguishing of the created human will in the presence of the will of God:

> Now if somebody asked me what is that, a poor man who wants nothing, then I would reply: as long as someone still feels that it is his will to perform the will of Almighty God, then that person still lacks the kind of poverty of which we speak. For this person still possesses their will, with which they wish to satisfy the will of God, and that is not true poverty. For, if we are to have true poverty, then we must be as free of our created will as we were before we possessed it. I say to you in all truth: as long as you have the will to do God's will, and have a desire for God and eternity, you are not yet truly poor. For a person is only truly poor who wills nothing and desires nothing. (ibid. II, 491f)

In fact so complete for Eckhart is this absorption of our will into that of God that he takes the somewhat extraordinary view that the presence of suffering is a sure sign that this process is as yet incomplete:

> If you wish to be free of all distress and pain, then turn

yourself wholly to God. Truly, all suffering follows from your failure to depend upon God alone. (ibid. V, 12)

Truly, if there were a person who suffered for God's sake and for God's sake alone, and if there came upon him all the suffering which mankind has ever known and all that the world knows, then that would cause him no pain and would not weigh upon him, for God would bear the load. (ibid. I, 37)

From this passivity of will there follows a certain quietism, or fatalism. We should not seek to change the way things are, for that suggests that God's will has not yet become our own:

It is good when our will becomes God's will, but it is far better when God's will becomes our will. When your will becomes God's will and you fall ill, then you would not want to become well again against God's will, but you wish that it should be God's will for you to become well again. And when things are going badly, then you wish that it might be God's will for things to improve. On the other hand, if God's will becomes your will and you fall ill – so be it! If your friend dies – so be it! God's will be done! (ibid. II, 9f)

If you are ill and you ask God for health, then health is dearer to you than God. Then he is not your God. He may be the God of Heaven and of Earth, but he is not *your* God. (ibid. 7f)

The acceptance of the way things are, and the detachment which allows one to remain impassive in the face of both suffering and joy is the sign, for Eckhart, of a holy life which is penetrated entirely by the presence of God. It is this theme of equanimity of mind which he discusses in a Latin sermon in two of his most beautiful passages:

The whole of human perfection therefore is to become distant from creatures and free from them, to respond in the same way to all things, not to be broken by adversity nor carried away by prosperity, not to rejoice more in one

thing than in another, not to be frightened or grieved by
one thing more than another . . . and although this may
seem to be a hard and a great thing, it is easily achieved
and is necessary. It is easy in the first place because when
we have tasted of the Spirit, all things are dear to us.
The immensity of the sweetness which God inspires in us
extinguishes all other delights. Secondly, because the true
lover is outside God and beyond him, as if outside being,
all things are a pure nothingness. Thirdly, because the one
who loves God loves him equally in himself and for himself
and has no love for anything else, then all other things will
give him cause to rejoice or not to rejoice equally. (LW,
69f)

Now someone who loves God truly loves him in all things
and receives God, receives all things, as having been willed
by God, whose will is in itself the cause of delight to the
one who loves God. It is as great in one thing as it is in
another, in the least of things as in the greatest, in one as
in all, in evil as in good, in adversity as in success, in things
bitter as in things sweet . . . (ibid. 66)

One consequence of the immense stress which Eckhart lays
upon the interior life in our day-to-day spirituality, upon
intention in our actions, upon what we are rather than what
we do, is that the intrinsic value of good works is questioned
except in as far as these reflect our inner being. The late
Middle Ages liked to emphasize the outer forms of religious
life and practice to a degree intolerable to the modern world,
and here Eckhart is striking an authoritative and much
needed note which will prove to be greatly influential. Nevertheless it would be unfair to say that Eckhart was criticizing
works *as such*, rather he is pointing to their sole justification
in the inner sphere:

People do not need to think so much what they should do,
but rather how they should be. If we are good, then our
works are radiant. If we are just, then our works also are
just. We should not think to found sanctity on doing things,

but rather on a way of being, for works do not sanctify us, rather we sanctify works. (DW, V, 197f)

Many people think that they should do great works in external things, such as fasting, walking barefoot and such like; things which we call penances. But the truest and best penance with which we make the greatest improvement, is when we turn inwardly from all things which are not God and are not divine, but turn wholly towards God in an unshakeable love so that our devotion and our desire for him are great. (ibid. 244f)

If someone has one hundred marks and gives them to God to build a convent, then that is a great thing. But I say that it is a much greater and better thing if someone despises themselves and regards themselves as nothing. (ibid. III, 67f)

Indeed to say a single Ave Maria with this attitude of mind, in which we strip ourselves of ourselves, is more useful than saying the entire psalter a thousand times without this attitude of mind. (ibid. V, 227)

For God does not see what the works are, but only the love, the devotion and the attitude of heart with which they are done. (ibid. 247)

SUMMING UP

As fertile and as controversial as ever, Meister Eckhart remains today a major landmark in the history of Christian spirituality. It might be appropriate to begin an estimation of his work with a glance at the justification for the condemnation of his twenty-eight propositions included in Pope John XXII's Bull *In agro dominico*.[16] We can identify some seven principal areas of dispute in that document. The first of these (propositions 1–3) is Eckhart's teaching on the creation which, in as far as it can be shown to state the co-eternity of the world with God would be heterodox and not authentic Christian teaching. The discussion above shows clearly however that Eckhart's concern with the creation was largely from the Creator's point of view, who stands outside time and who can therefore act only in eternity. In his defence Eckhart specifically denied that he believed in the eternal *existence* of the world (from our point of view), as distinct from its eternal *creation* from God's point of view (BL, 265). While acknowledging the boldness, even rashness of Eckhart's language and its potential to mislead, it can be argued legitimately that the condemnation of Eckhart on this point was the result of a misunderstanding on the part of the commission, itself a consequence either of their failure to place Eckhart's individual pronouncements in the context of his complete work, or of the considerable factional tensions, not least between Dominicans and Franciscans, which exercised the Avignon papacy.

Similar misunderstanding surrounds a second area of difficulty concerning the importance of external works (16–19). We have already seen how Eckhart stressed the *intention* which underlies our actions, and certain of his characteristically hyperbolic statements to this effect, in which it might appear that he is suggesting that works are not necessary in the spiritual life, attracted condemnation (that is, 'God does not specifically call for external works', by which Eckhart clearly meant that God calls for our inner conversion of which works are the natural fruit). A third area of difficulty was that of the identification of the individual believer who experiences the 'birth of God' in his or her soul with the person of Christ himself (10–13, 20–22). In his defence Eckhart withdrew his direct analogy between Eucharistic transubstantiation and the divinization of man, making clear that he thought of the faithful not as 'saviours' of mankind but as 'co-heirs' with Christ (BL, 268). None of Eckhart's statements as to the close union of the believer with Christ exceed the Pauline concept of filiation, or union with the Son.

A fourth area of dispute was Eckhart's view that 'all creatures are a pure nothingness' (26). Ostensibly of course this clashes with the Christian view of the creation whereby things have being from God. The evident meaning of Eckhart's statement however is that when compared with the absolute Being or Nature of God, the being of created things vanishes into nothingness. He himself quoted St Jerome and St Augustine in support of his view, and numerous quotations could be taken from entirely orthodox Christian mystics which express the same idea. It is found even in scripture: 'and my substance is as nothing before you' (Ps. 39:5 Vulgate, 'et substantia mea tamquam nihilum ante te'). Similarly when speaking of the Oneness of God and the absence of distinction within him, Eckhart can be said to be doing no more than stressing the unity of the Godhead (23–25). Further, when Eckhart speaks of God as intellect and of God as being, he is not suggesting distinctions within the Godhead but, as a modern scholar has stated, 'one refers to God in himself; the other to him as creator'.[17]

A sixth area of condemnation was Eckhart's teaching on the existence within the soul of something that is uncreated and uncreatable. Such a view is at first sight pantheistic and erases the distinction between the Creator and the created. He amended this position in the sermons by stating that there was something within the soul which, if it constituted the substance of the soul to the exclusion of all else, would mean that the soul was uncreated and uncreatable. He added that such however was not the case. In his defence Eckhart repeats this argument, stressing that the element to which he refers is intellect, and that if the soul of man were pure intellect, then man would no longer be man. The value of this defence is uncertain, and it is this point in the condemnation which has attracted most scholarly discussion. Koch, for instance, has argued that Eckhart's theory of analogy, according to which all being remains in God, precludes pantheism, and Haas has recently written that the theory of the 'spark of the soul' is only representative of our innate orientation towards God.[18]

In the light of our initial remarks on Eckhart as being fundamentally a mystical theologian, it seems that another approach can be adopted. This is that when Eckhart stresses that the higher or essential intellect is 'uncreated' and 'uncreatable', what he means is that its highest function is beyond the created realm. Eckhart is not putting forward an emanationist theory of the soul as being of the same essence as God; indeed, he shows little explicit interest in such an idea. What he means is simply that there is accessible to the human

person a state of transcendent knowledge, beyond the world
and its temporal and spacial limitations, in which we experience in our deepest interior a sense of oneness with God. That
he should have expressed this belief in the soul's capacity to
experience such a transcendence in the image of an 'uncreated' organ or power within the soul is the result of his
Dominican intellectualist inheritance. Nevertheless this
should not obscure for us the fact that Eckhart is primarily
using the image of the soul's spark in order to articulate what
is a *datum*, experientially given, of his, the mystic's, experience
of God. The 'divine spark', then, and the 'birth of God in the
soul' are images drawn from the Christian tradition which
Eckhart employs in order to embody and convey his own
highest experience of God as divine Nothingness. Although
more obviously theological in form, these images may be
compared in kind with that of the ascent of Mount Carmel,
for instance, with which St John of the Cross expresses his
own spiritual dynamic.

A final area of difficulty was the suggestion that man
through his sins glorifies God. We do not possess the works
from which these condemned quotations were taken. In the
light of the fact that Meister Eckhart may himself never have
edited the extant German sermons, such statements might be
the result of mistakes in the copying down of his words and
therefore not representative of his authentic teaching. Alternatively they may exist in works which have been lost. Although
we cannot find exact statements such as the condemned proposition 'Whoever blasphemes God praises him', there are
passages in the sermons where Eckhart stresses that our will
must become entirely subsumed into God's will. We will then
find it impossible to feel regret for the sins we have committed
in the past, as that would be contrary to the total passivity
which results from the complete union of our will with that
of God. It is possible that passages of this kind, once again
employing extravagant expression, served as the basis for the
condemned propositions (4–9, 14, 15).

It is the consensus view of modern scholarship that the
thought of Meister Eckhart is fundamentally orthodox and
that in the light of the totality of Eckhart's thought and in
the light of his own acceptance of the judgement of the Holy

See prior to the event, the propositions condemned in 1328 do not constitute a substantial threat to Christian orthodoxy. The fact of his condemnation must be explained in part by the failure of his judges to understand the signficance of certain statements in the light of Eckhart's entire ontological theology, in part by their failure to identify the 'poetic' or representational character of certain of his most telling images, the activity of factions hostile to his own religious order and, finally, his own use of extravagant and potentially misleading language, which led him on at least two occasions to moderate his position when challenged as to its orthodoxy. The boldness and vigour of his style was certainly something of which he was himself well aware, as can be seen from his remark in the General Prologue to the *Tripartite Work* that much in what was to follow might appear 'monstruosa, dubiosa aut falsa' but that all would be explained.

Although the daring and lively character of Eckhart's preferred mode of expression remains fresh for us today, and is generally an appealing feature of his work, the modern reader is inclined to wonder why a man of such intelligence took such evident risks in the face above all of the heresies which affected most particularly the areas of northern Europe where Eckhart worked and taught. Eckhart was himself in Paris in the year following the condemnation of the Beguine, Margaret Porette, authoress of the *Mirouer des simples ames anientes*, who was burnt at the stake in 1310 for persistently holding heretical views, views which were not entirely dissimilar to those imputed to Eckhart some twenty years later. Eckhart lodged in the same building as her inquisitor and he cannot have been unaware of her fate.[19] Eckhart was also in Strasbourg during the papal campaign against the Beghards of that city, between 1317 and 1319, and his own Cologne had been in recent years the scene of a vigorous campaign led by Archbishop Henry of Virneburg, Eckhart's own accuser, against the flourishing Beghard communities. We can only speculate on the reasons for this extraordinary fact: perhaps it was a result of his own natural ebullience, or of the immediacy of his vision of God, or perhaps it was in part the result of a certain *hauteur* which is occasionally perceivable in his sermons: the aloofness of a man who possesses abundant knowledge of many and sublime things.

But the chief cause of Eckhart's difficulties with the ecclesiastical authorities must be sought in the influence of the heretical group known as the Brethren of the Free Spirit.[20] They exercised their greatest influence among the Beguines and Beghard communities of Germany, and they believed that the complete union with God which their *perfecti* enjoyed allowed them and their disciples total freedom from moral constraint. Their communities were marked in particular by sexual excesses. They also seem to have denied the incarnation of Christ and the authority of the church. The heresy was particularly strong in Cologne, and it was in fact first described around the year 1270 by Albert the Great, who had founded the Dominican *studium generale* there.

Over a period of several centuries the church viewed the heresy of the Free Spirit to be the most dangerous and pervasive threat of all precisely because it did not seek to erect an alternative church but proved a persistent, though elusive, presence within the no-man's land of the *Béguinages*. There can be no doubt that Meister Eckhart's emphasis on a radical and liberating personal encounter with the Godhead, which appeared to transcend (although not to contradict) the moral and ecclesiastical order, can only have appeared to some to be particularly dangerous language. As we have seen, Henry of Virneburg, who initiated the attack against Eckhart, had been unremittingly and indiscriminately zealous in his assault upon the Beghards of Cologne. Certain tenets of Eckhart's teaching, though innocent enough to us, must have appeared in the eyes of his judges in Avignon to come perilously close to supporting the pervasive heresy of the Free Spirit with which the church believed itself to be at the time locked in mortal combat.

The Bull *In agro dominico* halted the dissemination of the Latin works of Eckhart, but it appears to have had less effect upon the popularity of his German sermons. The reasons for this are not difficult to find. He expressed himself in a gripping style and was capable of producing passages of the greatest spiritual beauty. Above all, Eckhart offered to ordinary people the heights of contemplative experience. He freed the heart of scholastic speculation from its rigid and academic exterior, thus allowing the common folk to feast upon the dramatic and inspiring perspectives of the highest philosophy, and in a language they could understand. In addition to this, Eckhart's message was a simple, pure and basic one, which moved from the heart of Christian experience and piety. In an age which stressed the external and visible aspects of religion, and which took these to new heights of complexity, Eckhart spoke of a spiritual state of mind, a state of *being* which appeared to sum up the Christian experience of the ages. Nor was this dependent upon ecclesiastical intermediaries or complex theories. Eckhart taught his listeners that all we need do is to grasp that before God we are nothing, that God has implanted within us a special element whereby we may come into intimate knowledge of him, and that this unmediated encounter with the highest Godhead is possible for each and every one of us, whatever our position in society and whatever our learning. It was a message which could not fail to move the hearts of many, and that is precisely what it did.

The spirituality of Meister Eckhart represents a tradition rarely encountered within mainstream Christianity. His stress on the cognitive nature of our experience of God *in this life* and the soul's capacity to become united with God through an existential, cognitive act is very different from the vocabulary of a Christian mystical tradition founded upon the love of the creature for his or her Creator and a union with God established by love and by grace. The evidence, as we shall see, is that in general those who came after him failed to understand the thrust of Eckhart's message, although many were inspired by his profound mystical sense of the immediate experience of God and more still (often unwittingly) took up elements of the vocabulary of his mystical theology in order, within their own distinct traditions, to delineate aspects of the inner life. Eckhart left a tradition of self-stripping, of self-reduction to an essence in which the soul enjoys a peculiar intimacy with God, and a stress upon the intention of works rather than their enumeration, which was to prove influential indeed.

His immense emphasis upon cognitive union with God, however, has pushed Meister Eckhart rather to the margins of the Christian tradition, which is one reason perhaps why he has so often been misinterpreted (and still is today). He lends himself perfectly as a bridge figure, and has provided valuable service in the wider ecumenism of dialogue with oriental religions with their innate preference for a spirituality of the mind. This has been the object of several comprehensive studies. Eckhart's theory of the 'nothingness' of creatures, of existential detachment and the passivity of the human will, and his belief in a transcendent intellective state, which can be arrived at instantaneously (an idea particularly congenial to the Zen tradition) have all played their part in this fertile and on-going dialogue.[21]

The study of Eckhart does however raise other fundamental questions. One of these is the extent to which a spirituality of this kind is fully reconcilable with the Christian revelation. At least one modern Catholic theologian has suggested that it is not.[22] Certainly Eckhart rarely refers to the Christian experience of divine love and grace, and we will look in vain in his work for the warmth of the person of Christ. His use of Christian doctrine although fundamentally orthodox sometimes takes on something of the nature of a cypher, a sign which points to something other than itself, rather than mediating what Hans Urs von Balthasar calls the 'form of Christ'. To regard the Eckhartian way as a distillation of the Christian experience is dangerous, and fundamentally contrary to the Christian understanding of the role of the historical Christ in our salvation. Rather, what is required is to draw Eckhartian spirituality into the Christian tradition; to identify its presence above all in Holy Scripture, which must be the normative horizon for all Christian theology. In this way, while the limitations of Eckhart as a systematic Christian theologian can be acknowledged, his extraordinarily profound spirituality can enrich and enlighten.

As we have seen, both the thought and the context of Meister Eckhart are complex phenomena. It is no surprise therefore that not all his disciples understood it and that even in the hands of those who did, it was subtly adapted and changed.

3

Johannes Tauler

We possess as few solid facts about the life of Tauler as we do of his great Dominican predecessor.[1] He was born in Strasbourg around the year 1300, and there is some indication that he may have been from a prosperous family some of whose members were local dignitaries. It is believed that he entered the Dominican Order in Strasbourg when still a youth, perhaps in 1315, and to judge from remarks he makes in the sermons Tauler might have had poor health which prevented him from following the ascetical practices of his brethren. If, in the light of his health, his studies followed the usual course, then he would have spent one year in the novitiate, three years studying logic and two years on the natural sciences, followed by one year studying Lombard's *Sentences*. It is not known whether Tauler then proceeded to the Dominican *studium generale* in Cologne, where he would certainly have enjoyed close association with Eckhart, although he would clearly have come under his influence in earlier years, while Eckhart was prior in Strasbourg. A likely reference in one sermon to Eckhart as 'a noble master' certainly argues for a personal association. It is striking that Tauler never regards himself as being an educated man with a higher degree and, indeed, shows a certain suspicion of learning, a fact which argues against a period of advanced study in his case either in Cologne or in the Dominican house of St Jacques in Paris.

Tauler is likely to have been ordained around the year 1325, and towards 1335 he was active in Strasbourg as a preacher and spiritual director, working among the many Dominican and Beguine houses there. By 1339 however

Tauler's own Order, the Dominicans of that city, became involved in the conflict between Pope John XXII and the Emperor Ludwig of Bavaria. In 1314 Ludwig had crowned himself emperor against his rival Frederick of Austria, whom he defeated in battle in 1322. He did not consult the Pope, whose prerogative it was to crown the emperor as part of the delicate balance of power and influence between church and state. In retaliation the Pope, who had previously been neutral, demanded that Ludwig should submit to him, or face excommunication. Ludwig replied by proclaiming the Pope a heretic on account of his current dispute on poverty with the extreme wing of the Franciscan Order, and by convening a council. In addition Ludwig laid claim to papal possessions in Italy where he eventually had himself crowned emperor and where in 1328 he established a short-lived anti-Pope, Nicolas V. During John XXII's campaign against Ludwig the city of Strasbourg supported the emperor while the Dominicans, after some hesitation, sided with the papacy. The Pope took the extreme and dubious measure of laying an interdict upon those areas which supported the emperor, thus depriving them of all ecclesiastical offices except the ministry to the dying. The Dominicans of Strasbourg, including Tauler, were consequently forced to withdraw to Basle, which had remained faithful to the papal cause.

In the same year of 1339 Tauler appears to have travelled briefly to Cologne, although the purpose of his visit is unknown. He did not return to Strasbourg with his brethren in 1343, but remained for a few years in Basle and visited Cologne again in 1346. Two further journeys, one to Groenendael to visit Ruusbroec and the other to Paris, are disputed. Tauler fell ill in 1360 and, according to one tradition, was cared for by his sister, a Dominican nun. He died on 16 June 1361. His tombstone can be seen in the Lutheran church in Strasbourg situated near the cathedral, which was built on the site of the original Dominican church that was destroyed by fire in 1870.

The details of Tauler's life are admittedly sparse, but we do know that this popular and impressive preacher travelled a good deal, delivering sermons both in communities and public churches, and undertook spiritual direction in a number of places, including Strasbourg, Basle, Cologne and a convent at Medingen, where Margarete Ebner, a particularly gifted woman, was a nun. An extraordinary legend in a work known as *The Book of the Master* speaks of a radical conversion in the mid-point of Tauler's life as a result of a conversation with a saintly layman who was a member of the group known as the *amici Dei*, or *gotesvrunde* ('Friends of God').[2] These were a loose association of devout folk, lay people and clerics, who were inspired in particular by the writings of Eckhart, Tauler and Ruusbroec. Tauler certainly moved in such circles, as can be seen from his frequent references to 'the Friends of God' in his sermons, who are distinguished by their authentic piety. They were widespread as a movement in Alsace, Switzerland, the Lower and Upper Rhine areas and in the Netherlands, focusing particularly on Cologne, Basle and Strasbourg. No credence is given today however to this attractive story of the manner of Tauler's conversion, and the author of *The Book of the Master* is generally believed to be Rulman Merswin, a pious and colourful Strasbourg banker who retired from his professional life in order to devote himself to religion and who came under Tauler's spiritual direction around the year 1347.[3]

A sign of Tauler's humbler status as a scholar is the fact that he appears to have written nothing in Latin, the language of the medieval scholar. What we do possess – some eighty-four sermons – is in German; and clearly these were composed both for the nuns under Tauler's supervision and for congregations of common folk who would have gathered in the great churches of Strasbourg and the surrounding areas to hear the celebrated Dominican preach. None of these however was written down in their present form by Tauler himself; the only writing we have from his own hand is an affectionate letter in which he speaks of the gift of cheese he is sending to Elisabeth Schaeppels and to Margarete Ebner in Medingen. The sermons have survived in the form of transcriptions, known technically as *reportationes*, which were made by persons present. The fact that these are of a consistently high literary quality has been seen by one critic to argue for Tauler's own possible revision of at least a number of such transcriptions.[4]

The sermons of Tauler enjoyed considerable popularity during his own lifetime, and it remained undiminished after his death. One of the signs of his popularity is the rapidity with which works by other authors became attached to his name. From the earliest days his sermons were gathered into single volumes rather than surviving as scattered folios, which had been the case with Eckhart. This corpus of some eighty-four sermons was first printed in Leipzig in 1498, together with the apocryphal *Book of the Master*, and it was reprinted in Augsburg in 1508 (this was the edition which was read by Luther).[5] The identical Basle editions of 1521 and 1522 added forty-two more sermons by Tauler and appended fifty-six further works by other authors. In both these cases the original Low German, that is to say dialect, text was translated into the standard Middle High German, and in both cases a number of sermons were included by Meister Eckhart, three in the former edition and fourteen in the latter. A further edition appeared in Cologne in 1543 under the auspices of the Carthusian monastery there. This was the work of St Peter Canisius, a zealous upholder of the Catholic cause, in which he was clearly eager to defend Tauler's Catholic orthodoxy from the claims of Protestant enthusiasts by excising anything which was open to Protestant interpretation. This edition added another twenty-five texts by Tauler, and it included the very influential, though apocryphal, compilation *The Prophecies of the Enlightened Dr John Tauler*. This was known later as the *Institutiones divinae* or the *Medulla animae* ('The Marrow of the Soul'), four chapters of which appear in the similarly influential *Book of Spiritual Poverty* (see below), which was likewise falsely attributed to Tauler. The industrious Carthusian monk Laurentius Surius, who also translated Ruusbroec and Suso, produced a Latin version of Tauler's works in Cologne in 1548, based on Canisius's edition. It was this version which gained the greatest popularity and was most influential, serving as the basis for further translations into vernacular languages (including German!). This edition, of course, played the important role of presenting a significant number of sermons by Eckhart under Tauler's name; and it was in this edition too that Tauler's thought was transmitted to Spain.[6] It was Surius also who produced the *Exercitia piissima super vitam et passionem Christi* ('The most pious exercises on the life and passion of Christ') mistakenly under the name of Tauler, which was another great success. In 1621 the Protestant publisher Daniel Suder-mann produced in German the *Book of Spiritual Poverty* (under the title *The Imitation of the Poor Life of Christ*) in Frankfurt under Tauler's name, likewise mistakenly. As a consequence of the lively Protestant interest in Tauler, especially as shown by the young Luther, works by Tauler found their way temporarily on to Pope Sixtus V's index of forbidden books during the latter part of the sixteenth century.

Modern critical interest in Tauler can be traced to the mid-nineteenth century, when interest in the whole field of German medieval mysticism began more generally. C. Schmidt and J. W. Preger began the process of discerning what was authentic Tauler in the corpus at this time, but it was not until 1910 that the first tentative critical edition of Tauler's work appeared at the hands of F. Vetter, who was able to use only five manuscripts out of a possible eighty or more. A two-volume edition by A. L. Corin followed in 1924 and 1929.[7] This represented an improvement although it too was inadequate as it was based upon only two manuscripts held in Vienna. Remarkably therefore Tauler still awaits a satisfactory edition of his work, and at the present moment the best edition available is probably the translation into modern German by G. Hofmann, published in 1961.[8] Tauler has been likewise ill-served by English translators who to date have produced only selections of his work.[9]

When Meister Eckhart died in 1328 or 1329 he left to Christendom the inheritance of a sublime and inspiring system of thought. The Eckhartian system however contained elements which the church judged to be heterodox, or likely to be understood in that way. Eckhart himself had held administrative positions of the greatest consequence in his Order and, through his teaching office in particular, not least during the final period at Cologne, must have exercised a direct influence on many of the finest minds from the North European countries. The immediate problem therefore faced by his disciples was how to propagate Eckhart's thought without themselves running the risk of appearing to advocate

dangerous views. Johannes Tauler is justly regarded as being
one of the first to confront this problem and to do so most
successfully. Though we find in his work passages which are
'pure Eckhart' in their feel, Tauler's sermons convey the
picture of an independent and gifted mind who, while holding
to much of the terminology of Eckhartian doctrine, nevertheless added a good deal to it and, in a sense, placed it in a
new context.

METAPHYSICS AND THE SOUL

Tauler, like Eckhart, believes in the immediacy of God's
presence for man. This, for Tauler as for Eckhart, is founded
upon a deep and inexpressible *correspondence* between God and
the human soul. God is present to us in a most actual manner
at the centre of our being. It is striking however that Tauler
avoids the difficult word *selenvünkelîn*, or spark of the soul, to
express this idea, which bears pantheistic undertones, and
prefers the notion of a *bild* or 'image'. Echoing St Augustine,
Tauler believes that there is an image of the Holy Trinity
eternally imprinted on the human heart:

> No one can speak of the nobility of this image, for God is
> in this image, and he himself is the image in a manner that
> transcends the knowledge of the senses. (H.200)

> This image means not only that the soul is made in the
> image of God, but it is the same image that God is in
> himself in his own pure and divine Being; and here, in this
> image, God loves, knows and enjoys himself. God exists,
> dwells and acts in the soul. (H.277)

Tauler even speaks of the likeness of the soul to God in the
profound union which it may enjoy with him but, mindful of
the judges of Avignon, he stresses that this is an appearance
and is the result of divine grace:

> The soul takes on the form and nature of God. Through
> grace it becomes all those things which God is in his own

nature because, by becoming united with God, by sinking into him, it is raised above itself into God. And then it is wholly coloured by God so that if the soul could see itself, it would think that it was itself God. Whoever could see it would see it clothed in God, coloured by him, contained in his nature and manner of Being, all by grace, and such a person would be blessed by this sight, for in this union, which happens not by nature but by grace, man and God are one. (H.277)

Tauler speaks also of Eckhart's *selenvünkelîn*, the soul's spark, but returns to one of its more traditional meanings as the desire for God implanted in the soul by God himself: 'The soul bears within itself a spark . . . whose thirst even God, who can do all things, cannot slake unless it be by the gift to the soul of himself' (H.246). A more important borrowing, for Tauler, is that of the 'ground of the soul' (*grunt der sele* or *selengrunt*) which, for Eckhart, was largely synonymous with the spark or divine element within us. Tauler speaks of it in more general terms, as the highest point of the human soul, that which is closest to God, equating it with the 'concealed abyss' of the soul, 'the hidden domain . . . where the precious image of the Holy Trinity lies hidden, the highest part of the soul' (H.155). Tauler proclaims that he is quoting Augustine when he goes on to speak of the wonderful union with God which takes place in the *grunt*. Augustine did, of course, refer to the *abditum mentis*, the 'abyss of the mind' in his *Confessions*, but Tauler has introduced an apophatic strain here which is essentially Eckhartian. It is worth noting though that added to this is a sense of *devotion* (that is, 'fire of love') and of grace, which are Tauler's injection of a love or desire mysticism into Eckhart's terminology:

St Augustine says of this ground that the soul of man possesses a hidden abyss which has nothing whatever to do with time and this world and which is raised far above the part of us which gives life and movement to our body. The delight of which we have spoken descends into that noble, blissful abyss, into that hidden domain which is its resting place for all eternity. There we become so still, so

true to ourselves, so clear in judgement, so detached and
so inward . . . Our spirit fuses wholly with God, burns in
all things and is drawn into the fire of love which is God
himself according to his essence and his nature. (H.167f)

In the abyss the spirit of man loses itself so utterly that it
is no longer conscious of itself: neither of its words nor its
ways, its impressions or feelings, its knowledge or love, for
everything is pure, undivided God, one inexpressible abyss,
one essence, one spirit. God gives through grace to the
human spirit that which he is by his nature, and unites with
the human spirit his own Being, without name, manner or
form. (H.185)

Elsewhere Tauler again has recourse to Eckhartian language
but this time he applies his own inimitable gift for representing in everyday, recognisable sense-imagery matters of
exceptional conceptual subtlety. The passage quoted below
equals Meister Eckhart at his most sublime:

The faculties of the soul cannot enter this ground, they
cannot approach even within a thousand miles of it. The
sense of space which is revealed in the ground possesses
neither form nor image, nor any manner of being. There
is no here or there in the ground for it is an unfathomable
abyss which hovers freely, unfixed, as waters that lap and
ripple, only in the next instant to disappear into an abyss
so that it seems that there is no water present at all. And
yet, in a moment, there is a rushing noise, and it seems as
if the water wants to submerge everything. So too it is in
this abyss, which is God's dwelling place, where he lives
more truly than in Heaven or in his creatures. Whoever
can enter that place will truly find God and find themselves
united with him, for God will never part from them but
will remain always present. Eternity can be experienced
there and enjoyed, for in the ground of the soul there is
neither past nor future.

In this same passage Tauler develops the idea of the 'ground'
as the dwelling place of God, pointing to its correspondence

with the ground of God himself, and he introduces a further apophatic motif drawn from Eckhart, when he stresses that it transcends all thinking:

> No created light can penetrate this ground, for God alone dwells here. The whole of creation could not fill this abyss, nor reach its innermost depths. It could not satisfy it, for no one can do that but God alone in his infinity. Only the Divine Ground corresponds to this ground of our soul. 'Deep calls upon deep'. If we are attentive to it, then this ground acts upon the faculties of the soul. It seizes and draws the higher and lower powers back to their beginning, their origin, if only we are attentive to it, keep our own company and listen to the precious voice that calls out in the solitude, in this ground, drawing more and more into it. There is such solitude in this wilderness which no thought can ever penetrate. Truly they can't! Of all the rational thoughts which someone might ever have had about the Holy Trinity – and some people are very concerned to think about such things – not a single one can penetrate that solitude. No, certainly not. For this is so inward, so deep within us, beyond time and place. It is wholly simple and without distinction, and whoever manages to enter it will feel as if they had always dwelt there, united with God, although such moments are short. And yet these moments are experienced as if they were an eternity. (H.336f)

Tauler borrows also the image of the *Gotesgeburt*, or 'birth of God in the soul', in order to express the union of God with human kind. As is the case with Eckhart, this birth takes place in the ground of the human soul:

> Truly, in this ground the heavenly Father gives birth to his only begotten Son a hundred times more quickly than is a single moment in our reckoning, and in the sight of eternity. It is always completed anew and in its own inexpressible radiance. If we wish to experience this, then we should turn within ourselves, far beyond the activity of our outer and inner faculties and images and beyond all that has its

origin in the world, and we should sink into and become
one with the ground. Then the power of the Father will
come and call us into himself through his only begotten
Son, and as the Son is born from the Father and returns
to the Father, thus we too are born from the Father in the
Son and return with the Son to the Father and become one
with him. (H.202)

The birth of God in the soul does not enjoy the dominant
position in Tauler's work which it does in Eckhart, and it
is infrequently mentioned. The *grunt* itself however, and its
possession by God, becomes the chief keynote of Tauler's
thought. He alludes to it frequently, so that it becomes principally an image of interiority and of our inmost, most private,
spiritual life. He tells us for instance that God *must* enter the
ground of our soul when it is rightly prepared (H.17), but
that we cannot prepare it ourselves. Rather, Tauler argues
against those who strive to win God through their own ideas
and devotions. Such people, he says, only 'disturb the ground'
and thus prevent God from entering it and working within
it. They are very different from those who understand that
they must yield to God wholly and in all things:

> The difference between these people and the others is that
> they allow God to prepare their ground and do not wish
> to do it themselves.

> But the others, that is the noble ones . . . allow God to
> possess their ground and give themselves entirely to God,
> stripping themselves of all that is their own in all things.
> They keep nothing of themselves in anything, neither in
> works nor in the manner of their devotions, neither in
> activity nor in passivity, neither in joy nor in suffering.
> They accept all things from God in humble fear of him and
> give him themselves in naked poverty of self, in willing
> detachment, and bend humbly before the divine will. They
> are content with whatever God wills in all things, whether
> in peace or in distraction, for they have no thought for
> anything but the will of God in which they find their good
> and their pleasure. (H.37)

The ground is the place within ourselves to which we may withdraw and in which we locate what is best within ourselves and what is closest to God. Thus, Tauler advises us, if we lose a sense of God's presence in our lives, then it is to this that we should turn:

> If we become aware that we have strayed from God, then we should leave all things and go quickly to the Temple, which means to say that we should gather all our faculties in our inner Temple, in our deep ground. When we have fully withdrawn there, then we shall without doubt find God and know him again. (H.59)

Although we do find passages in Tauler where he shows the same *speculative* character as Eckhart, an interest in the nature of the Godhead itself or in the transcendence of all images and distinction, these are untypical. Nor do we find in him the same theology of total union with God, uncompromisingly stated. Tauler seeks to hedge his understanding of mystical union with statements such as 'if the soul could see itself, it would think that it was itself God', and he speaks frequently of grace and of the 'created' entering the 'uncreated'. Most particularly, Tauler introduces a pneumatic theology, a theology of the Holy Spirit, into his teaching of the 'ground'. This serves to emphasize the activity of grace within the human soul and removes the need for the dominant emphasis upon the Son, and our identification with the Son to the exclusion of all distinction, which was one of the causes of Meister Eckhart's difficulties. Tauler writes:

> This turning away from involvement in things in the expec-tation of the Holy Spirit differs from person to person. Some receive the Holy Spirit with their senses in a way that is conceivable to the senses, while others receive him in a much nobler way with their higher powers, with their rational powers and in a rational way which is much above that of the senses. But a third group receive him not only in this way but they also receive him in their hidden abyss, in the secret domain, the ground where the precious image

of the Holy Trinity is concealed, the highest part of the soul. (H.155)

Indeed the Holy Spirit takes on a vital significance in Tauler's thought. It is fitting that in one passage he speaks of the Holy Spirit in an image of the Rhine, that magnificent river which flows through the heart of Tauler's homeland as a great artery, bringing it life. It is a river which in its massiveness caught the imagination of many of Germany's greatest poets, including Goethe, Hölderlin and Heine, and anyone who has stood beside of the Rhine when it is swollen with Alpine snow-melt and in full flood, will well appreciate the force of Tauler's comparison:

> This precious Holy Spirit entered the disciples and all those who were open to him, bringing such wealth, such abundance and superfluity and overflowed them inwardly. It was as if we were to allow the Rhine its way, removing from its path all hindrances. As if it were to break its banks with its mass of flooding waters, roaring and threatening to submerge all things, filling all the valleys and inclines. So too did the Holy Spirit come upon the disciples and all those who were open to him. And so he still does today unceasingly: he fills and floods the grounds of our souls, our hearts and minds, whatever he finds. These he fills with great wealth, graces, love and indescribable gifts. And he fills the valleys and the depths which are opened up to him. (H.170)

THE SPIRITUAL LIFE

Tauler follows Eckhart in basing his teaching on the spiritual life on the concept of *abgescheidenheit* or 'detachment'. He does not follow Eckhart however in envisaging this as an intellective state in which the individual attains in a liberating vision to the realization of a reality which is beyond the created order and which frees the individual from any attachment to the world. Nor does it signify for Tauler a state of complete union with God in which the individual ceases to act and to respond as a created entity in the world. There may be elements of both these principles in Tauler's thinking, but his own emphasis is overwhelmingly in the direction of self-abnegation and self-denial. *Abgescheidenheit* is for Tauler not a matter of sudden spiritual insight, but principally one of long moral purification in which the soul achieves a state of creative passivity before God and enters into its own ground. This switch of emphasis is one of the key areas of distinction between the two men:

> Now what does 'true detachment' mean . . . ? It means that we should turn and detach ourselves from all that is not God alone, that we should examine with the light of reason all our works, words and thoughts to see whether there is not something in the ground of our soul which is other than God and which does not hunger for God in all things, in activity as in passivity. And should we find something which is directed at something other than God, then we should cut it off and cast it out. (H.154)

> If you want to be taken up into God's inmost nature, to be transformed into him, then you must free yourself of yourself, of your nature, your inclinations, your actions, your self-opinion, in short of all the ways in which you have had possession of yourself. For with these it cannot work. Two beings, two entities cannot occupy the same space. If warmth is to enter, then the cold must leave. Is God to find a way in? Then created things and all that is your possession must make a space for him. (H.220f)

Tauler takes from Eckhart other concepts which derive from this all-important idea of detachment. He refers in one place, for instance, to the 'nothingness' of creatures, combining with the idea of our non-existence as creatures before God a sense of our own moral worthlessness: 'he who looks upon his nothingness, his non-being, his helplessness, in him truly the grace of God is born' (H.324). Or, as we find it in a longer passage: 'If you hold your pious actions or exercises to be of importance, then it would be far better if you were to do nothing at all but turn inwards to your own pure nothingness, to your good-for-nothingness, your helplessness' (H.390). The emphasis which Tauler lays upon the nothingness of creatures can be seen from the following quotation, where this idea comes to represent the needful passivity towards God which is the foundation of the spiritual life:

> When God wanted to create all things, there was only Nothingness. From that he made a Something; he made all things from the Nothingness. If God is to work in his own special way, then he requires only that this Nothingness should be present. Nothingness is more suited than anything that is to experiencing the action of God in a passive manner. Do you want always to be open to those things which God can grant his friends and which he can accomplish in them and in their lives? Do you want him to overwhelm you with his gifts? Then struggle above all to understand that in the ground of your soul you are truly *nothing*. For our self-love and our lack of renunciation prevent God from completing his noble work within us. (H.420f)

Coupled with the nothingness of creatures is the Eckhartian notion of spiritual poverty (*armuot*), in which Tauler again plays down the philosophical aspect in favour of the moral dimension:

> We must distinguish between an outer and an inner form of poverty, which is the essence of true poverty. The outer form is not for all people, and not all are called to it. But we are all called to the inner form of poverty, all of us who wish to be friends of God, that is who want God to possess our ground entirely and who want to be possessed by no other thing at all and to possess no other thing except in the way that God intends, that is in poverty of spirit. As St Paul says 'like those who possess nothing and yet have all things', which means that we hold nothing so dear, neither an object nor a friend, neither body nor soul, neither desire nor profit, that we would not gladly give it to God with praise, entirely in the way that he wants, if he should ask it of us. (H.55)

So far we have been looking at the areas of Tauler's spirituality in which his teaching is based at least upon Eckhartian terminology. There are places however where Tauler presents a point of view which contrasts with Eckhart's teaching. So complete had been Eckhart's vision of our union with God, for instance, that suffering had appeared to be quite peripheral to the life of one who had experienced the birth of God in the soul. If we are aware of our own suffering, then this can only signify that our union with God is not yet perfect. There is no trace of this idea in Tauler. Rather, Tauler stresses that suffering is a preparation of our 'ground'; it is through suffering and the acceptance of the suffering that falls to us as being in accordance with God's will that we are purified. It is here also, when speaking of suffering, that Tauler shows his live pastoral concern and his deep understanding of the human heart:

> If you want to become perfect and to achieve the best that you are capable of, then keep these two points in mind. The first is that you should free your inner heart of all created things, including yourself, and that you should control your inner and outer man so that you do not obstruct the work of the Holy Spirit in you. The second is that you should accept difficulties, whatever their cause, be they inner or outer, and whatever their nature, as coming from God and in no other way, for God thereby wishes to make you for himself and to enable you to receive his great gifts, which are supernatural and wonderful and to which you could never attain except by suffering patiently the effects of the enemy and of hostile men. (H.174)

> This is the shortest and most immediate way to the birth of God in the soul . . . Outer suffering often befalls the outer man. Perhaps something is said behind our back or concerning us which seems to us to be unfair, and thus we feel oppressed by the world. But if we can hold our injury within ourselves and allow it to hurt for the sake of God's wounds, neither complaining nor seeking revenge, then our pain will turn to great peace and joy. (H.311)

Here Tauler is speaking of the spiritual value of the suffering which befalls us in our everyday life. Elsewhere, however, he speaks of a distinct form of spiritual suffering which, he believes, belongs to the very essence of the spiritual life. The suffering of which he speaks is the *withdrawal of God* as a stage on the spiritual journey. We have already seen that, for Tauler, our innermost relationship with God is both active and passive. We both 'seek' and 'are sought': we seek God, through devotions and the like, but he no less seeks us, as an active agent, in the depths of our being. In the three-stage division of the spiritual journey which Tauler sets out, God again is the active force who first reveals himself, withdraws and then finally takes up the human soul into himself. This is certainly one of the earliest occurrences in Christian spiritual literature of the idea that God intentionally withdraws from us at a certain stage in our development, so that we may be purified and may come to know him more deeply. It is an idea which proved most influential. It appealed greatly to Luther who identified it with his sense of alienation from God, and it came to its fullest expression in the work of St John of the Cross and his Dark Night of the Soul. Tauler's very real understanding of this acute spiritual suffering is transparently evident in the two extracts quoted below:

I wish now to speak of three degrees of the mystical life which we may know as the lower, the middle and the highest form of that life. The first degree of an inner life of virtue, which leads us directly into the presence of God, occurs when we devote ourselves entirely to the wonderful works of God, the revelations of inexpressible gifts and to the outflow of the hidden goodness of God. This results in a state of mind which we call *iubilatio*, or rejoicing. The second degree is that of spiritual poverty and strange withdrawal of God, who leaves the soul in agony and nakedness. The third degree is the development of a divine life in which the created spirit enjoys union with the uncaused Spirit of God. (H.303)

And then we are so abandoned that we have no further knowledge of God, and we come into such distress that we do not know if we have ever been on the right path, we do not know whether God exists or not, or if we ourselves are alive or dead. And thus there comes upon us such a strange pain that the whole wide world seems to oppress us. We have no more experience or knowledge of God, but all else is abhorrent to us, and so it seems to us that we are caught between two walls, that a sword threatens us from behind and a spear from in front . . . (H.305)

In the light of such passages as those above in which Tauler shows his deep understanding of human suffering, it is scarcely surprising that he possessed a deep devotion to the life and passion of Christ. He refers frequently to the passion, holding it up as a constant model and inspiration for authentic piety:

Now they say this to me: 'Sir, I meditate on the suffering of our Lord every day, how he stood before Pilate, before Herod, how he was flayed at the pillar, I see him in this place and in that.' Let me teach you something concerning this: you should not see your God only as a man but you should see him as the greatest, most powerful and eternal God who created Heaven and Earth with a single word and who can destroy them again; you should see him as beyond all being and knowledge. Now consider that God wished to be broken for his poor creatures and then blush for shame that you, a mere mortal, have ever thought of honour, advantage and vanity. Bend before the cross, from whichever direction it comes, from outside or from within. Bend your proud mind before the Saviour's crown of thorns, and follow your crucified God with a humbled spirit, in true abnegation of yourself, both inner and outer, for your great God was broken, condemned and crucified by his own creatures and suffered death. In the same way you should suffer patiently and in all humility imitate his suffering and unite yourself with him. (H.392f)

SACRAMENTAL LIFE AND THE CHURCH

Tauler is at one with Meister Eckhart in his repeated mistrust
of the value of external works as compared with the inner life
of the spirit. He stresses that the value of outer works can
only derive from the extent to which they foster an inner
commitment to God:

> Just as a modest penny is insignificant when compared
> with a hundred thousand gold florins, in the same way
> external prayer is insignificant when compared with true
> union with God, which is the sinking of the created spirit
> into the uncreated Spirit of God and its fusion with him.
> (H.101)

In fact it is frequently characteristic of those whose 'ground'
is given to God that they are frustrated in their desire to
perform outer works of penance. God himself intervenes so
that they are called to turn to him inwardly, without recourse
to ascetical practice. Here once again Tauler shows his acute
understanding of human ways:

> Those however who are God's true witnesses rely upon
> God in the good and the bad and they rely stoutly upon
> his will, whether he gives to them or takes from them. They
> do not hold to their own intentions. And so if they think
> that they can perform great things and begin to count upon
> that, then God will frequently shatter whatever it is that
> they do because he means well with them, and thus things
> frequently happen which were not desired. If we wish to
> stay awake in vigil, then we must sleep against our will, if
> we wish to fast, we must eat, if we wish to remain in silence
> and in peace, then things happen quite differently. Thus
> every form of fixity is broken, and we are turned back
> upon our own nothingness, and are dependent upon God,
> acknowledging him in simple, humble faith and renouncing
> all fixity. (H.146f)

In an age which suffered not from a lack of penitential
consciousness and practice, but from its excess, Tauler is

outspoken against those who attribute exaggerated importance to their feats of penance:

> But there exists also a form of inner Pharisaism. In whatever they do, Pharisaic people think only of themselves. This is true also of some religious who think that they stand well with God. But if we examine their work rightly, we see that they love only themselves and think in essence only of themselves, whether it is a question of prayer or of anything else. But they are not aware of this . . . Such people do many works which appear to be great ones; they make a dash for every indulgence, they pray and beat their breasts, contemplate the fine pictures in the churches, drop to their knees and run from one church to the next in the town. And for God it is all in vain, for their hearts and minds are not turned to him. They are turned rather to creatures, for it is there that they find their pleasure, their well-being or comfort, their desire or profit, within or without. That is not the meaning of the commandment that we should love God with all our heart, with all our soul and with all our mind. And that is why God takes no notice of any of this. (H.397)

The distinction between the true church, who are the authentic followers of Christ, and the false Christians who develop a selfish involvement in their ascetical acts or intellectual accomplishments becomes a dominant theme in Tauler's sermons to which he returns time and again. It is a characteristic of these false Christians that they attack the true followers of Christ, who Tauler calls the 'Friends of God' (*gotesvrunde*):

> But there is an external feature which distinguishes them from the true friends of God: they like to stand in judgement on other people and the friends of God. But they do not judge themselves; whereas the true friends of God judge no one but themselves. (H.71)

When we speak of the 'scribes', we mean those intellectual people who apply their judgement to all things or who draw them into the field of their senses. They apprehend

things through the senses and apply their reason to the
object of their apprehension so that they come to understand great things. Thus they win fame and speak
eloquently, but the ground of their soul, which should be
the source of their wisdom, turns out to be empty and
shallow . . . they regard their own way of doing things and
their own will and habits as divine command and the divine
will, and they scorn and condemn the noble friends of God.
(H.61)

In a passage of enduring wisdom, Tauler speaks of a further
distinction between these two kinds of Christian in their
response to suffering:

We can tell whether someone has the true love of God
when great sufferings befall him. The friends of God take
them to God and suffer them for his sake. They accept
them as coming from him so that they suffer them with
him or in him. Or they so lose themselves within him,
because God unites himself so inwardly with them, that
suffering in God ceases for them to be suffering at all, but
becomes a joy and a delight. But if suffering befalls the
false friends of God with their Pharisaic ways, then they
do not know which way to turn but run all about the place,
seeking help, council and consolation. And when they do
not find them, then they go to pieces and fall into despair.
(H.71)

So exercised is Tauler by this distinction between the true
and the false Christian, and the latter's inclination to stand
in judgement on the former, that it is tempting to conclude
that he himself suffered much undue criticism, possibly from
his Dominican brethren. The spirituality which Tauler
espoused is certainly non-clerical, and he repeatedly makes
the point that God sees no distinction between those in
religious orders and those in the world. But Tauler is not
criticizing the existence of religious orders here, rather he is
voicing a view familiar to us in the modern age that true
religious piety knows no fixed place or identity. Tauler is
keenly aware of the laity, and he speaks at one point of a

man who has been a ploughman for over forty years and who is 'the greatest Friend of God of all' (H.364). Nor indeed would it be true to say that Tauler is condemning the devotional practices of the church, rather it is their abuse, when their use becomes idolatrous, that he castigates. The attitude of Tauler towards the sacramental life of the church is summed up in his remarks on the mass. He stresses that devout Christians should attend mass frequently, ideally every day, and that they should receive communion, for the Eucharist is the 'best and most beneficial' of the sacraments and it possesses an immense transforming power. It is typical though that even here, at the heart of the church's sacramental life, Tauler links the sanctifying quality of the Eucharist with the characteristics of the *Wesensmystik*, the mysticism of self-stripping:

If you wish to be transformed into God, then you must strip yourself of yourself. For our Lord said: 'Whoever eats this bread will have eternal life'. Nothing is more profitable to this end than going to the most sacred sacrament. For that frees you from yourself, and to such an extent that both inwardly and outwardly the old man in you completely dies away. Transforming and dissolving our human nature, and sending its own power coursing through our veins, so that it has one life and one being with us, this divine food frees us from ourselves. (H.211)

But those who find the ground of their souls and their senses to be pure and who rise up to God receive the noble fruit of the mass most fully. They do not turn from God, whether he gives to them or takes from them, but trust him and believe in him in good and in bad. They are born in God, and he in them. If they encounter an obstacle, whether an inner or an outer one, then they turn quickly from it and do not dwell upon it with long complaints. They love God and think only of him. They sink themselves into him and do not see his gifts but him alone. They accept all things as coming from him and bear them in him. In such people the Blessed Sacrament effects a noble and wonderful transfiguration, and for them the mass is the shortest and most immediate way to God. (H.241)

SUMMING UP

Speaking at one point of a 'noble master', by which he evidently means Eckhart, Tauler states that this master had advocated a way of sanctity which was 'without guidance on uncharted paths'. He added that many people had crudely misunderstood this message and had become 'poisoned' by it. This is the reason, he says, why it is very much better that his audience should follow the well-trodden path under guidance to sanctity and to truth (H.104). At every stage of Tauler's own path we are aware of the presence of Eckhart, principally in the use Tauler makes of his terms and in his belief that a deep, unmediated encounter with God is possible in this life. It is undeniable that Tauler has borrowed a good deal from the master, although it would be wrong to suggest that in the transference Eckhart's thought remained unchanged.

Let us look first at the points in common, for it is these, largely, which are to prove so very influential over the course of the following centuries. The first and most immediate point in common is the belief that the human soul can in this life enjoy a very profound union with God, so intense in fact that the normal borders between the Creator and the created are blurred. In Eckhart there is no distinction, and he can leave himself open at times to the charge of pantheism. In the case of the more circumspect Tauler, the soul is so taken up into the nature of the Godhead itself that it would appear to an outside observer to be one with the Divine. Secondly this union is arrived at, and itself fosters, a state of *detachment*, in which the soul is no longer occupied with or possessed by material created things. Here we encounter the *via negativa*, the 'negative theology', of Pseudo-Dionysius according to which we enter into the Godhead only by a process of self-stripping. We must abandon all within us and within our world which is not God. Thus we enter into a kind of 'divine darkness' of which both Eckhart and Tauler, following

Pseudo-Dionysius, speak. This immense emphasis upon detachment from 'things' and upon the inner life of the soul leads both Tauler and Eckhart into a deeply individualistic and inward spirituality in which actions and practices have no value in themselves except in so far as they support and foster inner devotion, detachment and abandonment to the divine will. It is this aspect of their thought which, understandably enough, has most attracted their Protestant interpreters, and has led to them both being proclaimed as forerunners of the Reformation. We have already seen however in Eckhart's fidelity – even when under strain – to the Roman Church, and in Tauler's spirituality of the sacraments that such a view of them carries only limited conviction.

But if we must acknowledge Eckhart's influence at every step, we are also constantly aware of the immense difference in temperament which divides the two. It is not merely a question of Tauler's obvious need for caution in the immediate aftermath of the Bull *In agro*, although that is sufficient to explain his frequent *caviats* and circumlocutions. The difference between the two men is deeper, and when Tauler urges caution upon those who become 'inebriated', those who question the value or possibility of petitionary prayer or those who discuss things beyond the understanding, then, although Tauler would have had the heretical Brethren of the Free Spirit in mind, we are forced to reflect that these criticisms contain a grain of truth with regard to Meister Eckhart himself. Above all, Tauler studiously avoids formulations which are either open to misinterpretation or which might appear audacious and shocking, even when the content of his statements is close to Eckhart's own teaching. His constant reiteration of the need always to follow God in a spirit of 'humble fear' and his scrupulous avoidance of ever appearing to present himself in a positive light also leave us with the impression that he was a most attractive man of deep personal humility.

Following a difference in temperament, there is also a clear distinction in spiritual vision. Tauler follows Eckhart in his conviction that a genuine and dynamic union with God is part of the spiritual life and is available for all who seek it;

nor need we be a priest, a nun or a friar in order to know God in this way. We may know him furthermore in a church or in the marketplace, for this knowledge has no limits, spacial or temporal. Tauler follows Eckhart also in the terminology with which he sets out this union. The key Eckhartian terms *abgescheidenheit* and *gelâzenheit* both appear in Tauler's sermons, as well as the 'Birth of God', the 'Divine Spark' and the 'nothingness' of creatures. But in Tauler's hands their sense is subtly changed. For Tauler the way to God is not instant but long; he thought it impossible for someone under the age of fifty to achieve full union with God (H.137). The path is long and it involves deep and constant meditation on the life and passion of Christ. The 'images' from which we must seek escape are not a particular state of consciousness, but areas of attachment that embody forms of moral disorder. Detachment itself is not a sovereign indifference to pain and joy, but is a long process of effort and purification through suffering in which we are at every stage dependent upon the grace of God. If Eckhart produced a system of speculative metaphysics which still enthralls minds tuned to his own uniquely intellective vision, then Tauler clothed it in the tried and tested vestments of traditional devotion. He drew it towards the historical mainstream. We might even say, in a sense, that he 'christianized' it.

Johannes Tauler is generally seen as being the guardian and transmitter of Eckhartian thought to posterity. This is to do him a disservice. As we have seen, although Eckhart was Tauler's inspiration, Tauler refashioned and changed him, turning his high speculation into a system which was altogether more earthly and accessible to common folk. The vision which Tauler transmitted was one that centred on an inner choice of God, a commitment to a life of detachment and self-abnegation, founded upon a real and all-consuming experience of God. The Bull *In agro* effectively stopped the knowing dissemination of Meister Eckhart's work, whereas Tauler's sermons achieved ever greater popularity and, when the age of print arrived, were extensively published. We have seen that essentially his voice was his own.

It would not be fair to conclude a discussion of Tauler's work without giving a particular example of his unique gift for stating sublime truths in the most striking and homely form. It is doubtlessly this skill, and the deep understanding of what it is to be human which informs it, which defines Tauler's 'voice' and goes a long way to explaining his enduring popularity. In the first passage he speaks of our sins:

> The horse drops dung in the stable. Although the dung is unclean and evil smelling, the same horse laboriously pulls the same dung to the fields where fine wheat and good sweet wine grow from it, which would never grow so well if the dung were not there. Now your dung is your own faults which you cannot rid yourself of or overcome. These you should carry with much effort and labour to the field of God's will in true detachment from yourself. Scatter your dung on this noble field and without any doubt there shall spring up noble and delightful fruit. (H.43f)

In a wonderful extended image drawn from the world of viti-culture, a craft which is everywhere to be seen in the green and steep-sided valleys of the wine-producing Rhine and Mosel areas, Tauler speaks in this second passage of how the devout God-loving soul grows gradually into the love and blessedness of God:

> What noble and precious fruit God grows from the person who cultivates their vine in such a way that the divine sun can work upon it and penetrate it! Then the sun shines and works upon the grape and brings it to glorious fruit . . . Then the sun shines more brightly still and casts its heat upon this fruit and makes it more and more transparent, the sweetness in it grows and the skin of the fruit becomes ever thinner so that God is close to it constantly. However often we look at it, we always find that it is illumined by the divine sun from within, more clearly than any sun ever shone in the sky, and thus all our ways are transformed into God so that we neither perceive nor delight in any thing nor know any thing more truly than God, though in a manner which transcends the powers of reason and rational knowledge. And then the leaves are stripped off so that the

sun can shine upon the fruit fully. In the same way all obstacles will fall away from such a person and they will receive everything without hindrance . . . (H.50f)

4

Suso and the Theologia Deutsch

HENRY SUSO: LIFE AND WORKS

Of all the mystics of our period, more biographical material surrounds the figure of Henry Suso, also known by his German name of Heinrich Seuse, than any other.[1] The source in question is the *Life of the Servant*, a biographical work which, it is claimed in its prologue, was written down by Elsbeth Stagel, a devout nun who prompted her spiritual director to divulge extensive details of his own spiritual life. We are told that when he later discovered the existence of this 'spiritual theft', he burnt part of it but, after a message from heaven, refrained from burning the rest which then became the substance of the *Life of the Servant*. Although it was long regarded as genuine, this work has not altogether passed the stiffer examinations of the modern critical age. Opinion is divided on it. All acknowledge it to be a highly literary construction in the medieval manner, full of accounts of visions, miracles and trances, but some scholars (including Bielmeyer and Gröber) feel that it is substantially autobiographical and hence to be taken virtually at face value. Other scholars (Rieder, Lichtenberger and Ancelet-Hustache *inter alios*)[2] have expressed doubts on the grounds of contradictions and intrinsic unlikelihood, and they see it as being the work of two or possibly three hands who have inextricably interwoven aspects of medieval fiction and colouring around a bare skeleton of fact. James M. Clark is however almost certainly right when he says: 'However much these tales were coloured by the imagination of the author or authors, one feels that they may be substantially true.'[3]

Whatever the actual status of the *Life of the Servant*, we can assert with confidence that Henry Suso came from the South German province of Swabia, as it reports, and that he was born around the year 1295, probably in the beautiful lakeside city of Constance or in nearby Überlingen. One later tradition suggests that he may have been of the noble family von Berge, and that he chose to use the maiden name of his pious and gentle mother rather than that of his worldly and irreligious father. Suso himself says that he was a sickly child 'marked with woe', and the *Life of the Servant* reports that he entered the Dominican friary in Constance at the age of thirteen, which is to say two years before the normal minimum age of acceptance. It is likely that Suso gained a dispensation on the grounds of a substantial donation which his parents made to the monastery at this stage. The circumstances surrounding his entry into religious life later caused him some considerable unrest until his mind was set at ease by the personal counsel of Meister Eckhart. Constance possessed a *studium particolare*, and it is there that Suso would have completed his early studies, although he may also have studied for a while in Strasbourg. From Constance Suso went on to the Dominican *studium generale* in Cologne around the year 1325, although he never took a higher degree and, like Tauler, whom he may or may not have known, showed a certain distance towards the world of higher learning.[4]

We do not know the motives surrounding Suso's early entrance into religious life, but we are told in the *Life of the Servant* that he underwent a conversion experience at the age of eighteen. Soon afterwards he fell into ecstasy while kneeling in the choir and tasted the joys of heaven. He adopted strikingly austere practices of physical mortification, cutting the initials IHS on his own chest, for instance, so 'the blood flowed copiously out of the flesh and ran down over his body and down his chest'.[5] These practices lasted for sixteen years when, as a result of a vision, Suso threw all his ingenious instruments of mortification into the Rhine. But it was revealed to him in a vision that other innumerable sufferings were to befall him, principally his misuse and misunderstanding at the hands of his brethren. Indeed Suso seems to have been taken to task, probably for his pro-Eckhartian views, by a general chapter of the Dominican Order, perhaps in Maastricht in 1330. The followers of St Thomas Aquinas were at the time waging a major compaign for theological supremacy in the Order.

It was probably as a result of this event that Suso ceased to be *lector* (the friar responsible for the education of his brethren) in Constance and began to concern himself with the apostolate and with the spiritual direction of Dominican sisters. He travelled a good deal, visiting in particular the convent of Töss, in the eastern part of Switzerland, where Elsbeth Stagel was a nun. Suso was moreover involved in the same papal interdict as Tauler when, as a result of the conflict between Pope John XXII and the Emperor Ludwig of Bavaria, the Dominicans who took the side of the Pope and supported the interdict had to leave the city of Constance, which had sided with the emperor. Although Suso had been elected prior of his community, his tribulations did not cease. The *Life of the Servant* narrates his many illnesses, how he was repeatedly the victim of anti-clerical feeling among the common people and how he was himself unjustly accused by his own brethren, envious of his pastoral success, of having fathered an illegitimate child. Suso is likely to have been that prior of Constance who was deposed by the general chapter in 1348, although his innocence was established by another chapter in 1354. Suso left Constance and moved to Ulm. It was there, towards the year 1360, that he produced an edition of his own works known as the *Exemplar*. He died on 25 January 1366 and was buried in the Dominican church of Ulm. This church was rebuilt in the seventeenth century, and no trace of his grave has been found. On 16 April 1831 he was pronounced blessed by Pope Gregory XVI, and his feast day falls on 23 January.

The *Exemplar* which Suso produced around the year 1360 began with the *Life of the Servant*, followed by the *Book of Eternal Wisdom*, written between 1334 and 1340, and the *Book of Truth*, his earliest work produced between 1327 and 1330 in which he makes a spirited defence of some of the teachings of Meister Eckhart. The fourth and final work is the *Little Book of Letters*, which is a selection of letters Suso wrote to Elsbeth Stagel and others under his direction. Apart from the *Exemplar*, there is a large *Book of Letters* which yielded the smaller selection, some four possible sermons published under the name of Tauler or Eckhart and a minor work of doubtful authenticity called the *Minnebüchlein* or *Book of Love*. More important is the *Horologium Sapientiae*, a Latin work that is parallel to the *Book of Eternal Wisdom* and which Suso wrote around the year 1337.[6] The precise relationship between the two has been the subject of much scholarly concern, and the *Horologium Sapientiae* was long thought to be a simple translation of the *Book of Eternal Wisdom*. The prevailing view is that both versions depend upon an earlier Latin text, consisting of notes and sermons, which in German translation formed the basis of the *Book of Eternal Wisdom* and which was incorporated in its original form into the *Horologium Sapientiae*. A collection of a hundred meditations on the passion of Our Lord, which was appended to the German work and not to the Latin, is believed on the grounds of its independent manuscript tradition to be anterior to them both. Both the *Book of Eternal Wisdom* and its counterpart, the *Horologium Sapientiae* (the *Clock of Wisdom*, so-called because it was divided into twenty-four parts) attained enormous popularity during the Middle Ages. The *Horologium* exists in some five hundred manuscripts, and it even compares with the *Imitation of Christ* in the extent of its favour and influence.

The works of Henry Suso were much copied during his own lifetime, and a first printed edition of his work, including some apocryphal items, appeared in Augsburg in 1482 and 1512. In 1555 this same version formed the basis for a translation into Latin by the indefatigable Laurentius Surius of Cologne, and was reprinted in 1588 and 1615. It was translated back into German in 1661. On account of his traditional Catholic piety, Suso never attracted the attention of the Protestant reformers, although Daniel Sudermann did produce an edition of the more neutral letters in 1622. In general Suso suffered the decline in interest which affected things medieval and it was with the renaissance of late eighteenth-century interest in *medievalia* that his own star rose again. The distinguished German philosopher and cultural historian Johann Gottfried Herder, who was a major figure in the early German Romantic movement, wrote a poem to his memory and, in 1829, Melchior Diepenbrock published an improved text drawn up by the popular Catholic activist Görres with a preface by the Romantic poet Brentano. Suso thus excited the interest not so much of philosophers as those who were discovering in German medieval history a source of inspiration for the political and cultural ideals of their own age.

The Diepenbrock edition was reprinted several times during the course of the nineteenth century. It was partially superseded in 1880 by an incomplete edition from the outstanding Dominican scholar Denifle (who was in fact named 'Heinrich Seuse Denifle' after the mystic), but it was only in 1907 that Bihlmeyer produced a first-rate standard edition, which has served as the basis for the numerous modern translations of Suso's German work.

THE BOOK OF TRUTH

A glance at one of the early printed editions of Suso's work, with extensive and highly-worked woodcut illustrations, immediately reveals that he belongs more to the world of medieval piety, with its trances, visions and tears, its mortifications and pungent imagery than he does to the precise instruction of Eckhart or Tauler in the deepest ways of an abstract, timeless mysticism. Suso, it is frequently said, was a poet who had absorbed all the refinements and devices of the *Minnesang* tradition (a German variant on the Courtly Love poetry of the troubadour poets of Provence) of which he made able use in order to express his own vision, which was one firmly embedded in the popular piety of the age. We see, for instance, in the one hundred meditations on the passion of Our Lord which conclude the *Book of Eternal Wisdom* a clear affinity with such practices as the Way of the Cross, a creation of the early fifteenth century, and the devotional meditations of the rosary, which was also reaching its mature form at this time.

It appears strange to us today that a spiritual figure such as Suso, who was so steeped in the richly embroidered medieval cultural idiom, should have defended the theology of a thinker whose uncompromising and austere negative theology stands at the opposite pole to all that Suso espoused in the greater part of his own immensely popular writings. The answer is doubtlessly to be found in the personal relationship which must have existed between Suso and his teacher and in the very real affection and respect which Suso appears to have felt for Meister Eckhart. Ample evidence of this is to be found in the account given in the *Life of the Servant* of how Eckhart left his abode among the blessed in heaven in order to visit his pupil. But we will look in vain for more than passing reference to Eckhartian spirituality in the *Life of the Servant*, whatever the value of that work might be, which the French scholar Bizet called 'le document psychologique le plus conséquent que le moyen âge ait laissé',[7] as spiritual autobiography. Although we do find elements of Eckhart's 'detachment from creatures' in the *Book of Eternal Wisdom*, which Denifle similarly called 'the finest fruit of German mysticism',[8] the dominant idiom of that book is altogether different in tone with its emphasis upon an abundance of religious imagery and works. Rather, it is to the modest early work, the *Book of Truth*, for which Suso in all probability faced the strictures of his Order, and to his letters that we must turn in order to consider his absorption of Eckhart's message.

We find in the *Book of Truth*, which is framed in the form of a dialogue between 'the Disciple' and 'Truth', a clear defence of certain of the positions for which Meister Eckhart suffered condemnation. Suso begins by echoing the apophatic language which is so typical of Eckhart, and, significantly, he hedges it with the names of other scholars:

> Now it is evident that the nature of the simple essence mentioned above is infinite, immeasurable and beyond the comprehension of reason. That is why all learned scholars are agreed that this essence, without more precise definition, has no name. And therefore Dionysius says in his book on the divine names that God is non-Being, or Nothingness . . . (BM, 328f)[9]

Following Eckhart's teaching, Suso stresses the unity of the divine:

Truth answered: this multiplicity is a simple unity according to its ground and base.
The Disciple: What do you call the ground and origin and that which is not the ground?
Truth: I call the ground the source and the origin from which the emanations spring.
The Disciple: Lord, what is that?
Truth: That is the nature and the essence of the Godhead, and in this abyss-like ground the Trinity of Persons sinks into its unity, and there every form of multiplicity is in a certain sense lost to itself. There is no alien activity at work there, if we may put it that way, but there is only a still and unmoved darkness. (BM, 330)

Suso repeats Eckhart's distinction between God and Godhead, and points out that this is not a real distinction at all:

Truth: Yes, God and Godhead are one, though the Godhead does not act or give birth, only God does that. But this difference only follows from the names which our reason applies. In essence they are one . . . (ibid.)

We find the same concept of the preexistence of creatures in eternal and archetypal form within God, although Suso presents the view, contrary to Eckhart, that the existence of creatures in the created world is of higher value than their existence in God:

Truth: the essence of the creature in God is not creature, but the createdness of every creature is nobler and more profitable to it than the essence which it possesses in God. For what does a stone, or a person or any creature possess more in its created essence for having been eternally God in God? (BM, 332)

This contrasts with his view expressed elsewhere concerning the nothingness of creatures:

But whoever wishes to 'leave' themselves in the correct way

should look upon their inner selves in a threefold manner. Firstly, in such a way that he, sinking into himself, gazes upon the nothingness of his ego, mindful that his ego, like the essence of all things, is a nothingness, having come forth and being cut off from Being, which is the sole active force. (BM, 335)

The keynote of Suso as an apologist is caution. Nowhere is this more apparent than when he discusses the possibility of union with God in this life, removing it, unlike Tauler, from the experience of all but the elect:

One teacher says that there is a kind of select person who is experienced in the spiritual life and who is so pure and Godlike that their virtue appears divine, for they have been destroyed and recreated in the unity of the first model and, somehow forgetful of transient and earthly life, they are transformed into a divine image and are made one with it. But it must be added that this state is only possible for those who possess this blessedness in high degree and for the few and most pious people in this life. (BM, 338)

Suso agrees with Tauler however in placing Eckhart's practical spirituality within a decidedly christological context. This may be seen first from a quotation taken from the *Book of Truth*, in which he makes the Eckhartian 'breakthrough' dependent upon Christ's redemption of humanity; and secondly in a quotation from Suso's Tenth Letter:

The Disciple: . . . I would like to hear something about the breakthrough by which, through Christ, we return to God and attain his blessedness.
Truth: You must remember that Christ, the Son of God, had something in common with all men as well as being quite different. What he has in common with all men is his human nature, so that he was also truly man. He did not just become a person, but took on human nature . . . and whoever therefore seeks a true return to God and to be themselves a son of God in Christ, must turn from themselves to him; then he will attain his goal. (BM, 333f)

And this is the source of true perfection, which rests on the union of the highest powers of the soul with the source of Being in a state of high contemplation, in the most passionate love, in delight in the highest good, as far as the weakness of our bodies, which pull us earthwards, permits. And since our souls cannot attain to the absolute Good by a path without images on account of the weakness of our wearisome bodies, we must have an image which will lead us there. And the best one according to my understanding is the precious form of Jesus Christ. (BM, 390f)

Again like Tauler, Suso is keen to attack the Brethren of the Free Spirit, who had misappropriated certain of Eckhart's teachings in order to justify their lawless and immoral way of life. In the sixth chapter of the *Book of Truth*, Suso introduces the 'Wild Man', who is a personification of the sect of the Free Spirit. The first error which Suso counters is that of pantheism, which the 'Wild Man' claims permits him unbounded freedom. Suso points to correct distinctions and to the natural and moral order. He counters the 'Wild Man's' claim that the nothingness of the human spirit allows him total moral licence by stressing that 'nothingness' as applied to God is a term for superabundant being and that the human spirit in union with God always remains itself. Thirdly he answers the 'Wild Man's' claim that a certain 'Master' had taught that we become indistinguishable from Christ by quoting a passage from Eckhart himself in which Eckhart specifically denies this. The heretic finally submits and asks the disciple for instruction in the truth.

The *Book of Truth* is a short work which contains many passages of some considerable difficulty. There have been careful analyses of Suso's theology, showing for instance that although it reflects Eckhart's own thought in the main, there are grounds for suggesting that Suso's position owes something to Nominalism, the philosophy of William of Ockham, which was fast gaining ground in the fourteenth century. The passage concerned, in which Suso speaks of the greater value of the existence of things in the world rather than in their archetypal form in the Godhead, has been seen as contrasting the modern trend, which lent greater value to individual

phenomena, with the traditional Platonic approach, which
sought their essence in the Godhead. Coming to Suso from
Eckhart and Tauler however, it does appear that too much
has been claimed for Suso as a thinker. He shunned the world
of higher learning, his use of language is a good deal looser
than that of his two contemporaries, and his handling of
ideas is incomparably weaker than is the case with Eckhart.
Whereas Tauler was deeply influenced by Eckhart's teaching,
to which he returns time and time again, Suso was only
superficially so.[10] Above all, Eckhartian method is clean
contrary to Suso's preferred spiritual idiom, which embraces
imagery rather than transcends it and which won him great
popularity during the late Middle Ages. As for his relevance
today, it has to be said that Suso's undeniable achievement
within the cultural traditions of his own age does not translate
easily to our own. Although he will continue to excite scholars
tutored in the style of the medieval *Minnesang*, his message
for the modern age is much less accessible than that of
Eckhart and Tauler. It is by no means clear that Suso was
even an important transmitter of Eckhartian thought after
the Bull *In agro;* there are only a handful of manuscripts of
the *Book of Truth*, including only two copied independently of
the *Exemplar*. Interest in the *Book of Truth* seems therefore
to have been insignificant in comparison with the immense
popularity of his other work. Nevertheless the personal testimony of a saintly man such as Suso, who personally knew
Meister Eckhart, is a matter to posterity of no little
significance.

THE THEOLOGIA DEUTSCH

The thirteenth- and fourteenth-century mystical movement
which flourished particularly in the German-speaking areas
of the Upper and Lower Rhine valley and which found its
highest expression in the work of Eckhart, Tauler and Suso
entered deep into the consciousness of the age. German mysticism had begun with what the Germans have called *Nonnenmystik* (literally 'nuns' mysticism') in the women's convents
of the twelfth century. This movement included some figures

of genius, such as the formidable Hildegard of Bingen,[11] who made a substantial contribution to the life of the church and to the current state of scholarship, as well as achieving distinction as a composer and poetess. Elisabeth of Schönau, prioress of a Benedictine convent near Trier, was another woman of standing, whose visions recorded by her brother show an affinity with the 'bridal mysticism' popularized by St Bernard of Clairvaux. It is only in the work of Mechthild of Magdeburg, however, in the thirteenth century that we find the first signs of what we might term a 'mysticism of being'. Although written in Low German dialect and surviving only in a High German translation, Mechthild's work *The Flowing Light of the Godhead* is the first major piece of mystical writing in the German language. It generally reflects a 'nuptial' type of spirituality, but there are passages, in particular the forty-fourth chapter, in which Mechthild speaks of an unmediated union of the soul with God through a process of self-abandonment. This has justifiably attracted much attention as being an anticipation of developments to come. Mechthild herself ceased to be a Beguine late in life and joined the Cistercian convent of Helfta in 1270 where Mechthild of Hackeborn was active and the future St Gertrud the Great, another celebrated visionary who had much to do with the development of devotion to the Sacred Heart, was still a child. Without doubt, the achievements of Eckhart, Tauler and Suso can be seen to owe a great deal to the request made by Pope Clement V in 1267 to the Dominican Order to undertake pastoral responsibility for the many women's communities which had sprung up since the Crusades. It was this which brought the wealth of scholastic learning within the Order into contact with the acute spiritual sensibilities of the women religious. All three of the great Dominicans were at some time or other involved in pastoral care of this kind. Indeed there are abundant signs of the fruit of this interaction in the thought of Dominican thinkers before Eckhart and his school, in particular in the work of figures such as Johannes von Sternengassen and Dietrich von Freiberg. The former was *lector* in Strasbourg and Cologne and may have taught Suso and Tauler, and we have already seen something of the mystical theology of the latter and his undoubted influence upon Meister Eckhart.[12]

Mysticism in the fourteenth century in the German-speaking areas of the Upper and Lower Rhineland was not confined to a few erudite men and women, but was a long-term phenomenon that put roots deep into the local population. Apart from the major writings of the period there are a great number of lesser works, spiritual manuals, books of counsel and the like, which attest to the popular transmission of certain of the key ideas which had been generated or popularized by Meister Eckhart and his school. We have seen the network of relationships involving clergy and laity alike which passed under the name of the *gotesvrunde* or 'Friends of God'. These were a popular movement who sought their inspiration in the writings of the Dominicans, propagating their works and their mystical ideals. The latter part of the fourteenth century however saw a return to the 'nuptial mysticism' characteristic of the thirteenth century. Margarete Ebner, her cousin Christine and Elsbeth Stagel all wrote down collections of 'revelations', as did Adelheid Langmann and Katrin von Gubwiller.

Of the works which were written and widely copied in Germany in the period following the great flowering of Dominican spirituality in the early fourteenth century the *Book of Spiritual Poverty*[13] and the *Theologia Deutsch* stand out. Until the mid-nineteenth century, the former was thought to have been written by Tauler himself and was first published by Sudermann in Frankfurt in 1621 under the title *Imitation of the Poor Life of Jesus*. It is generally believed to have been written at the beginning of the fifteenth century and it certainly does reflect the influence of Taulerian thought in its account of a life of virtue, spiritual poverty and mystical union with God. It is an interesting work in that it makes a clear association between inner spiritual poverty and the external poverty which was such a vital and contentious issue in the church at the time. Although it was widely copied, the *Book of Spiritual Poverty* did not have the popularity and the influence which came to the *Theologia Deutsch*, which was written at around the same time and which was likewise the work of an unknown hand.

Although his name is unknown to us, we do know that the author of the *Theologia Deutsch* (known also as the *Theologia Germanica*) was a priest and warden of the Knights of the Teutonic Order at Sachsenhausen, near Frankfurt am Main. This martial Order had originally been created in 1190 during the Crusades. By the late fourteenth century however it was entirely involved in the colonization and administration of Central and Eastern Europe. The date of composition is usually placed, on linguistic grounds, in the first part of the fifteenth century, around the year 1430.[14]

The textual history of the *Theologia Deutsch* is not without its complications. To judge from the paucity of manuscripts, it appears not to have been well-known prior to its discovery in truncated form by Martin Luther around the year 1515. Luther published this work in his Wittenberg edition of 1516, and this abbreviated form of the *Theologia Deutsch* is referred to as text A. In 1518, in Wittenberg and Augsburg, Luther published a complete text, known as B, which he had found in the Carthusian monastery at Erfurt. This manuscript was lost and Luther's edition of it became the most influential form of the work, being reprinted many times, including some twenty times in Luther's lifetime. It formed the basis for translations into French and Latin at Basle in the mid-sixteenth century, despite Calvin's emphatic opposition to the enterprise, and for Flemish translations published by Plantin around the same time. It is this text also which has appeared in two modern critical editions, that by Mandel in 1908 and by Siedel in 1929, and it has been the basis for most modern translations of the work. This particular text, which took the title *Theologia Deutsch* for the first time, contains many theses which are particularly close to Luther's own ideas at the time of his discovery of the manuscript. It was even mooted at one stage that the great Reformer may have interpolated additions which reflected his own theology into text A, thus producing the adapted but influential text B.

A further text of the *Theologia Deutsch* was discovered in 1843 by R. Reuss. This was a manuscript copied at the Cistercian abbey of Bronnbach in 1497. Pfeiffer published it in 1851 and it was produced in a critical edition by W. Uhl in 1912. This is known as text C, and it contains some significant differences in places from text B. There are therefore three extant texts of the *Theologia Deutsch*. One view which has been put forward is that A is the earliest text, and that B and C go back to a common defective source, following distinct manuscript traditions. Luther's corrections, it is suggested, were incorporated into his text in the case of B and, in the case of C, there are a number of interpolations from an unknown source. Recent finds tend to confirm that B, Luther's second edition, is the purest copy of the text available.[15]

The *Theologia Deutsch*, no less than the other mystical works of this age, was surrounded by controversy during the turbulent years of the Reformation and its aftermath. In the case of this work the partisanship was particularly acute as at one stage it deeply influenced Martin Luther and, through him, other reformers such as Carlstadt, Johann Arndt (the author of *True Christianity*) and Philipp Jakob Spener, founder of the German Pietist movement. From the very beginning the *Theologia Deutsch* was identified in the young Luther's mind with the person and work of Tauler, for whom he felt an unbounded admiration. In a letter of 14 December 1516 Luther wrote to his friend Spalatin:

> If you wish to read some sterling theology, which is the equal to that of the ancients and written in German, then you should get hold of the sermons of Johannes Tauler of the Order of Preachers of which I am sending you an extract. I have never read in Latin or in German a more wholesome piece of theology or one more consonant with the Gospel.[16]

In his preface to the first edition of 1516 Luther attributes the work to Tauler himself and in his preface to the second edition of 1518, which quotes Tauler by name, he attributes it to one of Tauler's disciples. Luther writes that besides the Bible and the works of Augustine, he has learned more from the *Theologia Deutsch* than from any other book, although, in course of time, the reformer's attitude to mysticism was to change.

The *Theologia Deutsch* continued to enjoy high favour among the Protestants after Luther's time, particularly those contesting new forms of (Protestant) ecclesial authority by appealing to a form of religion based upon the individual and his or her experience. It was an especially popular work among the Pietists and the Anabaptists, and became 'a rallying point for those who were unhappy with the later development of the Reformation and for those mystical and spiritualistic groups who believed in a practical, undogmatic form of Christianity'.[17] In 1621, in confirmation of its standing among the Protestants, the *Theologia Deutsch* was included in the list of works proscribed by the Roman Church.

The *Theologia Deutsch* belongs as much to the fifteenth-century world of the *Imitation of Christ* by Thomas à Kempis as it does to that of Eckhart and Tauler. It contains little speculation and little sense of an immediate union with God; its message rather is one of simple piety and a life of virtue founded on divine grace. Though we do find traces of apophaticism, or negative theology, as when the author says:

> But this perfection is beyond the grasp and recognition of creatures and they cannot express it, in accordance with their nature as creatures. Therefore this perfection is called 'Nothingness', as it is not of their kind, which is why the creature as creature cannot recognise or understand it, cannot name it or comprehend it in its thoughts. (VH, 71f)

The author speaks also of the way of negative theology which passes beyond all images, but he speaks of it with caution, and leaves the reader with the overwhelming impression that his knowledge of it is second-hand:

> And if the soul is to reach that place, then it must be quite pure and free from all images and must have detached itself from all creatures and, above all, from itself. And there are many who say that this cannot be done and that it is impossible in our day and age. But St Dionysius thinks it possible; that is the impression his words give which he wrote to Timotheus . . . (VH, 79)

The author of the *Theologia Deutsch* feels altogether unsure of

God Within

himself in the field of speculation. Although he refers briefly
to the Eckhartian distinction between God and Godhead, and
to the unity of God, the anonymous author, known as the
'man of Frankfurt' or less happily in English as 'the Frank-
furter', responds to the question 'But what is the One?' with
the answer 'It is goodness' (VH, 81). God is for him the
'eternal, single, perfect good' (VH, 152), and it is upon this
'eternal good' that the life of the faithful is founded through
grace. They are *vorgottet*, which means 'made divine', for they
are 'illumined and permeated by the eternal or divine light
and are inflamed and consumed by eternal and divine love'
(VH, 130). Their characteristic is 'true, real and deep
humility' and 'spiritual poverty' (VH, 119). This latter phrase
has had a long career, as we have seen. It originated with
Eckhart as a psycho-spiritual state of luminous detachment
and became in Tauler a turning away from the world and its
passions. The book mentioned above under the title *The Book
of Spiritual Poverty*, which probably belongs with the *Theologia
Deutsch* to the early fifteenth century, illustrates the extent to
which this particular concept had become fixed and was
common currency in mystical circles. The underlying sense
of it in the *Theologia Deutsch* is that of a simple piety based
upon thorough-going and radical self-abnegation. The author
writes:

> But where there is spiritual poverty and true humility,
> things are very different. And this comes from the fact that
> we discover and recognize in truth that we are nothing in
> ourselves and in what we possess and that we can do
> nothing and serve nothing but transgression, wickedness
> and evil. Thus it follows that we find we are unworthy of
> all that God and his creatures have done for us or might
> do for us . . . (VH, 105)

The author has a direct and powerful vision of a simple
turning towards God and away from preoccupations with the
self:

> And when we then consider nothing, seek nothing and
> desire nothing but the Eternal Good and not ourselves nor

our own but only the honour of God in all things, then we will share in the joy, the bliss, the peace, the stillness and the consolation of the Eternal Good – and that is everything – and so we will be in Heaven. (VH, 85)

The 'man of Frankfurt' has a similarly direct idea of the nature of sin. It is *ungehôrsam* or 'disobedience' and the chief manifestion of this is *eigenwille* or 'self-will'. The spiritual life therefore is for him a constant process of practising obedience to the divine will:

This means that we should apply ourselves and accustom ourselves to such obedience to God and his commandments at all times and in all things that there is no longer any resistance to him in nature or spirit, but body and soul and all their members are ready and willing to do the will of their Creator as a person's hand is ready and willing to perform their will. For their hand is in their power, and they can turn it and use it at will. And where we find that things are not so, then we should set about putting them right, out of love and not from fear, and we should set our heart on God in all things, seeking his honour and praise. (JB, 264)

Among the ideas of this book which attracted the Reformers is the author's emphasis upon individual piety, although we do not find the specific questioning of the value of works which we find in Tauler, for instance. The author recommends an inward frame of mind: 'Whoever wishes to consider and understand the matter aright should recognize that true peace and calm do not come from the things outside ourselves' (JB, 154). A further point which drew their attention is the *theopathic* element. This means literally the 'God-suffering' experience of the believer, which is certainly an echo of Tauler's view of God as the initiator or active partner. Associated with this are certain passages in the *Theologia Deutsch* which have been interpreted as supporting Quietism. Quietism as a spiritual movement reached its fullest expression in the condemned writings of the Spanish theologian Molinos, and in the French Church of the seventeenth

century, especially in the life and work of Madame Guyon
and Archbishop Fénelon. It was a movement which argued
for the complete suspension of the human will and therefore
motive for action through the state of contemplative union
with God: 'For Madame Guyon and in Quietist spirituality
the soul abandons itself to God once and for all and is thus
dispensed from any further effort'.[18] In its extreme forms
Quietism dispensed with any active form of devotional or
religious practice. Eckhart and Tauler had stressed the extent
to which our human will is consumed and transformed in the
divine will, but they had done so within the context of a
powerful sense of mystical union with the Godhead. This is
lacking in the *Theologia Deutsch,* and the complete renunciation
of the power of the human will, outside an overwhelming and
unmediated sense of union with God, has a distinctly Quietist
feel.

The *Theologia Deutsch* has been acclaimed an outstanding
work of Christian literature and it has been described as
being merely an echo of the great Dominican writings of
the fourteenth century. Certainly it has excited minds and
controversy more than any other mystical text from this
period, and certainly it contains passages of considerable
spiritual beauty. But it fails to convince at a deep level when
it speaks of our union with God; we do not encounter the fire
and the radiance of personal experience in that area as we
do in Eckhart and Tauler. The 'man of Frankfurt' does
however share the pastoral concern of Tauler and Suso with
the ravages of heresy in the form of the Brethren of the Free
Spirit, who represented such a distortion of true spiritual life.
Though the tone of the work is not that of mystical inspiration
but of a rich and practical everyday spirituality. As such it
is particularly close to the *Imitation of Christ.* Nowhere is this
more clearly to be seen than in the author's comments on
suffering. This is not regarded as being a sign of our failure
to achieve full union with God (Eckhart), or as the potential
means of our sanctification (Tauler), but it is something
which is an unavoidable part of our everyday existence. We
might as well face that fact, the author tells us, and learn to
accept suffering in peace:

There is no one living on earth who always has stillness and calm, without troubles or frustrations, and for whom everything always goes according to their will. We have to suffer in this life, whatever people say. The moment we are free of a problem, there are two to take its place. So you should accept this fact and should seek to preserve true peace of heart which nobody can take away from you, in order that you should overcome all your troubles . . . (155)

Although suffering, too, is what links us with the life of our Saviour, and so we should relinquish our own will and take up our cross in imitation of him:

Above all we should deny ourselves and take our leave of all things for the sake of God and we should give up our own will and all our natural inclinations so that we may be purified and cleansed of all sins and vices. Then we should humbly take up our cross and follow Christ. (156)

By the late fourteenth and early fifteenth century, although there was still a good deal of religious fervour and natural piety, the mystical inspiration in Germany initiated by Eckhart and adapted by Tauler was coming to an end. The fresh and exhilarating concepts generated by Eckhart had become commonplace and had lost their context of immediate mystical experience. They remained influential, and would in later time greatly influence the philospher and conciliarist Nicholas of Cusa, and the seventeenth-century writer known as Angelus Silesius. The former possessed manuscripts of Eckhart's Latin works in his famous library on the banks of the Mosel river. His theory of the unknowability of God, and of God as the transcendence of opposites, owes much to Eckhart, and he warmly defended Eckhart against the attacks of Johannes Wenck.[19] It was Eckhart also who was indirectly the inspiration for the inscrutable poetry of Angelus Silesius, published in his *The Cherubic Wanderer*. Nevertheless a new impulse was required to maintain and support the North European school of mysticism, and it came finally from outside Germany, from Flanders, in the person and work of Jan van Ruusbroec.

5

Jan van Ruusbroec

The social and religious situation in the Netherlands during the fourteenth century had much in common with that of the German Rhineland. The languages were cognate, even more so than today, and the great river Rhine which flows through both areas supported a similar culture and trade. There were however distinct differences in certain areas of life. One of these was the Beguine movement, which in the Netherlands enjoyed unusual prominence.[1] The origins of this movement are in fact to be found in the Low Countries during the twelfth century when small groups of devout women began to found like-minded communities. The name 'Beguine' either reflects a popular association between them and the Albigensians or refers to the beige colour of their habits of untreated wool. Certainly they differed from earlier female foundations in their determination to lead an active spiritual life and to resist regularization by the church. They lived in celibate all-female communities, but their practice of remaining within the world in order to earn their living, through a trade such as embroidery or through begging, following the example of the mendicant friars, caused much concern to the institutional church. We have already seen some of the problems which this movement raised for the ecclesiastical authorities, and which resulted in the call to the established male orders to take the Beguines under their pastoral wing. The Cistercians however were reluctant to devote so much time to this activity in view of the considerable number of women's communities which had sprung up in this period, and so the Beguines and their male counterparts, the Beghards, suffered from a lack of supervision which led inevitably to them becoming fertile ground for the virulent heretical movements of the age, particularly that of the Free Spirit.

The history of the Beguines in France and Germany is marked by their quite severe persecution at the hands of the bishops (such as that meted out in Cologne by Henry of Virneburg, Eckhart's accuser), while the papacy in general attempted to protect the many doubtlessly faithful Beguine women from the bishops' zeal. The condemnation by the Council of Vienne in 1312 showed an awareness of the distinction to be made between the heretical and pious members of the movement. In the Netherlands, however, the situation was rather different in that the Dominican Order exercised considerable and effective pastoral care for the Beguines which made them more stable communities and more acceptable to the church authorities. The movement proved most durable in the Low Countries, and even today there still exists a *Béguinage*, for instance in Bruges.

The spirituality of the Low Countries was powerfully influenced by the spiritual currents at work among the Beguines, who espoused a deeply devout, often visionary and ecstatic form of piety. Indeed their particular devotion to the Eucharist and to the life of Christ was to result in the institution of the Feast of Corpus Christi, first sanctioned in the Beguine stronghold of the diocese of Liège. Two *Lives* from the early thirteenth century give us striking illustration of the character of the Beguine experience. Jacques de Vitry wrote the life of Marie d'Oignies in which he describes her many states of trance and ecstasy, and Thomas of Cantipré did something similar for the ecstatic known as Christina Mirabilis. Two later figures who hold an important place in the history of spirituality, Beatrice of Nazareth (Beatrijs van Nazareth) and Hadewijch of Antwerp, were also profoundly influenced by the Beguine movement.

Beatrice was the more traditional, and in a sense conventional, of the two.[2] She came from a pious, possibly noble family and received her initial training in a *Béguinage* in Zoutleeuw. Later she became a member of the Cistercian community of Bloemendaal (French: Florival), in modern day Belgium, where she specialized in the copying of manuscripts. Beatrice finally became prioress of the community at

Nazareth, which had recently been founded by her father, where she remained until her death in 1268. The last section of her biography, the *Vita Beatricis*, contains a vernacular work entitled *There are Seven Manners of Loving* (*Det sin seven manieren van minnen*). In this piece Beatrice fully expresses her own devotional character in which the love of God plays a predominant role. Although there are strong elements of a *Brautmystik*, such as we find also among visionary German nuns, Beatrice shows a highly evolved mysticism which is both speculative and based on love. This new and exciting motif which generates mystical imagery, and was to find its way into Ruusboec's work, can be seen in the following passage:

> But the blessed soul has a further manner of supernatural love, which moves it greatly from within. This is when it is drawn up above human things in love, above human thinking and reason and above all the works of the heart and is drawn by eternal love alone into the eternity of love, into the incomprehensible breadth, the unattainable heights and the immense abyss of the Godhead, which is all in all things and which is immutably the all-existent, all-mighty, all-comprehending and all-powerful in its deeds.

The works of the female mystic known as Hadewijch of Antwerp were only rediscovered in 1838.[3] Next to nothing is known about her life, although there is strong evidence from the surviving texts that she may have been the mistress of a Beguine community, writing between 1230 and 1250. There is also some evidence that she lost favour in her community and was expelled towards the end of her life. Her knowledge of Latin theological texts, the French language and the French troubadour tradition argue for a noble upbringing. Hadewijch's works include a series of letters addressed to her fellow Beguines, an account of visions and a number of poems written in stanzas and in couplets. She tells us herself that she first encountered the love of God when she was ten years old, and it is certainly this vision which occupies a central place in her life and thought. Her work is permeated with an intense experience of divine love, to which she seeks to conform with her whole being, and Hadewijch's writings abound in exhortations to her fellow Beguines to an ever greater love. This intense love-mysticism finds theological expression in Hadewijch's teaching on the Trinity. Drawing in particular upon the Cistercian William of St Thierry, Hadewijch speaks of the inner life of the Trinity as a love-ferment into which we ourselves are drawn; we are urged to live 'in the rhythm of the Trinity'. This was to prove to be an important influence upon Ruusbroec himself, although Hadewijch cannot be said to achieve anywhere the wonderful succinctness and power of expression which is characteristic of Ruusbroec at his best.

There is however one area of work in the Hadewijch corpus which strikes a rather different note from the generally diffuse treatment of love which characterizes the visions and the letters. The final thirteen poems of the 'Poems in Couplets' (*Mengelgedichten*) form a unity which is so distinct from the remaining poems that they are generally thought to be the work of another author, who has been dubbed Hadewijch II or Pseudo-Hadewijch. It is not known when these poems were written, although it may have been at a much later date. The emphatically Eckhartian tenor of their content suggests that they may have been written after the penetration into the Low Countries of certain of Meister Eckhart's sermons.[4] It must be stressed that no evidence for this influence exists, and it may be a question merely of a common spiritual atmosphere. Ruusbroec quotes from the work both of Hadewijch proper and Hadewijch II.

We have already seen that there is a greater emphasis upon *spiritual love* in the mystical life as conceived within the Flemish mystical tradition than is the case among the Germans.[5] This is not to say that the *Nonnenmystik* of St Elisabeth, St Gertrud and St Mechthild lacks this aspect, only that it achieves more developed recognition in the Beguine spirituality of the Low Countries. One reason for this distinction is the influence of Cistercian spirituality upon the tradition which gave birth to Ruusbroec. Not only was there a greater concentration of Cistercian convents in the Low Countries than in Germany, but the writings in particular of William of St Thierry were greatly influential.[6] William was born around 1080 in Liège, which is in present-day Belgium, and came much under the influence of the great St Bernard of Clairvaux, who gave profound theological expression to the dominant place of love in our sanctification. Following in particular the teachings of St Augustine, William stressed our mystical progression by incorporation into the inner life of the Trinity through a union of love. His work, the so-called *Golden Letter* (*Epistola aurea*), which was written for the Carthusian Order, sets out his teaching and gained wide currency during the thirteenth and fourteenth centuries in the religious houses of Flanders and the Netherlands (as well as England). We will find in the work of Ruusbroec a number of themes and phrases drawn from the mystical theology of William, which came to him either directly or through the writings of Hadewijch, whose inspiration he freely acknowledged.[7]

LIFE AND WORKS

Ruusbroec lived to a ripe old age and died peacefully in the odour of sanctity.[8] He became a figure celebrated for his wisdom and devotion, and the community at Groenendaal, of which he was a co-founder, became within his lifetime a centre of pilgrimage. It is no surprise therefore that the reliability of the two principal sources for Ruusbroec's life that we possess should be to some extent undermined by their decidedly hagiographic tone. The earlier source, a prologue to the first collection of five of his works written around 1360 by a Carthusian of Herne (Hérinnes) by the name of Gerard appears less hagiographic, however, than the later more extensive source, which was written some thirty to forty years after the death of Ruusbroec by Henricus Pomerius.[9] Pomerius was himself prior of Groenendaal in 1431, and his *De origine monasterii Viridisvallis*, which can be dated to between 1414 and 1421, shows his concern to present Ruusbroec in the best possible light, as a model of the life in God. It is upon Pomerius that we rely for most details concerning the circumstances of the mystic's life.

Following the usual medieval practice, Ruusbroec took the name of his birthplace. This was long believed to have been the small village of that name a few miles south of Brussels, although in recent times an alternative possible site, an area within Brussels itself, has been proposed. The year of his birth was 1293. In 1304 the young Ruusbroec went to Brussels to stay with a relative by the name of Jan Hinckaert, who was a canon of the principal church in Brussels, dedicated to the local saint, Gudule. He began to learn Latin at the chapter school there and embarked on his elementary studies in the *artes*. In 1317 Ruusbroec was ordained priest. It is not thought likely that he ever completed a course of advanced studies, beyond those required for his ordination.

During the course of his long life Ruusbroec wrote no less than eleven works on spirituality. Five of these were written during this early period in Brussels, and their composition was in part the result of pressure from the many individuals to whom Ruusbroec gave spiritual counsel and, in part, of his determination to counter the heresy of the Free Spirit. According to Gerard, Ruusbroec expressed some dissatisfaction with his first work, written around 1330 and called the *Kingdom of Lovers* (*Dat rijcke der ghelieven*). He regarded it as 'immature' and did not intend it to be copied. It was reproduced however without his knowledge, and a later work, *The Book of Clarification*, was written for the purpose of elucidating it for the Carthusians at Herne, who possessed the illicit copy. *The Kingdom of Lovers* is a lengthy interpretation of a line from the Vulgate: *Justum deduxit Dominus per vias rectas et ostendit illi regnum Dei* (Wisdom, 10:10), and it deals with union with God through the seven gifts of the Holy Spirit. We already encounter here Ruusbroec's characteristic preoccupation with the return to God, progressing through virtues to an unmediated union with God, and a Trinitarian mysticism, based upon the transcendent unity and dynamic diversity of the Three Persons. In addition Ruusbroec lays great stress on the *affective* aspect of this union, using words like 'savour' (*smakelijcheit*) and 'enjoyment' or 'delight' (*ghebruken*). It is one of the least read of his works, and has never been translated into English, but there are passages towards the end of the book, where Ruusbroec speaks of immediate union with God and of the outflow and influx of the Trinity, which are of great brilliance.

Ruusbroec's second work, *The Spiritual Espousals* (*Die gheeste-like brulocht*), is a more developed statement of his mystical theology and it attained considerable popularity in his life-time. The work is based once again on an interpretation of a biblical text ('See, the Bridegroom comes; go out to meet him', Matt. 25:6) which is analysed at three levels in order to illustrate the three distinct stages of the spiritual life. This division of our religious journey into the active, the inward or God-desiring life and the contemplative life was to prove the most fundamental aspect of Ruusbroec's system. The third book which Ruusbroec wrote during his period in Brus-sels is *The Sparkling Stone* (*Vanden blinckenden steen*). This again was written in response to a request for clarification and is a summary of the previous work. In 1336 Pope Benedict XII (who in a previous incarnation was the Cardinal J. Fournier who sat in judgement on Eckhart in Avignon) pronounced on the nature of the Beatific Vision. His intention was to counter the teaching of his predecessor, John XXII, who had taught that the Beatific Vision is enjoyed by the saints not immediately after death but only at the end of time, and it has been argued that traces of Benedict XII's teaching can be found in *The Sparkling Stone* where Ruusbroec emphasizes that the vision enjoyed in this life is inferior to that of the saints in the life to come. It is a short piece and is one of Ruusbroec's most accessible writings. The next book was *The Four Temptations* (*Vanden vier becoringhen*) which explores the spiritual and moral temptations which affect the lives of the Beguines: concupiscence, spiritual pride in mortification and learning, and indolence. His fifth book, *The Christian Faith* (*Vanden kerstenen ghelove*), is a simple work of catechesis which contrasts with the complex and richly allegorical *Spiritual Tabernacle* (*Van den gheesteliken tabernakel*). The latter was begun in Brussels and completed in Ruusbroec's new home of Groenendaal. This work depends on the allegorical method of reading scripture which was current in the Middle Ages and which is quite foreign to modern tastes. It was immensely popular however in Ruusbroec's own day, and was the most frequently copied of all his writings. Sensibly Ruusbroec did not circulate the second part of the work – which includes strident criticism of the many abuses current in the church of his day – until he had left the church of St Gudule and retired to his forest retreat.

In 1343 Ruusbroec, together with Hinckaert and another canon, Vranke van Coudenberg, left Brussels in order to found a community at Groenendaal ('Green Dale'), in the forest of Soignes to the south-east of the city. This had served since 1304 as the location of a hermitage, and the third occupant, Lambert, was persuaded to move to a neighbouring site in order to accommodate the new foundation. John (Jan) III of Brabant increased the original endowment with an additional portion of land in order to support the venture. The intention of the three men was evident. Only by physically vacating the city, where church life was heavily corrupted by materialistic values, and where noisy and disruptive building projects were constantly underway in their own church of St Gudule, could they establish a centre in the 'desert' where true and deep spiritual values could flourish. In this aim they appear to have been entirely successful, and, despite some initial resistance from Ruusbroec himself who may have been mindful of the pitfalls of community living, others soon joined them. Indeed Groenendaal became a place of pilgrimage for people from a wide area, from as far away as Paris and the Rhineland. Among these was Geert Groote, the founder of the Brethren of the Common Life (who were to be an influence in the early schooling of both Erasmus and Luther) and a key figure in the spread of the *Devotio moderna* in the Netherlands (which was to give the world Thomas à Kempis and the *Imitation of Christ*). As has already been mentioned, it is possible that Johannes Tauler himself may well have sought out the celebrated Flemish mystic in his home at Groenendaal.[10] In 1349 they 'regularized' their new way of life as a result of ecclesiastical pressure and adopted the Augustinian Rule. Van Coudenberg became provost and Ruusbroec prior of the new community.

Ruusbroec continued his writing at Groenendaal, and Pomerius leaves us a picture of the ageing prior creeping into the forest with his wax tablet to set down his thoughts. To these later years belong the *Seven Enclosures* (*Vanden seven sloten*) and the *Mirror of Eternal Blessedness* (*Een spieghel der eeuwigher salicheit*). The former work was written for a Poor Clare sister

by the name of Margareta van Meerbeke and is an extensive
guide to daily life in a convent. It combines an elevated vision
of the union of the soul with God with sound advice on
practical details of routine existence. According to the manuscript tradition, the *Mirror of Eternal Blessedness* was written in
1359, and was addressed to an unnamed Poor Clare sister,
in all probability the same Margareta van Meerbeke. Its
concern with the Eucharist gave rise to an alternative name
of *On the Blessed Sacrament*. This is widely regarded as a particularly successful exposition of Ruusbroec's thought, and it is
one in which he addresses curt remarks to those who espouse
the peculiarly noxious form of pseudo-mysticism of the Free
Spirit. A further treatise, *Seven Rungs of the Ladder of Spiritual
Love* (*Vanden seven trappen in den graed der gheesteleker minnen*),
returns to the same outline of a spiritual journey through
virtue to a Trinitarian love-mysticism. The *Book of Clarification*
(*Dat boecksen der verclaringhe*) dates from around 1363 and it
returns to the *Kingdom of Lovers* which so perplexed the
Carthusians at Herne. It is a short and lucid account of the
ideas presented in that book, and is an ideal introduction to
Ruusbroec's thought. His final work, *The Twelve Beguines*
(*Vanden twaelf Beghinen*), is an uneasy compilation of four treatises which is likely to have been made by his brethren when
Ruusbroec himself had reached a great age. It contains a
good deal of astrological and astronomical material which
might present some difficulty for the modern reader, although
there are also mystical passages of high quality.

In his eighty-ninth year Ruusbroec fell ill and was moved
to the monastery's infirmary. Two weeks later, on 2 December
1381, he died. Although at first buried in the chapel his
remains eventually returned to his old home of St Gudule
(now a cathedral church dedicated to St Michael). In 1909
he was pronounced blessed, and his feast day falls on 2
December, the anniversary of his death.

The process of translating Ruusbroec's work into Latin
began very early on, while he was still alive. But it was the
translation made by Laurentius Surius and published in 1552
in Cologne which became the standard version of Ruusbroec's
work. This *Opera Omnia* included some additional minor
pieces, and a work entitled *The Book of Twelve Virtues* (*Vanden*

twaelf dogheden), which is known today to have been written by Godfried van Wevel, a disciple of Ruusbroec. This particular text contains a close rendering of the *Talks of Instruction* by Meister Eckhart, and hence was one source by which authentic Eckhartian material was transmitted to posterity. Although the Surius translation is a reasonably accurate version and has served as the basis for many modern translations, it relies principally upon the *textus receptus* of Ruusbroec's work produced by his own community at Groenendaal shortly after his death. Distinct variations between this version and that of earlier manuscripts which were produced during Ruusbroec's own lifetime, point to the need for a modern critical edition. The four-volume edition of 1932–5, reissued in 1944–8 and produced by the *Ruusbroecgenootschap* ('The Ruusbroec Society') similarly relies upon the Groenendaal tradition. A new definitive critical edition began to appear in 1981, however, of which only two volumes have appeared to date.[11]

THE THOUGHT OF RUUSBROEC

We have already seen how the mystical element leads to certain difficulties in the elucidation of Meister Eckhart's thought. It possesses an inner dynamic, which results from his personal mystical vision and which leads to an exceptional fluidity of concepts. It is not a question of development as such, by which certain ideas take the place of other ideas; rather we are concerned here with a change of *focus* as seeming truths give way to the apprehension of a deeper reality. We will encounter something similar in Ruusbroec's work. Like Eckhart, Ruusbroec evidently enjoyed a deep personal encounter with the Godhead. He, too, will attempt to state a dynamic vision in static form, and in doing so will present ideas which appear almost paradoxical and resistant to the clarity of dispassionate enquiry. And yet, like Eckhart, Ruusbroec generated a vitality and a momentum in his work which spoke profoundly to those around him during his own lifetime, as it does to us today.

Before embarking on an exposition of Ruusbroec's system,

it may be appropriate to clarify the historical links which existed between the Flemish mystic and his great Dominican predecessor. Considerable work has been done on the dissemination of Eckhartian manuscripts in the Low Countries during the early fourteen century,[12] and it is known that a number of sermons were translated into Dutch at an early stage, together with van Wevel's Dutch reworking of *The Talks of Instruction* as *The Book of Twelve Virtues*. Ruusbroec certainly knew the sermon *Beati pauperes spiritu* for he refers to it in *The Twelve Beguines* (T, IV, 40–2) although he does so in a disparaging way. This reflects the fact that this particular text was generally associated with the Brethren of the Free Spirit in the Netherlands, and Eckhart, whose condemnation was known, was viewed as a highly subversive figure. Other Dutch religious leaders including Ruusbroec's own disciple Jan van Leeuwen, attack Eckhart by name. The fact that Ruusbroec does not do so may lend strength to the theory of the meeting between Ruusbroec and Tauler, who, we may imagine, would have spoken highly of the Meister.

It would be wrong however to read into such hostility an informed critique of Eckhartian thought; the image of Meister Eckhart in the Netherlands at this time was far too partial and highly charged for any ojectivity.[13] This is borne out, for instance, by the fact that the sermons translated were circulated anonymously and were often approved reading for nuns and lay brothers, despite the general admonitions against Eckhart which issued from several quarters of the spiritual establishment. Texts of this kind, together with Van Wevel's rendering of the *Talks of Instruction*, may well have influenced to a degree the evolution of the spirituality of the *Devotio moderna*, despite the warnings against speculation, in particular that of Meister Eckhart, which came from Geert Groote, one of the founding spirits of the movement. The *Devotio moderna* grew into a large-scale phenomenon in the Netherlands, which furthered the cause of individual piety and an internal anti-hierarchical religion. The *Devotio moderna* was the inspiration for one of the most popular and influential Christian works of all time, the *Imitation of Christ*, and it also led to the foundation of the Brethren of the Common Life. This religious congregation specialized in the field of education, and it was in their schools that Desiderius Erasmus, one of the greatest critical scholars of the late medieval period, and Martin Luther were to receive their early education. The precise extent however to which the seeming presence of such tendencies in Eckhart's work actually influenced the *Devotio moderna* is an open and much discussed question.

It was not however the teaching of Eckhart as the preacher of a simple, individual and muscular piety which interested Ruusbroec. Although he was almost certainly unaware of their ultimate source, we find throughout his work distinctly Eckhartian material. Ruusbroec employs specifically Eckhartian language in his insistence on the need to transcend all creatures and images in order to attain an 'imageless' state of naked being in which God can be encountered. He talks also of the 'spark' (in which however he follows St Thomas Aquinas's definition of it as 'the inclination to the good'), of the 'ground' of the soul and even occasionally of the 'eternal birth of God' in the soul's ground. Despite these apparent borrowings, it would be quite wrong to speak of Ruusbroec as being in any meaningful sense a disciple of Eckhart. The thrust and tenor of his thought are quite different, as we shall see, and what might be dubbed Eckhartian material becomes an organic part of his own distinctive system. It is unclear, also, how Ruusbroec might have come into contact with Eckhartian ideas. In the prevailing atmosphere of hostility towards him, it is unlikely that Ruusbroec would have dwelt at length on the few authentic works that existed in the Netherlands at the time. A more likely source is Hadewijch II, whom Ruusbroec certainly quotes in *The Twelve Beguines*, and who may herself have come under the influence of Eckhartian texts. A further possibility, of course, is Johannes Tauler. Although the earliest Dutch translations of Tauler's work date from the mid-fifteenth century,[14] there is a very real possibility, as we have seen, that Tauler may have visited Groenendaal during Ruusbroec's lifetime. The fact also that Ruusbroec sent a copy of his *Spiritual Espousals* to the Friends of God in the Rhineland in 1350 underlines at the very least the existence of a mutual awareness. It is also true to say that those Eckhartian elements which we find in Ruusbroec are all contained in Tauler and, further, that they bear Tauler's own stamp of inward devotion and enlightened morality.

HUMAN NATURE AND DIVINE GRACE

Jan van Ruusbroec stands in the tradition of a trinitarian love-mysticism which was conveyed to him principally by the work of Hadewijch and William of St Thierry and which has its remote origins in the thought of St Augustine. Just as was the case for St Augustine, therefore, the trinitarian principle of three in one becomes such a dominant idea for Ruusbroec that it appears at all levels of his thought and experience. He is fascinated both by the triune principle at work in all things and by the ideas of unicity and multiplicity which are contained in the notion of 'three Persons, one God'. The practical consequences of this for Ruusbroec's work are that he tends to think in threes and he likes to envisage what we might call a system of dual modality whereby the principle of multiplicity, diversity and activity alternates with that of unicity and rest. Ruusbroec's natural tendency therefore is to think in terms of a 'flux' or 'pulsation', as these two principles constantly yield one to the other. The further point which Ruusbroec inherits from the Augustinian tradition is his strong theology of grace. Nothing of the supernatural life can occur in us without the direct operation of divine grace, and Ruusbroec constantly draws our attention to the workings of grace within us at all levels of our psychological and spiritual being.

Thinking in triads and threefold unities was fundamental to medieval thinkers, who liked to see the reflection of the divine reality in all things and who reverenced number as a mystical sign of this ubiquitous presence.[15] It is however a little strange to us, and it is worth outlining the general features of Ruusbroec's system before beginning to analyse it in detail. He sees for instance the nature of the human being as tripartite. In the first place we exist as creatures, having much in common with the animals. At this level our activity and multiplicity are expressed in our bodily faculties and in the faculties of the lower mind, whereas the unity and coherence of this level is to be found in the centre of our physical life, or what Ruusbroec calls the 'unity of the heart'. The operation of grace in this sphere, which transforms it from the natural to the supernatural life, acts upon us from the outside in the form of the church and its moral commandments. The life of grace which it produces in us is the life of good works and external acts of piety. The second level of unity which exists in us is that of the faculties of the higher mind. Here multiplicity and activity are expressed in our memory, will and intelligence. These on the other hand find their unity in the 'ground' of the soul. The supernatural life is realized in this dimension of our being through the inward promptings of grace and through a life of inner devotion and charity. The central place of love in this life leads us on to the third stage, in which we encounter and activate the source of our own being as it is contained from eternity in the Godhead. We become involved in the inner life of the Trinity itself and are destroyed and renewed through the love generated by the Persons of the Trinity. In the final stage we become one with the flux of the Godhead in the Trinity, enjoying the blissful interchange of love which exists there and entering into the radiant stillness of unity as it exists beyond and within the divine Persons. This barest outline of Ruusbroec's work is intended only to highlight the idea of a movement between activity and rest, unicity and multiplicity, which is fundamental to all his thinking and is the key to its understanding.

Ruusbroec himself begins his tripartite division of man with the highest level of our existence, which is our existence within God. This is essentially the traditional medieval idea, Platonic in origin and given common currency in the West by St Augustine, that creatures exist not only in the world but also as an idea in the mind of God. This 'idea' is our divine 'blueprint', and it is the source of our being and existence. At the same time this ideal and divinized self is the goal of our spiritual journey:

Now take note: there is a threefold unity which exists in all people naturally and in all good people supernaturally as well. The first and highest unity is that which we have

in God, for all creatures depend on this unity for their
being, their life and their preservation, and should they be
separated from God at this level, then they would fall into
nothingness and become nothing. We possess this unity
both within ourselves and beyond ourselves as that which
is the source of our life and which sustains us in being. (E,
72; T, 144)[16]

Ruusbroec appears to think of this level of our being in terms
approaching Eckhart's 'ground of the soul', in which the
divine life within us is constantly renewed. He refers in fact
to the 'eternal birth' of God in this deepest region of our
being, stating that this occurs 'ceaselessly' and that God
'possesses' this area of ourselves, all of which images are used
by Eckhart in his own metaphysical vocabulary. This, the
highest unity, then is not only the source of our continuing
being but is also the guarantee of our likeness to God and of
our potential sanctification:

> . . . for the being and the life that we are in God, in our
> eternal image, is immediately and indivisibly united with
> the being and life that we possess essentially in ourselves.
> For this reason, the spirit, in its most intimate and highest
> part, in its bare nature, ceaselessly receives the imprint of
> its eternal image and of the divine radiance and becomes
> an eternal dwelling place of God. God possesses this
> dwelling place with his eternal presence and constantly
> comes to it afresh with new radiance from his eternal birth.
> (E, 117; T, 203)

Ruusbroec progresses from this unified 'essence' of the soul
(*dat wesen der zielen*) to discuss the 'activities' of the soul which
arise from the 'second unity' or the 'unity of the spirit or
mind' (*gheest*). In his description of these activities, which are
the higher faculties of the mind, Ruusbroec closely follows
the triad of memory, understanding and will which, for St
Augustine, constituted our 'mind':

> There is also a second unity in us by nature, which is the
> unity of the higher powers. This is a unity from which they

arise naturally as active powers and is a unity of the spirit or mind . . . We possess this unity within ourselves above the realm of the senses, and from it spring the powers of memory, understanding and will – all our mental activities. In this unity the soul is called spirit. (ibid.)

The third dimension of our being is the life of the body itself, and of our senses. Here the diversity of our bodily powers, those which we have in common with the animals, are founded on the 'unity of the heart', which is an image that expresses our corporal vitality. Here we speak not of the 'essence of the soul' or of the 'spirit' but of the 'soul' itself:

The third unity which is in us by nature is the ground of the bodily powers in the unity of the heart, which is the beginning and source of our bodily life. The soul possesses this unity in the body and in the vitality of the heart from which all the works of the body flow and of the five senses. Here the soul is simply called soul, for it is the form of the body and animates the flesh by giving it life and keeping it alive. (ibid.)

In a passage which follows from the one above Ruusbroec stresses the unity which these distinct levels of physical (emotional), rational and spiritual (essential) life form:

These three unities exist naturally in a person and constitute a single life and realm. The lowest unity contains a person's feelings and animal powers; in the second a person exists as a rational and spiritual being and in the highest a person is preserved in being in an essential way. All this is in everyone by nature. (ibid.)

This division of the person into three contiguous levels or dimensions plays a critical role in Ruusbroec's understanding of the spiritual path as a whole. We have seen the stress he lays on the fact that this is the *natural* condition of human kind ('Now take note: there is a threefold unity which exists in all people naturally') and, during the course of this chapter, we will see the process whereby this system of nature is

transformed by grace until these three divisions may be said
to exist in us 'supernaturally as well'. Thus the path to God
for Ruusbroec is a threefold one, according to this threefold
division of our nature. In a passage from the beginning of the
Spiritual Espousals, in which he expresses his intention to
discuss a line from scripture in three different ways, Ruusbroec touches on these distinct stages of spiritual growth:

> We wish to clarify and explain these words in three different
> ways. Firstly in a general way in which we speak of a life
> for beginners, which is called the active life, but which is
> one that all men need who seek salvation. The second way
> in which we wish to interpret these same words is according
> to an inward and exalted life of desire to which many
> people come through the practice of virtue and by the grace
> of God. The third way.in which we wish to explain them
> is from the point of view of a superessential life of contem-
> plation, which few people attain and enjoy because of its
> sublime and noble nature. (E, 42; T, 104)

Ruusbroec emphasizes that it is only through grace that we
are transformed and that what is 'naturally' present in us
becomes 'supernaturally' so. He speaks in the following
passage of God's transforming grace as we encounter him in
the first stage of our journey ('with intermediary') and in the
second ('without intermediary'):

> . . . the spirit must be either like God through grace and
> virtue or unlike him through mortal sin. This is because
> man is made in the likeness of God, that is, in the grace of
> God, because grace is a divine light which penetrates us
> and makes us like God, and without this light we cannot
> attain supernatural union with him. Although we cannot
> lose his image in us or our natural union with him, we can
> lose our likeness to him, which is the grace of God, and
> thus suffer damnation.
>   And so whenever God finds some facility in us for
> receiving his grace, then he wishes to give us life through
> his sovereign goodness and transform us into his likeness
> by his gifts. This happens whenever we turn to God with

the whole of our will, for in that very moment Christ comes to us and enters within us, with intermediary and without intermediary, which is to say with gifts and beyond gifts. And we come to him and enter within him with intermediary and without intermediary, that is with virtues and beyond virtues. And he imprints his image upon us and his likeness, that is himself and his gifts, and frees us from sin, making us like him. (E, 118f; T, 204f)

THE ACTIVE LIFE

In tracing the passage of the soul from its 'natural' life to a 'supernatural' life in God, we will begin with the lowest or initial form of this life of grace, to which Ruusbroec gives the name, among others, of 'the union with God by intermediary'. Broadly this corresponds to a Christian life of virtue lived out with reference and in obedience to the church. Although he describes it as the 'life for beginners', and shows a tendency to pass over it on the way to the other, more interesting stages of the spiritual life, Ruusbroec is always at pains to stress that it cannot be dispensed with the moment we attain the interior life of union with God, and that it remains essential for our salvation. A succinct description of this life occurs in the *Book of Clarification:*

> . . . all good men are united with God by an intermediary. That intermediary is the grace of God, together with the sacraments of the Holy Church, the divine virtues of faith, hope and love and a virtuous life led according to God's commandments. To this belongs a death to sin and to the world and to all the disordered desires of nature, and by this we remain united with the Holy Church, that is with all good men. Thus we are obedient to God and are of one will with him, just as a good community is united with their superior. And without this union we cannot please God nor be saved. (B, 110)

In terms of another passage, from the *Spiritual Espousals*, the active life is 'supernaturally adorned and possessed through the external exercise of perfect virtues in the manner of Christ and his saints. This is to carry the cross with Christ and to subdue our nature to the commandments of Holy Church and to the teaching of the saints, sensibly and according to our strength' (E, 73; T, 146). A further discussion from the *Spiritual Espousals* goes into greater depth on the nature of the virtues which characterize this kind of life: fear of the Lord, kindness, knowledge, fortitude, counsel, understanding, wisdom. These are in principle the traditonal 'seven gifts of the Holy Spirit', which were developed as a concept during the patristic age and rely upon a reading of Isaiah 11:1–3. Ruusbroec stresses that the virtues are founded ultimately upon purity or simplicity of intention, which is the 'end and beginning and adornment of all virtue':

> Now understand how we can meet God in each of our works, increasing in our likeness to him and more nobly possessing our blissful unity with him. Every good work, however small it may be, which is performed in God with love and a righteous, pure intention, earns for us a greater likeness to God and eternal life in him. A pure intention unites the scattered powers of the soul in the unity of the spirit and orientates the spirit towards God. A pure intention is the end and beginning and adornment of all virtue. A pure intention offers praise and honour and all virtue to God. It passes through itself, the heavens and all things and finds God in the purity of its own ground. That intention is pure which holds only to God and sees all things in relation to God. (E, 121; T, 209)

This 'outer' life is therefore one of simple virtue and goodness in which the moral commandments of Christianity are accepted and made our own. It is the realm of alms-giving and good works, of external piety and prayer. Ruusbroec's emphasis on purity of intention safeguards this spirituality of works from descending into hypocrisy and a shallow form of 'doing good'. There is no trace here of the Pharisaism which so afflicted the fourteenth-century church and against which Ruusbroec was so forthright in his condemnation. Nor, as we progress on our spiritual journey, is there any question of leaving the life of good works and virtue behind; rather, as we shall see, our deepening encounter with God in the ground of our being enriches and vivifies the devout labours and sacrifices of this outer man. It is said of the active life therefore that it 'begins here and lasts eternally' (B, 150). But this life is nevertheless a limited one. Essentially it is a life of conventional piety, neither sinful nor inspiring, and if we wish to progress further, Ruusbroec tells us, we will need to advance from simple deeds in themselves to the state of being which is their ground:

> And for this reason, if someone wishes to approach God and to raise their life and exercises to a higher level, then they must pass from works to the reason for them, moving from the sign to the reality. Thus they will become master of their works, knowing the truth, and will enter upon the interior life. (E, 124; T, 212)

The active life truly lived leads in fact to the threshold of a higher and more inward devotion to God, which Ruusbroec calls the 'interior life' or the 'union with God without intermediary':

> In this way we should live in the unity of our spirits in grace and in likeness to God, encountering God constantly through the intermediary of virtue and offering our life and all our works in purity of intention to him so that we shall at all times and in all our works become more like him. And so, on the foundation of our pure intention, we shall transcend ourselves and meet God without intermediary and rest with him in the ground of simplicity. There we shall possess the inheritance which has been preserved for us from all eternity. (E, 122, T, 210)

THE INTERIOR LIFE

We will be misjudging Ruusbroec if we imagine that each of the three lives which he describes as stages of the spiritual journey form distinct areas which do not overlap. The union with God 'with intermediary', 'without intermediary' and 'without distinction' form a continuum. Nor does one stage supplant the other; rather there is a movement of depth in Ruusbroec's thought in which one perspective opens out into a new, more radical dimension of union with God. Nothing is lost, but the simplest acts of conventional piety are retained even when the soul enjoys the deepest and most intimate encounter with the Godhead.

Nevertheless the 'interior life' represents a greatly heightened state of spiritual consciousness *vis-à-vis* the 'active life', in which an intense inner devotion to God and a radical, personal experience of his enlivening grace overwhelm the dimension of a largely external life of good works. The area of ourselves which corresponds to this form of life is that of the 'higher powers', of memory, intelligence and will. Working from the principle of the Trinity, St Augustine argued that this triad constituted the human mind. The virtues, therefore, which belong to this life of grace are the 'higher virtues' of faith, hope and charity. These are essentially 'source' or 'foundational' virtues which guarantee the internal disposition required for the external life of virtue and good works.

In his discussion of this stage, Ruusbroec stresses the inner life in its many forms. He places great weight on the quality of self-abnegation and the subordination of our own will to the will of God:

> From this obedience there comes the renunciation of our own will and our own opinions. Only a person who is obedient can deny their own will in all things for the will of another, for anyone can do outer works and yet hold to their own will . . . By renouncing our own will in deciding what is to be done, what not done and what is to be endured, the substance and occasion of pride is banished and humility is perfected in the highest degree. And God becomes master of a person's whole will, which becomes so united with God's will that they can neither will nor desire anything else. (E, 57; T, I, 125)

Our new interior life is revealed also in the way that we

respond to suffering. Rather than destroying us, suffering wisely handled becomes the source of a real interior joy:

> If a person is to be healed of this distress, then they must feel and think that they are not their own possession but that they belong to God. And therefore they must abandon their own self-will to the free will of God, allowing God to act in time and in eternity. If they can do this without heaviness of heart and with a free spirit, then at that very moment they will be healed and bring heaven to hell and hell to heaven. For however much the scale of love goes up and down, this person always remains perfectly balanced. For they who suffer without resentment remain free and balanced in their spirit, and they experience the union with God without intermediary. (B, 126)

> And they will turn all their abandonment into an interior joy, offering themselves into God's hands and rejoicing that they are able to undergo suffering for the glory of God. If they do this aright, then they will know a greater interior joy than ever before, for nothing is so great a cause of delight to those who love God than the feeling that they belong entirely to their Beloved. (E, 92; T, I, 170)

In the active or exterior life, grace is mediated to the outer man through the church, her practices and teachings. For the interior life however the source of grace is more inward, and arises from the soul's own ground in which its higher powers are unified and from which they spring:

> All grace and all gifts flow forth from this unity in which the spirit is unified without intermediary with God . . . This grace descends on us in the unity of our higher powers and our spirit from which these flow out in active virtue by means of grace and to which they return again in the bond of love . . . Now the grace of God, which flows forth from God, is an interior impulse or urging of the Holy Spirit which drives our spirit from within and urges it outwards towards all the virtues. This grace flows from within us and not from outside us, for God is more interior to us

than we are to ourselves and his interior urging and working within us, whether natural or supernatural, is closer and more intimate to us than our own activity. For this reason God works from within us outwards, whereas all creatures act upon us from without. (E, 74f; T, I, 147f)

This passage draws out the flux which we experience at this stage between our exercising of the higher functions of the mind and their virtues and our experience of the inner bond of unity in the ground of the soul, which is their foundation. The language which Ruusbroec uses in order to discuss this ground shows the distinctive influence of Eckhartian terms and imagery. He speaks of the 'bareness' of the soul and of its 'essence'. Above all, he speaks of an inward state of being which is beyond all images and all creatures: the *abgescheidenheit* or detachment which for Eckhart is the keystone of the spiritual life:

> If someone wishes to see in a supernatural way in interior exercises, then three things are necessary. The first is the light of God's grace in a higher manner than we experience in an external and active life without fervent inward zeal. The second point is the stripping of alien images and concerns from the heart so that we are free and imageless, delivered from attachments and free of all creatures. The third point is the free turning of the will and gathering of all the powers, both corporal and spiritual and unencumbered by any inordinate attachments, so that we flow into God's unity and into the unity of the mind. In this way the rational creature can attain the exalted unity of God and possess it supernaturally. (E, 71f; T, I, 144)

In another passage Ruusbroec develops more fully what he understands by this detachment and shows how he envisages by it a combination of the Eckhartian state of being, beyond all creaturely differentiation, and the moral detachment based upon humility and self-abnegation, as developed by Tauler:

> Whoever wishes to have a heart free of images should possess nothing with affection, nor associate with anyone,

holding to them with attachment of will. For all association and all attachment which is not solely for the sake of God's glory serves only to fill a person's heart with images, being born not of God but of the flesh. And so if a person wants to become spiritual, then they must renounce all corporal attachments and hold to God alone with longing and affection, possessing him in this way. Thus images and disordered affections for creatures are banished. By possessing God with affection, we are inwardly cleansed of images, because God is a spirit who cannot be represented by images. But in their exercises, a person should make use of good images, such as the passion of Our Lord and all things which stir us to greater devotion. But in possessing God, we must descend into the bare imagelessness, which God is. (SS, 157; T, III, 5)

It is certainly when Ruusbroec is speaking of detachment and the state of imagelessness that he is closest to the work of Meister Eckhart; but even here there are essential differences. In Ruusbroec's view, for instance, this state is achieved not through austerities of the will but by holding to God 'with longing and affection'. Essentially we are called to replace the images of our attachment to the world with images of the Christian revelation. These in turn, far from proving an encumbrance, inspire us with love for God and devotion to him so that we are led into a new knowledge of God, as he is in himself, bare and devoid of all images and representations. We perceive then another aspect of Ruusbroec's dialectic here, in an implicit alternation between the images of Christian devotion and the imagelessness of the highest interior life to which they lead.

The theme of detachment, which is an essential part of Ruusbroec's interior life, is therefore always linked with a fervent love for God. Detachment is moreover not something we attain, but rather the result of grace operating at this inward level of the soul, and it is a reflection of the bare essence of God himself. Our experience of this essence, in the interior life, is one of ecstatic and transforming love:

Sometimes a person who lives the interior life turns in

within themselves in a simple manner following their inclination to delight, and there, beyond all activities and
virtues, they look with a simple and inward gaze upon
blissful love. Here they meet God without intermediary.
And there shines upon them from the depths of God's
unity an undifferentiated light, which shows them darkness,
bareness and nothingness. Such a person is enveloped in
the darkness and falls into modelessness as if they were
quite lost. In the bareness they lose the perception and
distinction of all things and are transformed and permeated
by a simple Radiance. In the nothingness all their works
fail them, for they are overwhelmed by the activity of the
love of God that is deep without end. And in the inclination
towards delight of their spirit, they overcome God and
become one spirit with him. And in this union in the spirit
of God they savour an ecstatic delight, and possess the
divine Essence. (E, 132f; T, I, 223f)

There is nothing static however about this experience of union
with God, for it generates an intensity of love and delight
which floods back into the soul's higher powers, cleansing
and transforming them. They experience 'an embrace and
fullness of felt love' (ibid.). At all stages of Ruusbroec's
journey the experience of unity excites the powers of the soul
again, finding expression in inward devotion and virtuous
action and in an intense active love. This active love leads in
turn, by the principle of 'savorous delight' in God's being, to
an experience of unity within him and of union with him.
And so this cycle of moral goodness and divine delight is
completed time and again.

The stress Ruusbroec lays at all points in his system on
our delight in God is distinct from the German tendency to
emphasize his transcendence. Central to Eckhart's vision is
the sense of metaphysical space, the total absence of created
being, which the soul experiences in the Godhead by following
the path of detachment. For Ruusbroec, on the other hand,
the advance of the soul into the Godhead is a journey into
transcendence which, although it involves detachment, is
essentially a passage through love, ecstasy and delight.[17] And
it is when he discusses the love of God and our deep delight

in him that Ruusbroec attains his greatest eloquence, as can be seen in the following text. Here he speaks of the immense hunger of the soul for God which, not being satisfied, culminates in a great 'restlessness and deep fury (*oerwoet*) of love':

> And the soul lays open all her faculties in order to give God all that she is and to receive from him all that he is. But this is impossible for her. The more she gives and receives, the greater her desire to give and to receive. And she can neither give herself to God entirely nor receive God entirely. For all that she receives, compared with what she still lacks, is little and it seems to her to be nothing. Therefore she becomes tempestuous and falls into restlessness and a deep fury of love, for she can neither do without him nor acquire him, neither sound his depths nor scale his heights, neither embrace him nor abandon him. (SE, 182f)

But at this moment of our greatest impotence and failure, when we are seized by the 'helplessness' of this love, God himself intervenes:

> But where the human way is found wanting and can go no higher, there begins the way of God. That is, when we hold to God with intention, with love and with unsatisfied desire and cannot become one with him, then the Spirit of Our Lord comes like a mighty fire that burns, consumes and devours all that is in us so that we are no longer aware of ourselves and our devotions but we experience ourselves as if we were one spirit and one love with God (ibid.)

Sometimes developing imagery he finds in Beatrice, Ruusbroec speaks of this flux of love as a living and a dying, a cessation in the bliss of inner unity and a restoration in the vitality of action and multiplicity:

> Sometimes this person living the interior life turns actively and with desire towards God so that they can give God all glory and honour, offering him themselves and all their works, and thus they are consumed in God's love . . . Such a person has an inward perception and sensation in the

ground of their being, where all virtues have their beginning and their end and where they offer God all virtues with desire, and where love dwells. Here the hunger and thirst of love become so great that they surrender themselves at every moment and cannot work, but rather transcend their activity and are destroyed in love. They hunger and thirst for the taste of God and at each sight of him they are grasped by him and touched by him anew in love. So living they die, and dying they return to life. Thus the yearning hunger and thirst of love are constantly renewed in them. (E, 133f; T, I, 225)

You well know that I have already said how all the saints and all good people are united with God with intermediary. Now I want to go on to tell you how they are all united with God without intermediary. But there are few in this life who are able and enlightened enough to feel and understand this. And for this reason, whoever wishes to feel and experience within themselves these three forms of union with God of which I speak, must live for God with their whole selves so that they can respond to the stirrings and grace of God, and submit to him in all virtues and interior exercises. Such a person must become exalted through love and die in God to themselves and to all their works so that they yield with all their faculties and suffer the transformation of the unfathomable truth which is God himself. Thus they must go out, living, to the practice of virtue and, dying, enter into God . . . Because they thus hold and exercise themselves in the presence of God, love will master them in every way. (B, 122)

Ruusbroec thus envisages an internal state in which we are constantly renewed by an ecstatic impulse from God which we experience as his transforming love and which drives us to seek him in his depths with our own answering love. The idea of reciprocity and of the mutuality of this love is essential to Ruusbroec's vision. And there is no image better suited to express this wild, transcendent dialogue of love than that of a storm:

In the summer it is common to see two strong opposing

winds clash and storm together in the air, thus creating thunder and lightning, hail and rain, sometimes even tempests and plagues, here below. We can see the same thing in the storm and fury of love when the human spirit is raised up to union with the Spirit of Our Lord and each spirit touches the other with love and each makes invitation to the other and offers him all that he is and all that he can do. Then reason is enlightened and becomes clear and desires at all cost to know what love is, and what that touch may be that moves and wells up in the spirit. And desire wants to discover and savour all that the enlightened reason can know, which gives rise to a storm of love in the soul and great restlessness. But this the loving spirit well knows: the more it gains, the more it lacks. And the storm and fury of love which spring forth, burning and welling up within it, cannot be appeased, but from each mutual renewing touch come yet more storms of love. And these storms are just like thunderclaps from which there springs the fire of love, like sparks from gleaming metal and fiery lightning from heaven. (SE, 176)

It is the 'touch' (*gherinen*) of God which causes the storms of love in the soul. This image of the 'touch', which is felt in the 'innermost part of the spirit' (E, 112; T, I, 196) is fundamental to Ruusbroec and he returns to it on many occasions in order to express the idea that the inner dynamism of the Godhead acts upon us, sanctifying us and drawing us into a profound inner union with him. This tactile and affective image is at the heart of his spiritual vision.[18] The 'touch' moreover is for Ruusbroec the final intermediary between ourselves and the true depths of the Godhead. It leads us to a state where the immediacy of God's presence transcends the capacities of reason; and it is here, as becomes apparent in the second passage quoted below, that love takes its proper place as *Amor-Intellectus*, the higher manner of knowing God, which gives us entry into his mystery:

Thus similarly the grace of God floods into the higher powers like streams, driving and enflaming a person to the practice of all virtues. And it dwells in the unity of our

spirit like a spring, welling up in this same unity from
which it arises, just like a living vein welling up out of the
living ground of God's richness where neither faith nor
grace can ever fail. This is the touch that I mean.

The creature undergoes this touch passively for here is
the union of the higher powers in the unity of the spirit,
above the multiplicity of all virtues. And no one is active
here but God alone, in his sovereign divinity, who is the
cause of all our virtue and blessedness. In the unity of the
spirit, where this vein wells up, we are above all works and
above reason, but not without reason, for the enlightened
reason, and especially the power of love, feel this touch but
reason cannot grasp or understand the mode or manner of
this touch, or how or what it is. This is because the touch
is a divine work, the source and irruption of all graces and
all gifts, and it is the last intermediary between God and
creature. (E, 112f; T, I, 196f)

And those who, through the practice of virtue and interior
exercises, have fathomed the depths of their being to its
source, which is the door to eternal life, are able to feel the
touch. There the Radiance of God is so great that reason
and all the powers of understanding fail, having to suffer
and yield to the incomprehensible Radiance of God. But
the spirit who feels this touch in its ground finds that,
although its reason and understanding fail before the divine
Radiance and must remain outside the door, its power of
love wills to go further. Like the intellect, it has been called
and invited but, being blind, desires only to enjoy; and
enjoying is more a matter of savouring and feeling than
understanding. This is why love enters while understanding
remains outside. (E, 114; T, I, 198f)

Love, then, is the key to this higher knowledge, and the touch,
which is the highest intermediary between God and man, is
the point at which, through this dialogue of love, we come to
the threshold of that transcendent knowledge. This is the
thrust of a final passage of singular beauty in which for the
first time we encounter elements which properly belong to
the third stage of the spiritual journey, which is the life of

contemplation: 'And above this touch, in the still essence of this spirit, there hovers an incomprehensible Radiance, which is the sublime Trinity from which the touch comes. There God lives and reigns in the spirit, and the spirit in God' (E, 113; T, I, 197).

THE CONTEMPLATIVE LIFE

Strictly, Ruusbroec's own understanding of the 'contemplative' life, which he also calls the 'superessential' or 'divine' life and which is the highest point of the spiritual journey, is that it consists in a still and blissful gazing upon the transcendent unity of the divine Trinity. But we encounter elements of this experience before its full flowering, and it is possible to trace them at the stage where the interior life reaches such a point of inwardness and intensity that the soul is drawn through the 'touch' of divine love to the very threshold of the divine mystery, which is the Trinity. There it comes to a place in which reason, even reason clarified by the divine light, is made impotent and only love can allow the soul to advance into a deepening knowledge of, and union with, the Godhead.

In the passage which follows we can see how Ruusbroec conceives of the inner life of the Trinity as an eternal alternation between the dynamic mode of active inter-Personal love, and a static mode of still and transcendent unity:

And there we must accept that the Persons yield and lose themselves, whirling in essential love, that is, in a unity of delight, and yet they always remain according to their nature as Persons in the dynamism of the Trinity. And thus we understand that the divine Nature is eternally active according to the manner of the Persons and yet eternally at rest and without mode according to the simplicity of its essence. (B, 136)

It is important to note in this passage that Ruusbroec does not suggest that the state of unity in the Trinity is higher than its dynamic multiplicity, which would not conform to orthodox teaching. Rather, the idea presented here is that there exist within the Trinity what one French critic has called two 'moments dialectiques', that is, two constantly interchanging elements or modes.[19] Although Ruusbroec does not teach that one is higher than the other, he does suggest that we progress into an apprehension of the unity of the Trinity through our experience of the dynamic life of the Trinity in its inter-Personal love. He speaks at one point of its 'living life', which is an image used before him by William of St Thierry and Hadewijch, and which aptly portrays the dynamism of the Godhead into which the soul, by love, is drawn:

> You can thus see that the attractive power of the unity of God is nothing other than love without end which, through love, draws the Father and the Son and all that lives in them into an eternal delight. And we desire to burn and be consumed in this love for all eternity, for it is here that the blessedness of all spirits lies. Therefore we should found our whole life on a fathomless abyss so that we eternally sink into love and immerse ourselves in its fathomless depths. And in the same love we will rise up and rise above ourselves to an incomprehensible height. In this modeless love we will wander, and it shall bring us into the immeasurable breadth of God's love. There we shall flow forth and flow out of ourselves into the uncomprehended abundance of God's riches and goodness. There we will melt and be dissolved, eternally taken up in the maelstrom of God's glory. (SS, 159; T, I, 8)

A further passage continues the theme of the integration of the soul, through love, into the inner life of the Trinity, but here we find a new and distinctive note of the transformation which takes place in the soul as it encounters the uncreated light of God's radiance:

> Therefore God has given us a life above ourselves, and that is a divine life. It is nothing other than a contemplating and a gazing and a holding to God in bare love, a savouring and a delighting and a melting away in love, and a constant

renewal of all this. For there, where we are raised above reason and all our activities in naked vision, we are wrought by the spirit of Our Lord. And there we suffer the inworking of God and are illumined by divine light, just as the air is illumined by the light of the sun and as iron is permeated by the strength and heat of fire. Thus we are transformed and penetrated from splendour to splendour, in the very image of the Holy Trinity . . . There the Father finds us and loves us in the Son, and the Son finds us and loves us with the same love in the Father. And the Father and the Son embrace us in the unity of the Holy Spirit, in a blessed delight which is eternally renewed, ceaselessly, in knowledge and in love, through the eternal birth of the Son from the Father and the outpouring of the Holy Spirit from them both. (SE, 172)

The idea that we are united with this transcendent light of the Godhead at the culmination of our spiritual journey is repeated many times. In it Ruusbroec is expressing the ancient Christian understanding that the soul is empowered to know God directly, in the highest mystical experience, through the bestowal of his own radiance upon us. This is the highest form of grace that we can know, and it is this which transforms us, and illumines us, to an extent that we are able to apprehend God in his essence:

And all those who are raised above their createdness into a contemplative life are one with the divine Radiance, and they are this Radiance itself. Through this divine Light and their own uncreated being, they see and feel and find themselves to be the same simple ground from which the Radiance shines forth immeasurably and in a divine manner and in which, according to the simplicity of the divine Essence, it dwells modelessly and eternally. For this reason interior, contemplative persons proceed, in the way of contemplation, beyond reason and distinction, and beyond their created being. In an eternal act of gazing by virtue of the inborn light, they are transformed and become one with that same light with which they see and which they see. (E, 150; T, I, 246)

Paradoxically, the experience of this light is concomitant with a vision of God as darkness. Here again we encounter Ruusbroec's dialectic with which he seeks to express mysteries which transcend ordered rational discussion. At the heart of God, or more properly at the heart of our experience of him as he chooses to reveal himself to us, there is a light/dark pulsation, just as there is a twin modality of unicity and multiplicity, of dynamic movement and stasis. And so, having spoken of the *lumen gloriae*, the light of Glory, which flows from the ground of the Godhead, transforming us and illumining us, he is able to speak also of our vision of God as 'a dark stillness and a wild desert' (E, 100; T, I, 181). It is the infinite transcendence of God which is being communicated here, for he is also 'inaccessible height and unfathomable depth, incomprehensible breadth and eternal length . . . a fathomless sea' (ibid.). The theme of divine darkness is established in a passage from *The Book of Enlightenment*:

> And for this reason enlightened people have found within themselves an essential inward gazing above reason and without reason, and an inclination of delight passing beyond all modes and all essence, sinking away from themselves into a modeless abyss of fathomless beatitude, where the Trinity of the divine Persons possess their natures in essential unity. See, here the beatitude is so simple and without mode that in it all the essential gazing, inclination and distinction of creatures pass away. For all spirits thus raised up dissolve and are destroyed by their delight in God's essence, which is the superessence of all essence. There they fall away from themselves into a fathomless unknowing. There all clarity returns to darkness, where the three Persons yield to their essential unity and enjoy an essential beatitude without distinction. (B, 146)

This third stage is also marked by a sense of satiety where previously there had been the 'madness' or 'fury' of love as the ascending soul strained, impossibly, for union with the Godhead. Ruusbroec speaks of 'an essential forward inclination', which, in the highest forms of the interior life, is 'an essential distinction between the soul and the essence of God' although it is the 'highest distinction which we can feel' (B, 144f). This idea recalls one of the great theoretical debates of the medieval period, which was the question whether the will (that is to say 'love') or knowledge predominates in the final Beatific Vision. The Augustinian tradition, which found its greatest champions in St Bernard of Clairvaux and the Franciscan St Bonaventure, insisted on the primacy of love in our final union with God. St Thomas Aquinas, on the other hand, and Meister Eckhart himself, stressed the place of knowledge. Thomas argued that love draws us towards the object of our desire but that only by knowledge (made possible through the bestowal of the light of Glory) can we truly possess God in his essence. It is striking that Ruusbroec, surely writing from the basis of his own experience rather than a concern with this theoretical discussion, should begin to introduce images of love's satiety where his portrayal of union with God tips into darkness, stasis and pure contemplation. The word he uses to express our experience of God at this level is still *smaec*, or 'savouring', though he speaks no more of the turbulent affections of the spirit with its 'storms of love', but of the stillness and darkness of God: that paradoxical state in which we know him by 'unknowing' (B, 146):

> The possession of this is a simple, fathomless savouring of all that is good and of eternal life. And in this savouring we are taken up beyond reason and without reason into the deep stillness of the Godhead, which is never moved . . . We are therefore poor in ourselves but rich in God, hungry and thirsty in ourselves but drunk and satisfied in God, active in ourselves but empty and at rest in God. (SS, 172; T, III, 25f)

Ruusbroec's final vision is an anticipation of the next life in which the soul is set free to flow into the 'fathomless sea' of the Godhead, into the immensity of the uncreated being of God. Ruusbroec takes us in the following passage to the very edge of created experience and to the threshold of the world that is to come:

Now this active meeting and this loving embrace are in

their ground blissful and modeless. For the fathomless, modeless being of God is so dark and so without particular form or manner that it contains all the ways of God, the activity and characteristics of the Persons in the rich embrace of essential unity, thus creating a divine bliss in the abyss of the ineffable. Here there is a blissful crossing over and a self-transcending immersion into a state of essential bareness, where all the divine names and modes and all the living ideas which are reflected in the mirror of divine truth fall away into simple ineffability, without mode and without reason. For in this fathomless simplicity all things are contained in a state of blissful beatitude, while the ground itself remains completely uncomprehended, unless by essential unity. Here the Persons must yield, and all that lives in God, for here there is nothing but an eternal stillness in a blissful embrace of loving immersion.

This is that modeless Essence which all fervent spirits have chosen above all things. This is that dark stillness in which all lovers lose their way. But if we could prepare ourselves in virtues, we would at once strip ourselves of our bodies and flow into the wild waves of the sea, from which no creature could ever draw us back. (E, 152; T, I, 248f)

SUMMING UP

In a letter to a Carthusian of Herne written around the year 1400 Jean Gerson, the scholarly and influential Chancellor of the University of Paris, accused Ruusbroec of pantheism and of contradicting Pope Benedict XII's pronouncement of 1336 on the Beatific Vision by suggesting that it was possible to receive that vision fully in this life. This charge was easily deflected by Jan van Schoonhoven, a writer of ascetical works and a surviving disciple of Ruusbroec, and it had no substantial, if any, consequences.[20] But we may well ask ourselves, in the light of Ruusbroec's uninhibited delineation of the radical union with God which is possible for us in this life, why he did not face the kind of official opposition which the elderly and venerable Meister Eckhart was forced to endure. In addition, whereas Eckhart himself exercised little overt criticism of the church's hierarchy, Ruusbroec's critique of contemporary church practice was so animated as to require the editorial attentions of his brethren after his death. It might well be asked why the passionate utterances of this gentle Flemish forest monk, as bold in his vision of the union of the soul with God as any had ever been, did not suffer a similar fate.

The answer is probably to be found in the weight of Ruusbroec's condemnation of those very groupings within and outside the church which threatened its teaching and its unity on the basis of a vile distortion of the true unitive experience. The Brethren of the Free Spirit practised a fulsome form of moral licence, claiming all the while to be united with God and thus freed from any kind of moral restraint or censure. Eckhart ignored them, unwisely so, while from the very earliest times, Ruusbroec pursued them mercilessly. The second reason is likely to be the immense goodness of Ruusbroec's message and his teaching of what he named 'the common life'. This expressed his belief that the highest contemplative experience leads directly back to works of selfless devotion and to those things which could easily be identified as traditional Christian piety by those who failed to understand the higher flights of his thought. In addition, whatever similarities exist between the work of Eckhart and Ruusbroec, the Flemish mystic is a figure who is 'more affective, warmer and more down to earth'.[21] His theology of renewing, transforming love, and his emphasis on grace, place him securely within the Christian mystical tradition. Eckhart, on the other hand, appears at a remove from the warmth of conventional piety, and he is easily misunderstood. All manner of groupings, philosophical, cultural and spiritual, have claimed the 'real Eckhart' for their own, and they still do. Ruusbroec, on the other hand, is a figure whom it would be difficult if not impossible to pursue for other than devout Christian ends.

But it has to be said that Ruusbroec, in some ways, has not attained the influence which might have been expected of him. He is seen today as an influence upon the Dutch and Flemish writers who came after him, including Harphius and the prolific Denys the Carthusian, and, although it is an area fraught with difficulty, he may have been a presence among the great Spaniards including St Teresa of Avila and St John of the Cross. In the modern period however he is known and loved mainly in the areas of his own cultural provenance. Writing – at length – about matters which defy ordinary speech, and in a minority language, Ruusbroec has never attained the popularity of his countryman Thomas à Kempis. Nevertheless many of those who are familiar with spiritual writings have only superlatives for Jan van Ruusbroec; Evelyn Underhill said of him that he was 'one of the greatest – perhaps the very greatest – of the mystics of the church'.[22] It would be both a compliment and a tragedy if Ruusbroec were to be 'a mystic's mystic'; for he is truly an immense treasure-house of spiritual wealth to be explored and enjoyed by all Christendom.

After the death of Ruusbroec, the tradition of speculative mysticism in the Low Countries went into decline. As early as 1377 Ruusbroec was visited by the church reformer Geert (Gerard) Groote, whose dynamic sermons inspired many and who was to become a principal figure in the new spirituality of the *Devotio moderna*. Groote admired Ruusbroec and translated his *Spiritual Espousals* into Latin, but he rejected the speculative side to Ruusbroec's thought and was not above criticizing him for it. Groote prefered Ruusbroec's ascetical and practical writings, especially those in which he attacked the abuses of the contemporary church, in which he found an echo of his own spiritual temperament. Groote founded the Order known as 'The Brothers and Sisters of the Common Life' in his home town of Deventer in 1383. The Fourth Lateran Council of 1215 had forbidden the foundation of new Orders, and the status of the new group long remained uncertain. They did not take vows as such, but they lived together as a community, observing the rules of poverty, chastity and obedience. They earned their own living by work of hand, refrained from leaving the precincts of their community and followed a life based on prayer, devotional exercises and the sacraments. The brethren developed a particular concern with educational life, and in time become influential in this sphere in the Low Countries and in

Germany. The 'Modern Devotion' is an attractive movement, but it would be fair to say that there is little that is original in it. It was exceptional perhaps for the intense and great stress which its followers laid upon constant meditation on the life of Christ.

Another foundation of the *Devotio moderna* was more overtly monastic. This was the Windesheim Congregation of Augustinian canons, whose mother house was founded at the village of Windesheim near Zwolle in 1387. Despite a certain amount of at times vigorous church opposition, this house founded an enormous congregation extending through the Low Countries to Germany and France. By 1500 it embraced some eighty-seven houses including Groenendaal itself, and it was greatly instrumental in spreading reform throughout a number of established orders. Groote's simple message, and that of his disciples in the *Devotio moderna*, including Florens Radewijns, Gerard Zerbolt and Gerlach Peters, was 'a call to conversion, meditation, imitation of the life and death of Christ, death to the world, charity, and humility'.[23] The Modern Devotion is a movement which affected all levels of life in the Low Countries, including the work of Rogier van der Weyden and the Flemish Primitive painters, but its greatest literary achievement is the *Imitation of Christ* which, it is now generally agreed, was written by Thomas à Kempis during the third decade of the fifteenth century. The brethren devoted much time to their mutual edification, and Thomas's work is essentially a manual of spirituality written for the fellow members of his community. Thomas, originally from Kempen near Düsseldorf, was for seven years a pupil of Florens Radewijns at Deventer. From there he moved to the new monastery of St Agnietenberg where he was elected sub-prior. His book precisely reflects the concern of the Windesheim Congregation with the inner life of conversion and morality, together with its profound suspicion of speculation. 'Non enim omne altum sanctum' (Book II, ch. 10), 'Not all that is high is holy', is the stout warning which the author delivers to his readers, and he advocates instead a life of humility, self-denial and patient love. It is better to practise humility, he reminds us, than to know its definition. It is indeed remarkable within such a setting to find the line 'Nam verum pauperem spiritu

et ab omni creatura nudum quis inveniet?' ('Who can find
anyone who is truly poor in spirit and free of all creatures?'
Book II, ch. 11). Over the course of a century the revol-
utionary language of Meister Eckhart, which sought to
explore new dimensions of inner speculative experience, has
become entirely representative of selflessness and moral
detachment, embedded in a spirituality for which contemplative vision is alien and strange.

The speculative tradition of the Low Countries did continue
in some degree however in the work of a Franciscan friar
often known by his Latin name of Harphius (Henrik Herp).
His treatise, *The Mirror of Perfection*, was to prove influential in
its Latin translation among the sixteenth-century Spaniards.
Harphius was not an original writer but drew extensively on
Ruusbroec's work, whose thought he both popularized and
reduced. Another fifteenth-century figure, Denys the Carthusian, similarly lacked originality, despite the immense breadth
of his learning. His works – some forty-four volumes in their
modern edition – include a detailed page-by-page commentary on the Bible. In his treatise *De contemplatione* (*On Contemplation*) he shows that he is more in the tradition of Pseudo-
Dionysius and the ancient monastic spirituality than a
descendent of Ruusbroec and the achievement of the Flemish
school.

The English Mystics

The situation in England during the fourteenth century differed in a number of respects from life in the other countries of northern Europe at this time. The issue of the struggle between the papacy and Ludwig of Bavaria, for instance, did not reverberate in the same way it did in Germany and the Upper Rhineland, where it set up significant tensions between the new religious Orders. But there were traces of a significant conflict in England between the papacy and aspects of English political life, including the nobles, parliament and the common people. This conflict concentrated primarily upon the matter of taxation and the perceived foreign interest of the papacy in appointments to the English Church.[1]

The building of the papal palace at Avignon, and the Pope's Italian wars, had created a driving need at the centre of the church for efficient methods of raising finance. The move towards more stringent financial control had begun during the pontificate of Innocent III, who in 1199 and 1215 had instigated the use of taxation in order to finance the Crusades. In 1225 Honorius III had levied a tax which constituted one-tenth of all clerical incomes and instituted the 'annate', which was the value of the first year's income from a benefice newly filled. These new taxes, together with the traditional English offering to the Pope known as Peter's Pence, were to be the cause of repeated dissent by the English people, which was expressed in the parliamentary protests of the years of 1307, 1309, 1343, 1351 and 1353. Generally it was the commons and the nobles who found the Pope to be interfering and who became disgruntled. In addition to the Statutes of Provisions and Praemunire, which sought to restrict papal rights in England in favour of the Crown, the interests of the king himself were generally safeguarded within the relationship of mutual understanding that prevailed between the English Crown and the papacy.

There was a history of opposition to the levying of taxes in England, a process in which the concerns of the papacy were in the popular mind identified with purely material interests. The distinguished scholar and humanist, John of Salisbury, voiced complaint as early as the twelfth century, and some two hundred years later Robert Grosseteste, a Franciscan and one of the greatest scientific thinkers of the age, was to make similar criticism.

The keenest critique of the Catholic Church came however from John Wyclif and the Lollard movement, which gathered around him. Wyclif was an Oxford trained theologian who developed the view that moral depravity in the incumbents of ecclesiastic office wholly undermined their authority. A bad pope therefore was not a pope at all. He attacked also the church's belief in the Real Presence of Christ in the Eucharist. Wyclif's teaching was condemned in 1382, but he survived to write further polemical pieces against the existence of the clerical and religious Orders within the church. Wyclif died in 1384 (still in communion with the Catholic Church). The bald and anti-clerical message which Wyclif proclaimed met stern official resistence on all sides, but it was taken up by the Lollards, a group of largely poorly-educated clergy, who propagated it in some remote areas of the country. Wyclif's teaching was not without influence on Jan Hus and his followers in Bohemia, and it was to gain new vitality in the years of the Protestant Reformation.

Despite the great significance of the theological debate between John Wyclif and the Catholic Church for the later development of church history, it was not a phenomenon which had much effect upon England at large, except in its theological centres. The existence of the Brethren of the Free Spirit, such a vital influence upon the progress and fortunes of continental mystical thought, found no parallel in Wyclif and the Lollards.[2] It would also not be true to say that the English mystics belong to an 'Eckhartian school', although this has been claimed for them.[3] There is scant evidence for the existence in England of manuscripts of those who figure in that school during the period of the greatest flowering of the English mystical tradition (with the possible exception of Julian of Norwich, the latest of our English mystics, who lived into the fifteenth century). One of the earliest texts, and one which is perhaps least representative of the continental current, is Henry Suso's *Horologium Sapientiae*. All but two of the numerous Latin manuscripts in England of this work date from the fifteenth century, and there is no record of any fourteenth-century English translations.[4] The editors of *The Chastizing of God's Children* believe that the work, which contains extracts in translation from Book II of Ruusbroec's *Spiritual Espousals*, cannot have been written before 1373.[5] The *Chastizing* shows, moreover, a cautious attitude to mystical union, in which the dynamic quality of Ruusbroec's thought is subordinated to pastoral concerns, which makes it an unlikely source for mystical inspiration. The *Treatise of Perfection of the Sons of God*, which is a translation of Ruusbroec's *The Sparkling Stone*, had no following (it survives in only one manuscript), and is described by the editors as 'a mere literary curiosity'.[6] A further text which requires mention is the *Mirror of Simple Souls*, now known to be an English translation of a French original by the Beguine Margaret Porette.[7] It has been suggested that the authoress, who was burnt at the stake in Paris in 1310, may have exercised a certain influence upon Meister Eckhart, or at least that her work may have been known to him. Certainly it was known to Ruusbroec. The *Mirror* presents a philosophy of the annihilation of the creature by its union with God which is easily interpreted along quietist or antinomian lines (of a moral lawlessness). It was translated into Latin in the late fifteenth century by the Carthusian Richard Methley, and exists in English translation only in manuscripts dating from the mid-fifteenth century. It is not impossible, of course, that some oral interchange took place as travellers brought news to England of the new spirituality. But such influence would be likely to be confined to centres of commerce and travel, such as Norwich, rather than the North and the Midlands, which are the geographical points of origin for the majority of the native mystical texts.

Although we cannot find evidence for an early

dissemination in England of the works of the 'Eckhartian' school of Germany and the Low Countries, we do find abundant evidence of mystical sources of another, though related, kind. These include Pseudo-Dionysius, whose widely influential work, *Mystical Theology*, was actually translated by the anonymous author of the *Cloud of Unknowing*. A second vital influence upon the development of a specifically mystical English tradition was the work of William of St Thierry, whose profound influence upon Ruusbroec we have also noted. William's *Golden Epistle*, written in Latin and therefore easily accessible, was long thought to have been written by St Bernard himself. In this work William treats of an intense form of trinitarian love mysticism, whose origins go back to St Augustine, but which finds at William's hands a particularly powerful expression. The *Golden Epistle*, though written by a Cistercian, enjoyed immense popularity in the Carthusian Order, for whom it was written and to whom it was dedicated. The role of the Carthusians, who enjoyed considerable expansion in England during the fourteenth century, was noteworthy in the English Church. The trend towards the solitary life visible in Richard Rolle, Walter Hilton and Julian of Norwich, found its culmination in this austere and eremetical Order, and it has been argued more than once that the author of the *Cloud of Unknowing* may himself have been a Carthusian, preserving that order's tradition of anonymity.[8]

The origins of the English spiritual tradition go back to the strongly monastic writings of Abbot Aldhelm in the seventh century and to those of the Venerable Bede in the eighth.[9] Although much of the Anglo-Saxon genius finds expression in works such as the visionary *Dream of the Rood*, which conveys a profound devotion to the passion, the same monastic and ascetical stamp surfaces four centuries later in the work of the Cistercian monk and abbot, St Aelred of Rievaulx, although here it is combined with the passion of his distinguished continental *confrères* St Bernard and William of St Thierry. It was Aelred also who, around the year 1160, wrote the treatise *A Rule of Life for a Recluse*. This was to serve as a model for the celebrated *Ancrene Riwle* (or *Ancrene Wisse*), one of the earliest prose texts in the English language, which is believed to have been written in the West Midlands some time in the early thirteenth century.[10] This work sets forth practical guidelines for the anchorite, or recluse, touching on the devotional life, penances, prayers, spiritual rules and practices. Its character is decidedly ascetical and pastoral, free of theological abstractions, and the *Ancrene Riwle* sets the tone for much of the English spiritual literature that is to follow.

A key influence upon the majority of English monastic authors is the work both of St Augustine and St Gregory the Great. This ancient tradition preferred to stress the ascetical aspect of our lives for which contemplation was a distant goal, partially and fleetingly realized in our present lives. Thus St Augustine and indeed the whole western church emphasize that the mystical vision granted us in this life is far excelled by the joy we will have in heaven. For Augustine in the *Confessions* it is a 'foretaste', something of which he 'can perceive the odour' but not yet 'feed upon' (*Conf.* vii, 23). Although contemplation for St Gregory the Great is the goal and climax of the spiritual life, all that we may enjoy of true contemplation, true vision, in this life is a glimpse of the heavenly light as 'through a chink in a window' (*Mor.*, v., 52; *Hom. in Ez.*, ii, v, 16,18). Set within the context of ascetical endeavour and a sharp distinction between the knowledge we may possess of God in this life and the next, the very concept of *contemplatio* can even lose its sense of true and empirical *union* with God, which is reserved for the exceptional few (generally Moses and St Paul), becoming the 'contemplation on divine truth' and 'on the things of God', which we find, for instance, in St Thomas Aquinas, for whom contemplation consists in 'prayer, reading and meditation' (*Summa theologica*: 2–2, q. 180, 3).

RICHARD ROLLE

Richard Rolle is the first major figure of fourteenth-century English mystical life and he exemplifies a number of its strengths and constraints. He was born at Thornton Dale near Pickering in Yorkshire. A fine story records how he ran away from home with a makeshift hermit's habit, and indeed after a period of study of the *artes* in Oxford he is believed to have taken up the hermit life while still at a tender age. Rolle is the author of a number of Latin treatises on the ascetical life. These include his chief works, the *Incendium Amoris* (translated into English by Richard Mysin in 1434 under the title *The Fire of Love*) and the autobiographical *Melos Amoris*, as well as *inter alia* the *Emendatio vitae* (*The Mending of Life*) and the *Canticum Amoris de Beata Virgine* (*The Song of Love on the Blessed Virgin*). Rolle also wrote, in Latin and English, a number of commentaries on the scriptures, including works on the Song of Songs, on Job and the Psalms. Although preferring Latin, he left a number of letters, fragments and lyrics in English.[11] Rolle died at Hampole, possibly a victim of the Black Death, in the year 1349.

Although possessing much native wit and a striking ability to make good use of what little education he had received, Rolle stands outside a specific contemplative tradition which could have lent his work greater cogency and purpose. A tendency towards self-indulgence in style and thought, and his exaggerated self-evaluation follow from the absence of such a guiding current in his life which might have provided a conceptual horizon for his undoubted natural contemplative gifts. These may be summed up in the three related phenomena which Rolle describes and which are characteristic of his contemplative experience: *calor* (heat), *canor* (song) and *dulcor* (sweetness). The *calor* comes when 'the mind is truly set on fire with everlasting love, and the heart is felt to burn with love in the same way, not in imagination, but in actuality'. 'Song' is 'when the savour of everlasting praise is received into the soul already abounding in heat, and thought is turned into song and the mind abides in mellifluous melody'. It is a condition in which the soul experiences 'the infusion and perception of a heavenly or spiritual sound, which belongs to the song of everlasting praise and the sweetness of invisible melody'. From these two states a third sensation arises, that of an 'ineffable sweetness' which pervades his being.[12] Rolle's language thus remains at the descriptive, experiential level, shunning system and analysis, which both limits its scope and lends it the charm of naive immediacy.

The writings of Rolle proved very popular in the two

hundred years between his death and the Reformation. He gained and left a reputation for sanctity, although the actual process of his canonization never ran full course. His works passed in manuscript form to the Continent and, in the sixteenth and seventeenth centuries, editions were published in Cologne. Subsequently Rolle suffered a period of neglect until, in 1866, the Early English Text Society began to publish his work.[13]

THE CLOUD OF UNKNOWING

With the *Cloud* and its corpus, we arrive at a significantly more sophisticated level of mystical writing than that achieved by Rolle, with all his devotion. The *Cloud* is believed to be the first surviving work of the author, which was followed by a paraphrase of Pseudo-Dionysius's *Mystical Theology* under the title *Hid Divinity*, the translation of extracts from Richard of St Victor's treatise *Benjamin Minor*, the *Epistle of Prayer*, the *Epistle on Discretion of Stirrings* and the *Discretion of Spirits*, which is an adaptation of two sermons by St Bernard. The *Epistle on Privy Counselling* is thought to have been the author's final work.[14]

The authorship of the *Cloud* corpus, which is unknown, has long been the subject of academic debate. He has been variously described as 'a cloistered monk' though not a Carthusian, a hermit, a recluse, and a rural parish priest.[15] For some while the idea was seriously entertained that Walter Hilton himself was the elusive author of the *Cloud*, although this view has now been discredited.[16] More recently two particular positions have been strongly argued. In his study of the English mystics Dom David Knowles suggested that the author of the *Cloud* may have been a Dominican on the basis of his 'clear dependence on the Rhineland school of spirituality and his technically orthodox Thomism on the vexed and topical issue of grace'.[17] In the case of a writer from the late fourteenth century, we do not need to postulate 'Dominican associations'[18] however in order to account for Thomist influence, even if Thomas is accepted as the source for the, by no means unusual, thoroughgoing view of grace which we find in the *Cloud*. The view furthermore that the *Cloud* is dependent on the Rhineland school is unsupported, both in the light of the fourteenth-century manuscript tradition and the undoubted dissimilarity between the spiritual theology of the *Cloud*, which is based primarily upon love, and the noetic speculative mysticism wholly characteristic of Eckhart and still present in Tauler.

Whatever alternative theories may at different times have been put forward, there has been a persistent tradition that the author of the *Cloud of Unknowing* was a Carthusian. This view has been energetically revived by James Walsh who, in his recent edition and translation of the *Cloud* points to the stress on the Divine Office and to various historical details which support this view, and carefully dismisses a number of weak objections against it, adding: 'We are saying nothing more than that . . . all the objections against such identification can be answered, and that whatever external straws there are favour it.'[19]

Further powerful support for the ascription of Carthusian authorship to the *Cloud* can be drawn from a number of factors. As early as the fifteenth century a Carthusian by the name of James Grenehalgh, who worked in the *scriptorium* of the Sheen Charterhouse, wrote in the margin of a manuscript (Douce 262) that Walter Hilton had been the anonymous author. Grenehalgh also believed, wrongly, that Hilton himself had been a Carthusian, and so the question arises whether Grenehalgh may not have been party to an early tradition among the Carthusians that the author of the *Cloud* had himself been a member of their Order.

A second factor which is of importance is the highly developed sense of his own identity as a contemplative which the author of the *Cloud* communicates. It is not merely something he *does;* rather it is something which he *is*. It is inviting to assume that the strength of this identity is fostered by his membership of a religious Order which is unequivocally identified with the contemplative vocation, as distinct from one which merely tolerates it. The only Order of this kind in England during the fourteenth century were the Carthusians, who experienced a significant increase in houses and vocations during this period.[20]

A third element which argues for this theory is the likely sources and reading of the author of the *Cloud*. Walsh sets out his debt to Guigues de Pont and Hugo de Balma, both of whom were distinguished Carthusians.[21] In addition to these, there is strong evidence that the writer of the *Cloud* knew the work known as the *Golden Epistle* by William of St Thierry. This treatise was written and presented to the Carthusians of Mount-Dieu, and it remained a greatly favoured work in the Carthusian Order. The earliest recorded manuscripts of the *Golden Epistle* in England date from the fifteenth century, and many were in the possession of the Carthusian Order.[22] The sophisticated mystical theology which William presents and which, as we have seen, was such an influence upon Ruusbroec, is one which places love at the centre of our knowledge of God. This alone is enough to suggest a link with the *Cloud*. We find however in Chapters 38 and 67 a close allusion to a passage from the final chapter of the *Golden Epistle*. William speaks in these terms: '. . . when in an ineffable and unfathomable manner the man of God is found worthy not to become God, but to acquire by grace what God is by nature'.[23] This is taken up by the author of the *Cloud*, and it reappears first as:

> . . . what compassion and what mercy will God have for the spiritual cry of the soul welling up and issuing forth from the height and the depth, the length and the breadth of his spirit, which contains by nature all that a man has by grace . . .

and then as: 'It is only by his mercy and without any merit of yours that you are made a God in grace'.[24] The existence of a clear allusion to the *Golden Epistle* in the *Cloud of Unknowing* is a further indication of the likelihood that the author of the English work was a member of the Carthusian Order.

Other primary, non-Carthusian, sources include the *Mystical Theology* by Pseudo-Dionysius, and Richard of St Victor's *Benjamin Minor*, both of which were translated by the author of the *Cloud*.[25] Another influential figure is Thomas Gallus, whose paraphrase of the *Mystical Theology* (the *extractio*) is believed to be the book to which the author of the *Cloud* refers in the prologue to his own translation of that work. Walsh has argued however that the more important *explanatio*, in which Gallus develops his own emphasis upon love as a cognitive faculty, was unknown to the author of the *Cloud* and that Hugo, who was much influenced by Gallus, was the mediator of this particular point.[26]

The image of the Cloud of Unknowing

If the spirituality of Meister Eckhart is intellective in character, while that of Ruusbroec is trinitarian, being based upon the alternating modality of unicity and multiplicty within the Godhead, then we may describe the spirituality of the *Cloud of Unknowing* as being a remarkably single-minded mysticism of love. In contrast to his distinguished contemporaries, the author of the *Cloud* has written a work which has a profoundly monastic feel. This results precisely from the fact that it conveys such a single-minded vision in which all extraneous detail of the spiritual life is subordinated to the central concept of piercing the 'cloud of unknowing between us and God' by a 'sharp dart of longing love' (ch. 12). Nor does the author know anything of speculation or multiple, extended imagery. His spirituality is primarily a *lived* one, experienced in the deep emotive centre of our being and free of the sophisticated intellectual constructs which are characteristic, for instance, of Eckhart and Ruusbroec and of the later Spanish mystics. It is certainly this simplicity of conception which in some degree accounts for the accessibility of the *Cloud* and its appeal to the modern world.

The factor however which the author of the *Cloud* undoubtedly has in common with the other great figures of his age is his experience of contemplative union with God as being neither remote nor for the exceptional few (generally Moses, Job and St Paul). Although the addressee of the *Cloud* is called to the exceptional state of the solitary life, in which he will take his 'first loving steps to the life of Perfection' (ch. 1),[27] this is a vocation, a way of 'knowing' God, which belongs to very ordinary people. The key to this life is the intense desire for God, which has been placed in our will by the Father himself: 'Your whole life now must be one of longing, if you are to achieve perfection. And this longing must be in the depths of your will, put there by God, with your consent' (ch. 1).

Following in the tradition variously represented by St Gregory of Nyssa (almost certainly unknown to the author), St Augustine, St Gregory the Great, St Bernard, Thomas Gallus and the Victorines, St Bonaventure and the Franciscan school, and William of St Thierry, the writer of the *Cloud* believes God to be accessible to our 'capacity to love' (*louyng miyt*) rather than our 'capacity to know' (*knowyng miyt*). We are unlikely to find a more succinct and emphatic statement of this school than in Chapters 4 and 6 of the *Cloud of Unknowing:*

> He cannot be comprehended by our intellect or any man's – or any angel's for that matter. For both we and they are created beings. But only to our intellect is he incomprehensible: not to our love. (ch. 4)

> For though we through the grace of God can know fully about all other matters, and think about them – yes, even the very works of God himself – yet of God himself can no man think. Therefore I will leave on one side everything I can think, and choose for my love that thing which I cannot think! Why? Because he may well be loved, but not thought. By love he can be caught and held, but by thinking never. (ch. 6)

The longing for God which we experience becomes keen and leads us into a single-minded intent towards him, to the exclusion of all his creatures. It is at this point, as we pursue this 'spiritual work', that we enter 'darkness and, as it were, a cloud of unknowing' (ch. 3). The source of this key image of a cloud is ultimately the *Mystical Theology* by Pseudo-Dionysius, which he himself translated, where it is used to express the total otherness of God and the impotence of our higher cognitive powers in the face of his transcendence.[28] Much of this sense is retained in the *Cloud* although the image has an evolving significance as the author seeks to express the deepening reality of our communion with God. An initial distinction is apparent in the continuation of the very first passage dealing with the 'cloud', quoted above:

> When you first begin, you find only darkness, and, as it were, a cloud of unknowing. You don't know what this means except that in your will you feel a simple, steadfast intention reaching out to God. Do what you will, this darkness and this cloud remain between you and God, and stop you from seeing him in the clear light of rational understanding, and from experiencing his loving sweetness in your affection. Reconcile yourself to wait in this darkness as long as is necessary, but still go on longing after him whom you love. (ch. 3)

The dominant characteristic of the 'cloud' here is that it obstructs. It prevents us from either perceiving God 'in the clear light of rational understanding' or from 'experiencing his loving sweetness'. Elsewhere it is described as 'privation of knowledge' (ch. 4). And yet it is a place we inhabit because of our 'simple, steadfast intention' (*nakid entent vnto God*). The 'cloud' then is the locus of our desire for God and our upward striving towards him. Although at this stage it obstructs, or appears to do so, and prevents our perception of God, the 'cloud' nevertheless holds the promise of our fulfilment: 'Reconcile yourself to wait in this darkness *as long as is necessary*'.

Although the 'cloud' is itself generated by our 'bare intent toward God', by our desire for him, it is at the same time dispersed or lessened by the 'sharp dart of longing love' (ch. 12). The author urges us to seek out the cloud and to 'beat always' upon it with the darts of our desire.[29] Thus, although we cannot see God directly in this life, we may nevertheless be granted a real communion with him:

> Be quite sure that you will never have the unclouded vision of God here in this life. But you may have the awareness of him, if he is willing by his grace to give it to you. So lift up your love to that cloud. Or, more accurately, let God draw your love up to that cloud. (ch. 9)

Indeed the cloud can itself become paradoxically the place of our deepening 'knowledge' of God. Speaking of Mary, the sister of Martha, whom patristic and medieval exegesis traditionally see as representing the highest contemplative principle, the author states:

> I want to say this: no one in this life, however pure and however enraptured with contemplating and loving God, is ever without this intervening, high and wonderful cloud. It was in this cloud that Mary experienced the many secret movements of her love. Why? Because this is the highest and holiest state of contemplation we can know on earth. (ch. 17)

Here the 'obstructing cloud of unknowing' (ch. 28) between ourselves and God, which represents 'privation of knowledge', has become 'high and wonderful'. Something has happened to work this dramatic change. The cloud has ceased to represent our failure to comprehend God with our reasoning powers, or even our affective powers, and now *indicates our intimation of the presence of God within the 'divine darkness'* (ch. 8). The darkness therefore is no longer an absence of knowing, but is rather a darkness of the intellect which deepens as we progress further into a 'knowledge' of God which is of a wholly different kind. Thus, paradoxically, ignorance or intellectual darkness is generated by the sense of the immediacy of God's presence, which is a perception mediated to us not through the rational mind but, characteristically and uniquely, through the 'mind of love'. Thus the author is able to speak of the darkness which surrounds even the highest act of contemplation in which the immediacy of our experience of God is expressed by the oxymoron, 'blind beholding': 'But the highest part of contemplation – at least as we know it in this life – is wholly caught up in darkness, and in this cloud of unknowing, with a movement of love and a blind beholding of the naked being of God, himself and him only' (ch. 8).

The image of the 'cloud of unknowing' may be said to represent our own spiritual centre in which we are withdrawn from the world and in which we are sensitive to God's touch. It does not represent the exercise of our usual cognitive powers in this experience, but rather their eclipse on account of the entirely different way in which we 'know' God: a unique manner of 'knowing' which is based not upon intellect but upon a percipient love.

The element of withdrawal from the world, the exclusion of sense impressions and worldly preoccupations, is greatly emphasized by the author of the *Cloud*. He conveys this aspect of our spiritual life in the image of 'a cloud of forgetting' which we are to lay between ourselves and the whole of creation:

> If ever you are to come to this cloud and live and work in it, as I suggest, then just as this cloud of unknowing is as it were above you, between you and God, so you must also put a cloud of forgetting beneath you and all creation. We are apt to think that we are very far from God because of this cloud of unknowing between us and him, but surely it would be more correct to say that we are much farther from him if we have no cloud of forgetting between us and all the creatures that have ever been made . . . In a word, everything must be hidden under this cloud of forgetting. (ch. 5)

It is striking in this passage that the author is not urging us to free ourselves from selfish dependency upon creatures, or not that alone, but from creatures *per se*. The author is keen that there should be no misunderstanding on this point: 'I always mean not only the individual creatures therein, but everything connected with them' (ch. 5). We encounter this same idea again when we are told that the highest, most noble thought, although highly praiseworthy in itself, must nevertheless be set aside in the ascent of our mind to God:

> Indeed, if we may say so reverently, when we are engaged on this work it profits little or nothing to think even of God's kindness or worth, or of Our Lady, or of the saints and angels, or of the joys of heaven, if you think thereby that such meditation will strengthen your purpose. In this particular matter it will not help at all. For though it is good to think about the kindness of God, and to love him

and praise him for it, it is far better to think about him as
he is and praise him for himself. (ch. 5)

At this point the teaching of the *Cloud of Unknowing* recalls
that of Meister Eckhart for whom also the entire creation as
a cognitive dimension needs to be transcended as we enter
into deeper knowledge of the uncreated God. This is a
distinctly different note from that of moral *ascesis* which views
detachment from creatures purely in moral or affective terms.
In the case of the *Cloud*, the purgation that is required is a
cognitive one to do with modes of knowledge (although based
upon love and a prior explicitly moral purgation, as we shall
see later), as we seek by our own efforts, aided by grace, to
empty ourselves of the created world and to become filled
with the uncreated God. This, the self-emptying of created
images, is 'our travail, though aided by the grace of God' (ch.
26), and it is in this work that the author urges us to our
greatest efforts: 'See to it that there is nothing at work in your
mind or will but only God. Try to suppress all knowledge
and feeling of anything less than God, and trample it down
deep under the cloud of forgetting' (ch. 43).

A further point in which the teaching of the *Cloud* is reminiscent of Eckhart is the way that it subordinates all particular
manners of self-discipline and devotion to the central and
primary act of contemplation. Contemplative union with God
becomes the source of all virtue, and it is this which extirpates
the root and ground of sin:

Were you to fast beyond all measure, or keep vigil at great
length, or rise at the crack of dawn, or sleep on boards or
wear chains . . . this would not help you at all. The urge
and impulse of sin would still be with you.

More: however much you might weep in sorrow for your
sins, or for the sufferings of Christ, or however much you
might think of the delights of heaven, what good would it
do you? Much good, surely; much help; much profit; much
grace. But compared with this blind movement of love . . .
there is very little indeed it can do without love . . . Without
it all the rest is virtually worthless. Negatively, it destroys

the ground and root of sin, and positively it acquires virtue.
(ch. 12)

In contemplation a soul dries up the root and ground of
the sin that is always there, even after one's confession, and
however busy one is in holy things. (ch. 28)

The author turns to the two principal monastic virtues,
humility and love, in order to illustrate how these, in their
highest forms, can be generated by contemplative grace. Of
humility, for instance, he says that there are two kinds, one
'imperfect' and the other 'perfect'. The former is the result of
our own reflections upon the 'degradation, wretchedness and
weakness of man', while the second, or 'perfect', kind is
caused by the 'superabundant love and worth of God in
himself'. The first is the result of our own endeavours, operating, as ever, with the aid of grace, while the second kind is
a free gift of God. The author certainly does not advocate
that we should neglect 'imperfect humility' in our pursuit of
the higher 'perfect humilty', rather he warns us against doing
such a thing. And yet he is well aware of the advantages of
the virtue which flows as a gift from our experience of God
in contemplative union with him:

> But I am doing what I am because I want to tell you and
> to let you see how much more worthwhile this spiritual
> exercise is than any other physical or spiritual work, even
> when this is done under the inspiration of grace. How that
> the love of a purified soul, continually pressing into this
> dark cloud of unknowing between you and God, truly and
> perfectly contains within it that perfect humilty, seeking as
> it does nothing less than God. (ch. 14)

The contemplative life and the active life

We have already seen in our discussion of the authorship of
the *Cloud of Unknowing* the extent to which the author
possesses an emphatic sense of the contemplative vocation.
That vocation is essentially one in which the individual withdraws, physically, from the world and embarks on the highest

stage of the Christian life, which is that of 'perfection': 'But in his own delightful and gracious way he has drawn you to this third stage, the solitary one. It is in this state that you will learn to take your first loving steps to the life of perfection, the last stage of all' (ch. 1).

From St Augustine and St Gregory the Great, together with the monastic writers of the later Middle Ages, the author of the *Cloud* has inherited a precise sense of the distinctions between the active and the contemplative lives. He is keen at all points to stress the interdependence of the two lives:

> The lower part of the active life consists of good, straight-forward acts of mercy and charity. The higher part (which is the lower part of contemplative living) is made up of various things, for example, spiritual meditation, an aware-ness of one's own wretched state, sorrow and contrition, a sympathetic and understanding consideration of Christ's passion and that of his servants, a gratitude which praises God for his wonderful gifts, his kindness and works in all parts of his creation, physical and spiritual. (ch. 8)

> A man cannot be fully active unless he is partly contempla-tive, nor fully contemplative (at least on earth) without being partly active. (ibid.)

And yet the author is quite clear that the contemplative vocation is higher than the active one and begins a work which shall be completed only in heaven:

> Everything a man does in the lower part of active life is necessarily exterior to him, so to speak beneath him. In the higher part (the lower part of the contemplative) a man's activity is inward, within himself, and he is, so to speak, on the level. In the higher part of the contemplative life a man is definitely reaching above himself and is inferior to none but God. Above himself, undoubtedly, because his deliberate intention is to win by grace what he cannot attain by nature, namely to be united to God in spirit, one with him in love and will. (ibid.)

It is clear morever that when the author speaks in general of the contemplative vocation he does not simply mean those individuals who, whatever their call of life, are inclined to know God in the contemplative way; rather he means those who are called to join a contemplative and solitary Order (that is, the Carthusians). This view is supported by his remarks in Chapter 1 in which he refers to the addressee's progression from the 'common state of the Christian life' when he was 'living with his friends in the world', to the higher calling of the solitary life and to contemplation. It is supported also by the author's remark at the very begninning of his work that he does in fact regard contemplation as being a possibility also for those who 'though active by their outward mode of life, are, by the inner working of the spirit of God – his judgements are unsearchable – disposed towards contemplation' (Prologue). The phrase 'active by their outward mode of life' must mean here those living in the world, which is to say those who are not actually members of a contemplative Order. The author of the *Cloud* thus envisages contemplation as being a possible mode of knowing God for those who have not opted for the solitary life. He remarks however that such people will not enjoy the contemplative vision 'continually', as do 'true contemplatives' (ibid.).

The idea, which the author later develops more fully, that the 'cloud of unknowing' between ourselves and God is continually pierced by the sharp darts of our desire for him lies at the very heart of his 'system'. Whereas Eckhart had presented a model for our union with God which was rather a 'once and for all' affair, or at least an essentially uninterrupted process of cognitive union (the 'eternal birth of the Son in our soul'), the author of the *Cloud* envisages a series of surges, as the will rises up to God, penetrates the cloud, and falls back to earth only to rise again in desire. Perhaps no single other factor so clearly shows the disinction between the breakthrough into a timeless and secure vision of God which is the end of intellective mysticism and the ecstatic and fluctuating union that is the fulfilment, on earth, of a mysticism of the will and the affections:

So pay great attention to this marvellous work of grace within your soul. It is always a sudden impulse and comes without warning, springing up to God like some spark from the fire. An incredible number of such impulses arise in one brief hour in the soul who has a will to this work! In one such flash the soul may completely forget the created world outside. Yet almost as quickly it may relapse back to thoughts of things done and undone – all because of our fallen nature. And fast again it may rekindle. (ch. 4).

Numerous monastic writers before the author of the *Cloud* had stressed the brevity and the incompleteness of the contemplative vision. For this English Carthusian however, although the moment of 'breakthrough' rapidly passes, we may live continually in the felt presence of God, if only we seek God with 'naked' or 'single-minded' intent. The contemplative experience of God is at the very centre of his spiritual vision, and he questions the view that it is something which is reserved for the exceptional few:

There are those who think that this matter of contemplation is so difficult and frightening that it cannot be accomplished without a great deal of very hard work beforehand, and that it only happens occasionally, and then only in a period of ecstasy. Let me answer these people as best I can: it depends entirely on the will and good pleasure of God, and whether they are spiritually able to receive this grace of contemplation, and the working of the Spirit.

For undoubtedly there are some who cannot attain this state without long and strenuous spiritual preparation, and who even so experience it in its fullness but rarely, and in response to a special call of our Lord – we would call this special call 'ecstatic'.

On the other hand there are some who by grace are so spiritually sensitive and so at home with God in this grace of contemplation that they may have it when they like and under normal spiritual working conditions, whether they are sitting, walking, standing, kneeling. (ch. 71)

If the author of the *Cloud* has in common with other great mystical writers the belief that contemplation can be and is experienced by ordinary people, then it is also true to say that he has a keen awareness of that excess of 'enthusiasm' which leads to inauthentic experience of a 'mystical' kind. He warns repeatedly against a foolish and literal interpretation of spiritual counsel, which can only lead to an overwrought condition or, worse, to a state of heresy or pride. Such people he calls 'the Devil's contemplatives' (ch. 45). Their physical and emotional excess produces a 'glow' and 'warmth' which they imagine to be the 'fire of love'. The carefully chosen language of this section suggests that the author might have intended over-enthusiastic followers of Richard Rolle as the object of his polemic. It is likewise possible that the incipient Lollard movement inspired by John Wyclif may have been the object of his attack in a later passage when he accuses those who 'lean too much on their own learning' and who 'Burst out and blaspheme all the saints, sacraments, statutes and ordinances of Holy Church' (ch. 56).

Again, in harmony with the authentic mystical writers of the church, the author of the *Cloud* cultivates humility and shies away from the suggestion of mystical 'achievement' and exclusivity. He is at great pains always to show how the higher spiritual practices depend upon the lower, apparently more mundane, exercises, and emphasizes time and again that it is God, who is the end of our desire, who plants the yearning for him in our souls and who is the means of its fulfilment:

> So when you feel by the grace of God that he is calling you to this work, and you intend to respond, lift your heart to God with humble love. And really mean God himself who created you, and bought you, and graciously called you to this state of life. And think no other thought of him. (ch. 7)

Conclusion

Our brief survey of the spiritual teaching of the *Cloud of Unknowing* has highlighted some of those aspects which the author has in common with the mystical writers of the Rhineland and some of those in which he appears to represent a wholly distinct tradition. The social and temporal conditions of fourteenth-century England were not those of Germany and the Low Countries. Above all, the threat of organized heresy does not seem to have exercised such a powerful influence upon the chief representatives of the English tradition. Doubtless the reason for this is that the main threat to Church orthodoxy in fourteenth-century England, the Lollard movement, did not justify itself by recourse to direct mystical experience, as did the Brethren of the Free Spirit, and thus did not call for mystical refutation. The polemic of the *Cloud*, as of later English spiritual works, appears often to be directed against mere foolishness.

A second essential difference is that the author of the *Cloud* stands within a strongly monastic tradition, as did his contemporary Walter Hilton. This means to say not only that there is a great emphasis upon love, but also that there is a keen awareness of the ascetical dimension of spiritual living. The key monastic virtues of humility and love become the cornerstones of our moral life. And, if there is a tendency to stress the practical dimensions of spiritual living, there is a lack of interest also in the application of speculative structures in order to express the highest mystical experience. This is apparent throughout the English mystical tradition which, although it contributes many brilliant and expressive images (as we shall see also with Julian of Norwich), wholly lacks the sense of theological system, of theological *ontology*, which is the very foundation of the work, and genius, of Meister Eckhart and Jan van Ruusbroec. This is evident for instance in the scant interest which the author of the *Cloud* shows in our original likeness to God which, for both Eckhart and Ruusbroec with their respective theories of the 'ground of the soul' and the 'unity of spirit', is the dynamic foundation for our new life of grace and which is contained, in a mysterious potentiality, in the deepest region of our soul. Indeed the author of the *Cloud* appears not to possess any marked sense of interiority. At one point the author urges the contemplative to 'live at the highest, topmost peak spiritually' (ch. 37) but in effect he lacks any appreciable sense of the *tréfonds*, the inner depths of the soul. Rather, the author chooses to locate the 'cloud', that perfect symbol of inwardness, outside the self (contrary to Hilton), in a space above man and below God.

A final argument for the independence of the English tradition, as represented by the *Cloud of Unknowing* (and Walter Hilton), from the Rhineland school is the total absence of the key imagery drawn ultimately from Eckhart, which forms the common base of that school (being occasionally present even in Ruusbroec). We have already seen that the language in which Eckhart articulated his exalted teaching was enormously influential upon the Continent, although the message which he sought to communicate was at best only partially understood. Tayler, Suso and Ruusbroec know and make use of terms such as 'the birth of God in the ground of the soul' and the 'divine spark'. Although the images of interiority may be wholly out of keeping with the spiritual idiom of the *Cloud of Unknowing*, other images generated or adopted by Eckhart and transmitted by his disciples proved influential on spiritual movements of a wholly non-speculative kind. Thus the concepts of 'detachment' and of 'spiritual poverty' gained new meaning in the pietistic and ascetical context of the *Theologia Germanica* and the writers of the *Devotio moderna*. The complete absence in the English mystical literature of such terms which were so popular abroad points emphatically to its thematic and linguistic independence.[30]

WALTER HILTON

Following the abstract mysticism and high contemplation of the *Cloud*, the work of Walter Hilton largely represents a return to the simplicity and ascetical values of Richard Rolle. We possess no more knowledge of his life than we do of his contemporaries.[31] He shows a trained mind, and is referred to in some manuscripts as *magister*, which suggests that he might have been a doctor of theology. It is felt likely that Cambridge may have been his place of study on the strength of his many connections with Cambridge men. There is textual evidence to suggest that Hilton may himself have spent some time living as a hermit though, at some point, he became an Augustinian Canon of Thurgarton Priory in Nottinghamshire. At a point prior to entering the community at Thurgarton, Hilton wrote a letter to one Adam Horsley, encouraging him to become a Carthusian. In the light of the fact that Horsley did not leave his post at the Exchequer until 1385, it can be assumed that Hilton did not enter the Augustinian community before that year. Several manuscripts record 24 March 1395 or 1396 as the date of his death.

As is typical of popular mystical writers in the Middle Ages, some uncertainty surrounds the corpus which can definitively be attributed to Walter Hilton. Nevertheless the consensus view is that he is the author of two English letters (one on the 'Mixed Life' of a contemplative living in the world and the other on the 'Song of Angels', which is probably to be seen as a critique of Rolle) and four short English exegetical treatises. Hilton also wrote four Latin letters, including the letter to Horsley mentioned above (the *Epistola aurea*), and a treatise called *De imagine peccati (On the Image of Sin)*. Also attributed to him is a translation of the *Stimulus Amoris* under the title *The Goad of Love*. Walter Hilton is chiefly remembered however for the two books of his *Ladder of Perfection*. The fifty or so manuscripts of this work which have survived attest to its popularity. It was the favourite reading of Lady Margaret Tudor, the mother of Henry VII, and it was she who asked Wynkyn de Worde to print an edition of it in 1494.[32]

Central to Walter Hilton's work is a distinction, which first received its classic formulation at the hands of St Gregory the Great, between the active and the contemplative life. The active life of penance, good deeds and virtue is for all, whereas the contemplative life is for the few, although it can be given to any, whatever their walk of life. But it is only the solitary who can experience the latter in its fullness (73).[33] Hilton declares at the very beginning of the *Ladder of Perfection*, that he is concerned in the book to explain to the anchoress how she may best come to her 'enclosure of spirit and heart', which is the interior place in which contemplation is formed (64). Contemplation, for Hilton, rests upon the active life of virtue and is constituted in three stages. The first of these 'consists in the knowing of God and spiritual things' at the level of a bald discursive knowledge mediated by books. The second stage 'consists principally in affection' in which we receive from the Holy Spirit 'the fervour of love and spiritual sweetness'. This is a condition in which we spontaneously experience 'savour', 'delight' and 'comfort' and in which, through devotion, we are transformed into 'spiritual mirth and sweet song'. In the third stage a marriage is formed between the soul and God 'which shall never be broken'. We are made one with God and are 'conformed to the image of the Trinity by this ravishing of love'. This experience, he tells us, is a foretaste of the bliss of heaven (66–71).

In the few brief descriptions which Hilton gives of the contemplative life, it is evident that he is not at all a speculative writer in the tradition of Pseudo-Dionysiu or the Rhineland mystics. His view of contemplation is essentially that it is an intensification of the life of inner devotion, and his language owes more to the ascetical monastic tradition of Rolle, St Bernard and St Gregory the Great than it does to the school of Christian apophatic mysticism. It is not in his account of union with God that Hilton excels but in his description of the journey to that point. Much of the *Ladder of Perfection* is taken up with the long and arduous journey of faith, the gradual breaking up of the ego in an intensely felt Christocentric spirituality, which is the preparation for the contemplative state. And it is here, in the domain of interior spiritual growth that we find Walter Hilton's real achievement.

The *Ladder of Perfection* abounds in images of interiority. Hilton speaks of 'the enclosure of spirit and heart' (64), 'the ground of your heart' (156), 'the point of your heart' (133), the 'privacy of heart' (314) and 'the secret chamber' (ibid.). His most significant image however is that of an interior darkness. This is 'the dark and painful image of your own soul which has neither light, nor knowledge, nor feeling of love nor delight' (133). We begin to become aware of this inner darkness through a process of introspection, or prayer. As we turn our minds to Jesus and seek to fix them upon him, we encounter 'this image, this black shadow' which, Hilton tells us, 'you carry . . . around with you wherever you go' (134). This 'darkness of conscience' (135) or 'dark image of sin' (149) is 'a false, misruled love of yourself' (136). It is an image of our own inner mind, unillumined by grace, which becomes a place of purgatory for us. Hilton devotes several extended passages to the description of this inner darkness, describing it repeatedly as a 'nothingness'. He suggests that it is a place of vacancy or, to use a modern philosophical terminology, of inauthentic being. As we enter this place we find ourselves in a cloud of darkness which stems from our own shallowness and self-oriented being, in which to linger feels like 'a hundred winters' until some physical delight from the external world catches our interest again (135).

Hilton is emphatic that it is Jesus himself within us who gradually breaks down the image of sin, and that we have no other recourse but to turn to him:

> I hope that whoever suffers this pain for a while will steadfastly cling to a naked awareness of Jesus Christ and to the desire to have nothing but his Lord, that he will not easily fall away from these, nor seek any other outward comfort for the time being. For this pain doesn't last long. Our Lord is near and will soon give ease to the heart. He will help you bear this body full of corruption, and through the merciful power of his grace-giving presence, he will break down this false image of love in yourself – not all at once, but little by little, until you are somewhat reformed to his likeness. (183)

> Who will help you break down this image of sin? Truly, your Lord Jesus. By virtue of him and in his name, you will break down this image of sin. Diligently pray to him and desire it, and he will help you. (181)

For Hilton, Jesus is contained as a concealed presence within this interior darkness. His power is moreover a transforming one, and we need only suffer this period of dryness in our interior prayer, 'to labour and sweat within this darkened conscience' (135), in order to release his powers within us. It is through his power and not ours that the image of darkness is dispelled within us and the divine image, which is the 'image of Christ' (186), is restored:

> In this darkness you must be sure to hold Jesus Christ in your mind and think determinedly about his passion and

his meekness. Then, through his power you shall, in your
thought, rise up from this earthly darkness through fervent
desire for God . . . For Jesus in his joy is entirely hidden
within this nothing, and you'll never find him in your
search unless you pass through this darkness of your
conscience. (135f)

The *Ladder of Perfection* is divided into two parts, the second
of which clearly represents a greater maturity of thought and
a greater cogency than the first. It begins with a restatement
of the original integrity of our being at the creation, which
has been marred by Adam's sin and our fallen state. Hilton
then states that there are three ways in which this original,
God-like image can be reformed. The first of these is baptism,
which Hilton describes elsewhere as the reforming 'in faith
alone' (200), underlining the medieval reluctance to tackle
the problems of infant baptism. This first way of reforming
God's image in us is in any case 'sufficient for salvation'
(ibid.). The second way Hilton calls reformation of the image
'through faith and experience' (219). This is altogether better
than the first way for it leads to the extinguishing of the dark
image of sin within us. It is the way that is 'characteristic of
perfect souls and of contemplatives' and 'can only be obtained
through much spiritual labour over a long period of time'
(200). It is the 'highest state a soul may come to in this life'
(228). The third way is the consummation of the second, and
it is reserved for the bliss of heaven. It is the second way, of
course, which Hilton is concerned to discuss in the second
section of his book, and it is to this that he devotes the greater
part of his attention.

The reformation of the image of God within us, for Hilton,
depends both upon a good deal of 'spiritual labour', by which
he means penances such as meditation, keeping vigil and
fasting, and upon a quality he calls 'meekness'. It is this
'meekness' which prevents us from taking pride in our ascetical achievements and thereby cancelling their value. The one
who succeeds in penances and takes pride in them, believing
himself to be good and holy, courts failure because 'he can't
yet strip himself naked of all his good deeds, nor can he make
himself genuinely poor in spirit, nor experience himself as the

nothing he is' (236). True meekness, true humility, therefore, requires that we experience the nothingness of our creaturely selves, acknowledging our spiritual poverty in the face of the absolute existence of God in Christ. The notion of our nothingness before Jesus and of our spiritual poverty in following him is a theme to which Hilton returns time and again, and it stands out as a point of undeniable affinity with the writers of the Rhineland school.

In Part II of the *Ladder of Perfection*, Hilton's remarks on the darkness within take on a new tone. He speaks of a 'night' which is 'Nothing but the abstaining and withdrawing of the thought of the soul from earthly things through its great desire and yearning to love and see and experience Jesus and spiritual things' (249). It is a 'night' which is 'sometimes painful and sometimes easy and comfortable' (250), depending on the degree of purgation from earthly attachments it involves. Certainly, it is a 'light-shot darkness' and 'a rich nothingness' (310), for it holds the promise and is itself the way to a new transcendence. It is moreoever once again the place in which the saving presence of Christ is immanent:

> It (the darkness) drives out of the heart all worldly vanities and flesh-centred affections. This desire gathers the soul within itself and occupies the soul exclusively with thinking about how it can come to the love of Jesus and thus be brought into this rich 'nothing'. Truly, the 'darkness' is not entirely dark, nor is the nothingness, when the soul meditates this way. For though the soul may be darkened to false light, it is not entirely dark to the true light. For Jesus who is both love and light is in this darkness, whether it is painful or restful. He is in the soul as its labouring for light in desire and longing, but he is not yet in it as its resting in love, nor as its showing forth his light. (251)

This way of reformation of God's image in us culminates in the state of contemplation. Whoever is 'reformed in experience' is 'made able and ready for contemplation' (317). Hilton presents contemplation as the goal towards which the purgative way leads us:

This dying to the world is the 'darkness' I've been talking about. It and no other is the gateway to contemplation and to reforming in experience. There may be many different roads and various works which lead different souls to contemplation according to the diversity of their dispositions and the differences of their states of life (for instance, religious and men in the world) which require different exercises. Nevertheless there is only one gate. (262)

Although Hilton, following in the tradition of St Augustine and St Gregory the Great, in a sense marginalizes contemplation by stressing its exceptional and esoteric character, he is fully aware of its immediacy and power. This can be seen from one of the few, brief passages in which he directly addresses it:

Such a soul does not see God blindly, nakedly and without savour, the way a philosopher does in his philosophy – by the light of his naked reason alone. Instead, this soul sees him in his understanding so that he is comforted and enlightened by the gift of the Holy Spirit with a wonderful reverence and a secret burning love, with spiritual savour and heavenly delight, more clearly and more fully than may be written or spoken. This vision, though it be only brief and small, is so powerful and so worthy that it completely ravishes the affections of the soul and draws them away from the contemplation and awareness of all earthly things and focuses them on itself so that, if the soul could, it would rest in this vision for evermore. (282)

Walter Hilton does not share the high mystic vision of the leading figures of the Rhineland school and of the author of the *Cloud*. He replaces their speculative genius with solid moral and ascetical teaching which is based upon a mature and deeply felt Christocentric spirituality. Nevertheless there are certain aspects of his teaching which either point back to Eckhart, Tauler and Ruusbroec or forward to the great achievement of the sixteenth-century Spanish school. We have already noted Hilton's stress on the value of a true spiritual poverty before God. To this may be added his sense of the *true* follower of Christ, whom he calls, in an image reminiscent of Tauler, 'God's friend' (144). Hilton spurns the performance of external acts of devotion, stressing the greater value of acts of inner asceticism that turn on our love for our fellow Christians (151). Nor can God be 'won' by specific acts of devotion, but gives himself freely and graciously (235): an idea which approximates to Eckhart's influential notion of 'modelessness' in the inner life. Hilton also speaks of an 'essential nothingness' which should become the object of our meditation. Although this idea is only touched upon in passing and never assumes the proportions of the Eckhartian 'nothingness of creatures', it does seem to represent in Hilton a state of inner detachment, even imagelessness. Hilton's chief image of detachment from the world however is that of the 'night', which can either be one of painful withdrawal from the senses, or one of rest and delight. Certainly the English mystic here anticipates an idea which was to be fully developed by St John of the Cross and to become a prime *topos* of the mystical tradition of the western church.

JULIAN OF NORWICH

The scant knowledge that we possess concerning Julian's life is taken, or deduced, from her own work.[34] She states in the Short Text of her *Revelations* that the 'shewings' occurred to her on 13 May 1373 when she was at the mid-point of her thirty-first year. This would suggest therefore that she was born early in 1343. The year of her death is unknown, although this must fall after 1413, as in that year the author of the preface to the Short Text knows her still to be alive.

The considerable erudition which Julian shows raises the possibility of her early training in Latin as a member of a women's religious Order, although there is no firm evidence to support this. It was as an anchoress however in the city of Norwich that Julian became renowned as a counsellor of great spiritual gifts and as the authoress of the two-part *Shewings*.

The first part of Julian's work is a description with short commentary of the sixteen visions which befell her during a period of sickness. She informs us herself that she had formerly prayed earnestly for three things: knowledge of Christ's passion, bodily sickness and three wounds from God. She held the visions of Christ's passion which came to her to be a fulfilment of this prayer and, it is believed, wrote down the visions soon after receiving them. It was some fifteen years later, however, that she greatly expanded on the Short Text with a longer version which presented a deeply felt and quietly erudite commentary on the visions. Edmund Colledge believes this longer version, written between 1388 and 1393, underwent one further revision.[35]

We have had to discount any direct influence of the Rhineland school upon the English mystics: Rolle; the author of the Cloud; and Walter Hilton. Neither the date of their own work, their geographical location, the date of the earliest traceable presence of English translations nor, in general, the tenor of their spirituality supports the idea of such a pattern of influence. The situation with regard to Julian is, however, in some degree different. She was writing at a slightly later date than the others of the English school. Moreover Norwich was an enormous centre of wealth and learning during the fourteenth century. It was the home of a number of religious houses, including a Franciscan *studium generale*, and there was much movement of highly placed scholars and clerics between Norwich and the continental centres. Nevertheless Julian was an erudite woman well-read in many of the spiritual classics, and it would be foolish to suppose that Ruusbroec, Tauler or, at a remove, Eckhart was responsible for the development of her ideas. Edmund Colledge does suggest the influence of William of St Thierry,[36] particularly in the fifty-fourth chapter of the Long Text, and it is possible that there are echoes to be heard, here and there, of the *Chastizing of God's Children*. And yet it must be said that there is no real trace in Julian of 'the birth of God in the ground of the soul', characteristic of the German school, or of the peculiarly intense trinitarian mysticism which predominates in that of the Low Countries. This is not, of course, to reduce her status; rather, it is an acknowledgement that she belongs with Hildegard of Bingen and Mechthild of Magdeburg among the women visionaries of Europe, who were one of the great achievements of the Middle Ages. Above all, the thing which distinguishes Julian from the Rhineland movement is, as for Walter Hilton, the failure of the unitive vision to take prime place in her description of the mystical life. And yet her work is permeated throughout with a warm sense of intimacy with the Divine. Indeed this is the special quality of her *Revelations* which has won her a great following. God is not a remote magisterial figure; rather, Julian prefers to speak of his 'great friendliness' (*homelynesse*, 314).[37] God is so 'friendly' or 'intimate' (*hamlye*) and so 'kind' or 'courteous' (*curtayse*, 224). Julian communicates a sense of the tenderness of God with her tactile, feminine imagery, as when she says 'tenderly our Lord touches us and blissfully calls us, saying in our soul: Let me alone, my dear child, turn to me' (439). Julian stresses the accepting and loving nature of God, who forgives us when we fall: 'It is an expression of royal friendship on the part of our courteous Lord that he holds on to us so tenderly when we are in sin, and that, moreover, his touch is so delicate when he shows us our sin by the gentle light of mercy and grace' (454). There is 'found in him no wrath' (509).

Julian's experience of God as protector/protectress who envelops us in a sustaining and all-embracing love finds its fullest expression in her remarks on the motherhood of Christ. He 'carries us within himself in love' (169) and, in the redemptive act of Christ, an act of total love, he is in the truest sense our Mother:

So we see that Jesus is the true mother of our nature, for he made us. He is our Mother, too, by grace, because he took our created nature upon himself. All the lovely deeds and tender services that beloved motherhood implies are appropriate to the Second Person. In him the godly will is always safe and sound, both in nature and grace, because of his own fundamental goodness. (168)

The concept of the motherhood of Christ generates a further image, that of our childhood in him, which Julian sensitively explores:

His desire is that we should do what a child does: for when a child is in trouble or is scared it runs to mother for help as fast as it can. Which is what he wants us to do, saying with the humility of a child, 'Kind, thoughtful, dearest mother, do not be sorry for me. I have got myself into a filthy mess, and am not a bit like you. I cannot begin to put it right without your special and willing help.' Even if we do not feel immediate relief we can still be sure that he behaves like a wise mother. If he sees it is better for us to mourn and weep he lets us do so – with pity and sympathy, of course, and for the right length of time – because he loves us. And he wants us to copy the child who always and naturally trusts mother's love through thick and thin. (173)

To say that we find in Julian a homely, though deep, spirituality, rather than one that takes as its focus an elevated union with God expressed in abstract terms, does not mean to say, however, that she lacks a sense of prayer, The depth and authenticity of her prayer-life is evident throughout her work and, most particularly, when she speaks of prayer itself:

Then we can do no more than gaze in delight with a tremendous desire to be united wholly to him, to live where he lives, to enjoy his love, and to delight in his goodness. It is then that we, through our humble, persevering prayer, and the help of his grace, come to him now, in this present life. There will be many secret touches that we will feel and see, sweet and spiritual, and adapted to our ability to receive them. This is achieved by the grace of the Holy Spirit, both now and until the time that, still longing and living, we die. On that day we shall come to our Lord, knowing ourself clearly, possessing God completely. Eternally 'hid in God' we shall see him truly and feel him fully, hear him spiritually, smell him delightfully, and taste him sweetly! (129)

The English mystics we have considered all enjoyed considerable popularity during the medieval period, richly informing English spiritual life until the Reformation. During those turbulent years they were taken abroad by Catholic refugees and survived in the religious communities of the exile. There they greatly influenced the Benedictine monk Father Augustine Baker, whose work, *Sancta Sophia (Holy Wisdom)*, became a classic of the English post-Reformation age and who also wrote an important commentary on the *Cloud*.[38] Henceforth, never really becoming the possession of Protestant England, nor in the Catholic world progressing beyond the small enclave of English recusant society, it was only in the present century that the classics of the English mystical tradition began to reap the full measure of their status and popularity.

Conclusion

The Mysticism of Being: Then and Today

The mystical writers we have looked at in the course of this book represent one of the greatest flowerings of the Christian mystical spirit there has been. It seems legitimate to ask, at least tentatively, what there was in the conditions of fourteenth-century European life which generated, or encouraged, or tolerated such a phenomenon, to seek to place it in the context of the mystical tradition of the church as a whole and, finally, to ask what significance there remains in it for us today.

The fourteenth century, as we have seen, was a time not only of great natural disaster as the bubonic plague ravaged Europe, but also of spiritual decline in the central hierarchical structure of the church. It began with a period of conflict, between pope and emperor, and with the activity of tenacious heretical movements which sapped the strength of the church and, possibly, that of its religious orders. Certain of our mystics felt the tensions of their day, Eckhart keenly so, but others were virtually unaffected by them. All our mystics, however, speak out against corruption in the church, and are painfully aware of the lack of spiritual life in their *confrères* and superiors. But we would be wrong to imagine that they rejected the church *per se* on account of its corruption, for virtually all, if not all, of the mystics whose work we have considered were members of a religious community or were anchorites. The low standards prevailing in the fourteenth-century church at large can only explain the popularity of our mystics, their reception by the masses who were eager for the personal experience of God; it cannot explain the fact of their existence. The reasons why Eckhart, Ruusbroec and the author of the *Cloud* should have lived within a few decades of each other are as unfathomable as those which govern the coincidence of genius in Renaissance Italy or nineteenth-century Russia.

If we cannot in essence account for the existence of the great mystical writers of the fourteenth century, then perhaps we will be able to identify features they hold in common and which reflect the deeper concerns of the age in which they lived. We will not need to have recourse to a 'diffusion theory' in order to explain the existence of what might perhaps legitimately be termed a school. The careful exploration of the respective manuscript traditions argues strongly against any easy idea of transference. We have seen that prior to the publication of Tauler's works in the early sixteenth century, Eckhart's influence beyond his own home region was minimal. We have seen also that the spirituality of Meister Eckhart, Jan van Ruusbroec and the *Cloud of Unknowing* are thoroughly independent systems, conceived in an entirely various idiom. The influence of Eckhart was upon his own circle, as was that of Ruusbroec and the *Cloud*. Nevertheless we can distil common points of reference from their respective positions.

The first element they have in common is the Augustinian inheritance. For Meister Eckhart this is expressed in his theory of intellect, which understands the human intellect to be identical with the primal idea of ourselves as we exist in God. It, the innermost part of our soul, participates directly in the divine Nature and shares its cognitive character. The theoretical base for this position is a late Dominican adaptation of Augustine's theory of mind, according to which the human intellect enjoys unity with the divine Intellect, in combination with Augustine's strongly held belief in our pre-existence in the mind of God as *idea*.

Ruusbroec, probably through his reading of William of St Thierry, is animated by the same Augustinian spirit. This time however it is the great doctor's theory of love which becomes central and provides the means whereby the human soul is drawn into the life of the Trinity. But for Ruusbroec, too, our pre-existence in God as divine Idea, which is the essence of Augustinian exemplarism, is of fundamental importance and becomes the dynamic pathway of our return to the Godhead.

The author of the *Cloud* likewise taught a profound mysticism of love. He lacks the direct sense of our own inner divine Image which Eckhart and Ruusbroec share (and which is so strong in Hilton), and for him it is the perfection of human kind before the Fall which is the guarantee of our full spiritual potential. What the author of the *Cloud* has in common with Eckhart and Ruusbroec, however, is the knowledge that the path to God leads us *beyond creation itself.* We must progress beyond all creatures, not just our attachment to them, but their very essence, if we are to enter the darkness of the Godhead. His is a *Wesensmystik*, then, an existential mysticism of self-stripping and essence in which the soul is gathered into its own furthest, highest, most inward point, where God himself is manifest.

The experience of 'self-stripping' then is the underlying principle which binds these distinct thinkers into the rough unity of a school. Performed authentically, which is to say as a response to divine grace, the shedding of all that is 'creaturely' within ourselves, the discovery of a bare core of being at our very centre which is quickened by divine Life, is the way in which we return to the source of all being, which is the Godhead itself. The manner of the way for Eckhart is 'insight', the manner of the way for Ruusbroec is the dynamic energies of love and, for the *Cloud*, it is love's penetration.

The *Wesensmystik* which these writers have in common brings with it a host of characteristics, all of which can be seen to derive from its fundamental dynamic. Thus we find in all our mystics a marked tendency to relativize the value of spiritual 'techniques'. Neither do they dwell on the benefits of works, but stress intent. They advocate a profound inner *ascesis* in the uncompromising single-mindedness towards God on which we found our spiritual life, and they scorn outright the idea that progress in our intimate relations with God may be attained by anything other than a deep passivity, in which we allow God to work a change of being within us, far more radical than anything we might ourselves 'do'. It is, in Eckhart's terms, a 'letting-go', while for Ruusbroec and the author of the *Cloud*, we receive from God the love which leads us into him.

There are of course problems as well which are generated by the radical character of a thorough-going mysticism of being. One of these is the ease with which it is misunderstood and misappropriated, becoming pantheism, quietism (an outright fatalism) and antinomianism (the denial of all moral constraint). Eckhart alone, who has suffered most from misuse, does not dwell at length on the dangers of abuse, whereas Tauler, Ruusbroec and the *Cloud* all harangue the heretics (not least, perhaps, as a form of self-defence).

A second difficulty is the tension set up by a form of mysticism which seeks to transcend all imagery and yet which evolves from within the doctrinal field of a world religion which is more intensely image-based than any other. The author of the *Cloud of Unknowing* makes little explicit reference to Christ (although there is no sense in this work of any doctrinal or spiritual deviation from the Christian norm) nor, as Bernard McGinn has pointed out, does Meister Eckhart interest himself in the historical Jesus.[1] But in Tauler, Ruusbroec and Suso this tension is felt. We have already noted Suso's remark that we are to lay aside all images except, that is, the image of our Saviour (p. 107). Tauler also seeks to integrate his devotion to Christ with an apophatic spirituality: 'A detached person must be free of creatures, formed into Christ, and transformed into Divinity' (H, 174). It is Ruusbroec however whose development of an imageless apophaticism is most contained within the essential structures of the Christian religion. By making the bare, essential unity of the Godhead a dialectical moment within the Trinity, Ruusbroec secures the place of the image. He senses that the force of Christian doctrine requires that our imageless and transcendent vision of God be located not beyond or above the divine image, the 'form of Christ', but *within* it.

If the keynote of our fourteenth-century North European mystics is interiority, then it seems appropriate to place them within the context of the developing movement towards a more internal, even introverted, self-understanding which is characteristic of late medieval North European culture. It is a trend which, as one historian of art has said, can be seen in the tortured inner intensity of Albrecht Dürer's portraits.[2] It is traceable also in the incipient humanism of the German classic *Der Ackermann von Böhmen* (c. 1400), and it finds its fullest expression finally in the voluntarism of Martin Luther and the European Reformation. This *concern with the individual*, which will become paramount, for instance, in the portraiture of the Netherlands school in the fifteenth and sixteenth centuries with its psychological density and celebration of unaffected simplicity, appears to be, by and large, a North European affair; and as such it serves to distinguish the fourteenth-century mystical school from that of southern climes.

It is here however, within its historical context, that the mysticism of England, the Netherlands and the Rhineland takes on a certain ambiguity. Their stress upon interiority, upon the pure inward impulses of faith which must animate any external act of devotion if the latter is to be of value, has legitimately been seen to be an important anticipation, perhaps even one source, of this characteristic emphasis of the Reformation. And yet, as we have to some extent seen, the precise relationship between the deeper structures of the 'northern mysticism' and Protestantism is a complex one. One vital point of influence was certainly Eckhart's principle, mediated through Tauler to Luther, that creatures are in themselves *nothingness*. This must have appealed to the Reformer, for whom man is first truly constituted in his response through faith to Christ. Along with Eckhart's belief in the 'nothingness' of creatures, however, was his teaching of the soul's 'spark' or 'ground', an affinity to the Creator which inheres inalienably within the creature. This idea, that there should be anything remotely divine in the natural man, was entirely contrary to the direction of Luther's theology (who crossed out Tauler's 'spark of the soul' in his text and replaced it with 'faith'), and it is a point which serves rather to draw the northern mystics decisively towards the humanist camp.

Whatever their doctrinal character, great mystical movements have one thing in common: their belief that God can himself become in the most meaningful way the object of our experience. This is perhaps their greatest contribution to the life of the church. Not only do the mystics provide forms with which to encourage and embrace contemplative gifts but, most importantly, they serve, like the martyrs, to underline for all Christendom the empirical *reality* of the Christian religion.

The mystics we have covered, then, have performed a particularly valuable service within the western church. The heritage of St Augustine and St Gregory the Great was one which tended to stress the rarity of a deep and unmediated union with God. It became something that was both partial and fleeting and that was reserved for the chosen few. This contrasts rather with the tradition of the eastern church which, fostered by the patristic tradition of Evagrius, St Gregory of Nyssa and Maximus the Confessor, placed greater stress upon the possibilities of a unitive experience of God in this life. The altogether richer tradition of the East in this respect received further nourishment from the teaching of St Gregory Palamas (who also lived during the fourteenth century). Palamas encountered some opposition on account of his theory that we may know God directly in this life, through his energies, which sparked off a controversy not wholly dissimilar to that which surrounded Ruusbroec and even Eckhart. Palamas's views prevailed, however, and his Hesychast teaching is now a formidable force within the Orthodox tradition. The value of the North European mystics therefore was to keep before the eyes of the church, in the centuries before the great Spaniards, the potential of a deeper union with God that, in their own judgement, was a possibility held out to all.

But what is the value of these mystics for us today? I believe that it is considerable. We in the modern church are less inclined to take things on trust and like to know things for ourselves. It is not surprising therefore that a number of these mystics have only 'come of age' in the present century,[3] when an interest in the experiential side of religion has become more widespread. A balanced yet powerful mystical witness and theology, which springs from the heart of the Christian religion itself, can only enliven and enrich the whole of our Christian life. It powerfully contradicts the notion that Christianity is a system of intellectual beliefs, or even only a code of moral practice. The Christian religion must tap and foster the deepest spiritual needs of the human race, while remaining true to its own dynamic and world-changing nature. It is here that the mystical theologians we have considered have their part to play, for the *Wesensmystik*, besides being one of the deepest historical expression of human spiritual consciousness, is also relatively timeless. It is free of many of the cultural and historical encumbrances which make so much that is of value from the past difficult to assimilate. But the unitive knowledge of 'spiritual insight' and love, the profound experience of God as a divine Nothingness or a dark Brilliance that is beyond all rational comprehension, the reduction of the self to a bare point of being radiant with divine Life, is a language that all can speak.

Abbreviations

AISP	Archivio Italiano per la Storia della Pietà
B	Ruusbroec, *The Little Book of Enlightenment;* see Notes, ch. 5 n.16.
BL	Blakney, *Meister Eckhart.* 1941.
BM	Biehlmeyer, K., *Heinrich Seuse.* 1907.
DS	Dictionnaire de spiritualité
DW	Meister Eckhart, *Deutsche Werke.* 1936.
E	Ruusbroec, *The Spiritual Espousals;* see Notes, ch. 5 n.16.
EETS	Early English Text Society
H	Hofmann, G., *Johannes Tauler: Predigten.* 1979.
HCS	History of Christian Spirituality, ed. L. Bouyer. 1968.
JB	Bernhart, J., *Eine Deutsche Theologie.* 1950.
LW	Meister Eckhart, *Lateinische Werke.* 1936.
M	Ruusbroec, *A Mirror of Eternal Blessedness;* see Notes, ch. 5 n.16.
Q	Quint, J., *Meister Eckhart: Deutsche Predigten und Traktate.* 1977.
SC	Sources Chrétiennes.
SE	Ruusbroec, *The Seven Enclosures;* see Notes, ch. 5 n.16.
SS	Ruusbroec, *The Sparkling Stone;* see Notes, ch. 5 n.16.
T	Ruusbroec, *Werken.* Tielt, 1944–8.
VH	Von Hinten, W., *Der Franckforter (Theologia Deutsch).* 1982.
WA	Weimarer Ausgabe.
ZAL	Zeitschrift für deutsches Altertum und deutsche Literatur.

Notes

CHAPTER 1   THE MEDIEVAL BACKGROUND

1   W. R. Inge, *The Philosophy of Plotinus*, 3rd edn, I (London, 1929), pp. 2f.

2   See for instance the definition of mysticism given in the *Lexikon für Theologie und Kirche* (VII, 732); 'The concept of mysticism, which is difficult to define precisely, means in its strict theological sense the immediate experience of a divine or transcendent reality which goes beyond everyday consciousness and rational knowledge.'

3   HCS, II, p. 362.

4   For an excellent treatment of this period see Andrew Louth, *The Origins of the Christian Mystical Tradition*. Oxford, 1981.

5   A. G. Little and F. Pelster, *Oxford Theology and Theologians* (Oxford, 1934), p. 318.

6   Quoted in R. Klibansky, *The Continuity of the Platonic Tradition* (London, 1939), p. 21.

7   G. Leff (1968), p. 302.

8   See Appendix I in S. Tugwell, *The Way of the Preacher* (London, 1979), and C. H. Lawrence, *Medieval Monasticism* (London, 1984), pp. 203–12.

9   This selection of comments on the fourteenth century appears in the introduction to J. A. Wiseman (tr.), *John Ruusbroec*. New York, CWS, 1985. To these may be added Barbara Tuchman's work, *A Distant Mirror: the calamitous fourteenth century* (1978).

10   The name 'Beguine' may derive from 'beige', the colour of their chosen clothing of untreated wool or, alternatively, may have resulted from their association in the popular mind with the Albigensian movement. There is an extensive study of the Beguines by E. McDonnell, *The Beguines and Beghards in Medieval Culture*. New York, 1969 (1953).

11   G. Leff (1976), p. 9.

12 G. Leff, *Heresy in the later Middle Ages: the relation of heterodoxy to dissent, c. 1250–c. 1450* (Manchester, 1967), I, pp. 29f.

CHAPTER 2 MEISTER ECKHART

1 The fullest account of the life of Eckhart is to be found in Koch (1959 and 1960). See also Ruh (1985), pp. 18–30. For an account in English see Woods, pp. 23–40.

2 See Ruh (1985), p. 19.

3 See ibid. pp. 168f. For details of the trial see also Beckmann, in German, McGinn (1980) and Woods, pp. 151–77, in English. The documents concerning the trial can be found in Laurent, Pelster (1935) and Théry. Eckhart's defence is also published in Daniels, and a translation in Blakney, pp. 258–305, although a more reliable one is to be found in Colledge and McGinn.

4 Although one of those manuscripts was discovered in the library of Nicholas of Cusa, who was himself influenced by Eckhart in no small degree. Selections from the Latin works have been published in translation recently, by Maurer and by McGinn (1986).

5 J. Quint (ed. and tr.), *Meister Eckhart: Deutsche Predigten und Traktate* (Munchen, 1977) (1955), p. 13.

6 Although Quint leaves it out of his modern German translation of Eckhart's German works. A summary of the discussion on the authenticity of *On Detachment* can be found in DW, V, pp. 392–7. A good English translation is in Walshe, III, pp. 117–29.

7 Astonishingly, there has been some dispute on this point, and it is suggested in HCS, II, p. 391, for instance, that Suso, alone of the Rhineland mystics, enjoyed experiences of a mystical kind. Quint (1977), p. 22, is surely right when he says that a recognition of the experiential basis of Eckhart's philosophy is essential for its correct understanding, and Oechslin likewise when he speaks of 'une sorte de reflet' in Eckhart's work 'que l'on ne rencontre que chez les mystiques authentiques' (DS, 4^1, col. 113.)

8 Namely I. Degenhardt's excellent study, *Studien zum Wandel des Eckhartbildes*.

9 Rosenberg, *Der Mythus des 20. Jahrhunderts* (Munich, 1933); Karrer, *Meister Eckhart, das System seiner religiösen Lehre und seiner Lebensweisheit* (Munich, 1926); Bornkamm, *Eckhart und Luther* (Stuttgart, 1936); Della Volpe, *Il misticismo speculativo di Maestro*

Eckhart nei suoi rapporti storici (Bolonia, 1930). For the earlier studies, see Degenhardt's full bibliography.

10 LW, III, p. viii.

11 Among recent studies which draw out the latent Platonism, see B. McGinn, 'Meister Eckhart on God as absolute unity' in O'Meara (ed.), *Neoplatonism and Christian Thought* (Albany, 1982); Emilie zum Brunn and Alain de Libera, *Maître Eckhart: métaphysique du verbe et théologie négative* (Paris, 1984). See also n. 14 below.

12 See for instance Copplestone's *A History of Philosophy*, III, Part 1 (New York, 1962), pp. 202f, for an excellent discussion of Eckhart's doctrine of creation.

13 There is a good discussion of this point in Colledge and Marler, ' "Poverty of the Will": Ruusbroec, Eckhart and "The Mirror of Simple Souls" ' in Mommaers and De Paepe (eds), *Jan van Ruusbroec: the sources, content and sequels of his mysticism* (Louvain, 1984), pp. 17–24.

14 See B. Mojsisch, R. Imbach, M. R. Pagnoni-Sturlese and L. Sturlese (eds), *Dietrich von Freiberg: Opera Omnia* (Corpus Philosophorum Teutonicorum Medii Aevi, II, 1–4) (Hamburg, 1977–84; B. Mojsisch, *Theorie des Intellekts bei Dietrich von Freiberg* (Corpus Philosophorum Teutonicorum Medii Aevi, Beiheft I) (Hamburg, 1984); K. Flasch (ed.), *Von Meister Dietrich zu Meister Eckhart* (Corpus Philosophorum Teutonicorum Medii Aevi, Beiheft II) (Hamburg, 1984). Similar material is discussed in French in A. de Libera, *Introduction à la Mystique Rhénane d'Albert le Grand à Maître Eckhart*. Paris, 1984.

15 The Middle High German noun *abgescheidenheit* comes from the verb *abgescheiden* which means 'to cut off'. It is therefore an emphatic, active word which is better translated as 'detachment' rather than 'disinterest' as we find it in Blakney.

16 Although not a theologian, there is a good article by M. O'C. Walshe on the question of Eckhart's orthodoxy, 'Was Meister Eckhart a heretic?' in *London German Studies, I* (1980), pp. 67–85. See also the article by McGinn (1980).

17 G. Leff, *The Dissolution of the Medieval Outlook* (New York, 1976), p. 123.

18 Alois Haas (1979), p. 44.

19 See Colledge and Marler in Mommaers and De Paepe (1984), p. 15.

20 See G. Leff, *Heresy in the later Middle Ages* (Manchester, 1967), pp. 308–407; and R. E. Lerner, *The Heresy of the Free Spirit in the later Middle Ages*. Berkeley and Los Angeles, 1972.

21 See for instance Rudolf Otto, *East Meets West* (New York, 1960), in which he compares Eckhart's thought with that of the Hindu philosopher Sankara; and Suzuki, 'Meister Eckhart and Buddhism' in *Mysticism Christian and Buddhist*. New York, 1971.

22 Hans Urs von Balthasar, *Herrlichkeit*, 3/I (Einsiedeln, 1965). pp. 390–406.

CHAPTER 3   JOHANNES TAULER

1 For details of Tauler's life, see Cognet (pp. 106–13), and Scheeben's article, 'Zur Biographie Johannes Tauler' in Filthaut (ed.), pp. 19–74; also the introduction to the CWS translation of Tauler by Shrady (see Bibliography). There has been little recent work on him, even in German, although Richard Kieckhefer has an article on him in Szarmach (pp. 259–72); and Gosta Wrede, *Unio Mystica: Probleme der Erfahrung bei Johannes Tauler* (Uppsala, 1974) may be consulted. See also Steven Ozment, *Homo Spiritualis*. Leiden, 1969. The introduction by Alois Haas to Hofmann's translation (see n. 8 below) is useful, as is the preface by Haas to Shrady's translation. Hans Urs von Balthasar has also written interestingly on Tauler, stressing the place of suffering in his thought, in *Herrlichkeit*, 3/I (Einsiedeln, 1965), pp. 411–16.

2 There is no evidence that the 'Friends of God' formed anything more than a loose community of like-minded people who were drawn into fellowship by their enthusiasm for the message of a deeper more inward religion which Eckhart and his followers were offering. The origin of their name is biblical, going back to passages such as John 15:14–15, Exod. 33:11 and Jas. 2:23. Mechthild and Eckhart both used the term 'friend of God' to refer to the devout. A good evaluation of their significance (with bibliography) may be found in the DS, cols 493–500, which stresses the informal character of the movement.

3 A greater realism was first injected into the discussion and the fictional nature of the *Book of the Master*, first shown by the great Tyrolean scholar H. S. Denifle in his work, *Taulers Bekehrung kritisch untersucht* (Strasbourg, 1879). Rulman Merswin is also regarded as the author of the many other works attributed to the 'Friend of God from the Oberland'. See Clark (1949), pp. 75–97, for a fascinating discussion of Merswin. See also Thomas Kepler, *Mystical Writings of Rulman Merswin* (Philadelphia, Westminster Press, 1960)

4 Cognet, pp. 114f. Cognet believes that Tauler's sermons show

a higher degree of construction than those of Eckhart. It is certainly true that Tauler's sermons generally clearly follow the structure typical of the medieval sermon: *exordium* (introduction), *tractatio* (development) and *conclusio*.

5 The young Luther read the 1508 Augsburg edition of Tauler's work and was much impressed by 'such sterling theology, equal to that of the ancients' (letter to Spalatin of 14.12.1516, in WA Br.1, Nr.30, 58). Luther found affinity with what he believed to be Tauler's suspicion of works and of scholasticism, his emphasis on complete submission to the divine will and his remarks on the sufferings which befall the devout soul with which Luther identified his own sense of alienation from God. See Bernd Möller's contribution to *La Mystique Rhénane* (pp. 157–68); Ozment's article, 'Eckhart and Luther' in *The Thomist*, XLII (April, 1978), pp. 259–80; and the article by Heiko Obermann in his *Die Reformation von Wittenberg bis Genf* (Göttingen, 1986), pp. 45–89. See also p. 112 below and the discussion of the *Theologia Deutsch*.

6 The question of the influence of Tauler, as of the Germanic mystics in general, in Spain is a complex one. It has been the object of a number of studies (P. Groult, *Les mystiques des Pays-Bas et la litterature Espagnole du seizième siècle* (Louvain, 1927); Joaquín Sanchis Alventosa, *La escuela mistica alemana y sus relaciones con nuestros misticos del siglio de oro.* (Madrid, 1946). The influence of Tauler dates from the Surius translation, for which the German Carthusian was rewarded by Phillip II. Alois Winklhofer, in Filthaut (ed.), pp. 400ff, points to the presence of explicit Tauler, or Pseudo-Tauler, quotations in the work of Juan de los Angeles, and believes that St John of the Cross also knew Tauler in Surius's translation (see also J. Orcibal, *S. Jean de la Croix et les mystiques rhéno-flamands* (Paris, 1966).) The Germanic mystics have also been viewed as being an influence on the Spanish Quietists, the *Alumbrados* (see *La Rencontre du Carmel Thérèsien avec les mystiques du Nord* (Paris, 1959) for a full discussion of this controversy).

7 Carl Schmidt, *Johannes Tauler von Strasbourg* (Hamburg, 1841); Wilhelm Preger, *Geschichte der deutschen Mystik im Mittelalter* (Leipzig, 1874–93), III. See bibliography for details of the editions by Vetter and Corin.

8 G. Hofmann, *Johannes Tauler: Predigten.* Einsiedeln, Johannes Verlag, 1979.

9 Susanna Winkworth (London, 1857); E. Strakosch, *Signposts to perfection: a selection of the sermons of John Tauler* (London, 1958);

see bibliography for more recent translations. The French however have been better served with E. Hugueny, G. Théry and A. L. Corin, *Sermons de Tauler*, 3 vols. Paris, 1927–35.

CHAPTER 4   SUSO AND THE THEOLOGIA DEUTSCH

1   I have chosen not to follow the German practice of using the name 'Seuse' rather than the Latin form 'Suso', more familiar to English and French ears. Both names have been used in the past, and it was Denifle (who himself bore the first names Heinrich Seuse) who popularized the use of Seuse in the German. This name goes back to the medieval form of the mystic's mother's maiden name, which was Süs or Süse.

2   A history of the discussion is given in the article on this theme by J. Ancelet-Hustache in *La Mystique Rhénane* (Paris, 1963), pp. 193–206.

3   James M. Clark (tr.), *The Life of the Servant* (London, 1952, p. 73.

4   The precise nature of Suso's relations with Tauler are unknown. Certainly Tauler had in his possession a copy of Suso's work the *Horologium Sapientiae*, which Heinrich von Nördlingen, their mutual friend, sent to Margarete Ebner. And certainly both visited Cologne, Suso perhaps around the year 1325. And yet there is no evidence that they ever actually met. On several occasions Suso speaks of a particular and devout companion, but we possess no evidence to show that this was Tauler.

5   Clark (1952), p. 25.

6   Clark points out that an additional reason for presenting a Latin version was its dedication to Hugo de Vaucemain, the General of the Dominican Order. Suso would clearly have been keen to avoid further doctrinal difficulties with his Order. Hugo de Vaucemain, being a Frenchman, could not have read German (Clark, 1949, p. 64).

7   J. A. Bizet in DS, 7[1], col. 235.

8   Quoted in Clark, op. cit. p. 62.

9   My translations are taken from the standard edition of the works of Suso by Bielmeyer, 1907.

10   This is the view also of Künzle, the editor of the new critical edition of the *Horologium Sapientiae:* 'Suso retained a sense of gratitude towards his Cologne master all his life, as towards a good father, who had strengthened him in his spiritual life and endeavours and had inspired him to the pursuit of yet higher

goals . . . We should not speak of him as a "disciple", who adopted the teaching of his master in its particularity, but we should think of Suso more as a follower of Eckhart in the sense elucidated above' (p. 98).

11 The medieval women mystics have attracted some considerable attention in recent times. One of the best general works which can be consulted is the excellent Elizabeth Petroff, *Medieval Women's Visionary Literature* (Oxford, 1986). For the lesser known figures, see F. W. Wentzlaff-Eggebert, *Deutsche Mystik zwischen Mittelalter und Neuzeit* (Tubingen, 1947).

12 See Filthaut (ed.), pp. 111–16, and see above pp. 53ff for Dietrich.

13 The critical edition of *The Book of Spiritual Poverty* was by H. Denifle (Munich, 1877). There is an English translation by C. F. Kelley (London, 1954).

14 E. Schröder argues in *Die Überlieferung des 'Frankforters'* (Göttingen, 1937) for a date at this point due to the absence of the Middle High German word 'minne' ('love') from the *Theologia Deutsch*. It must be said that the whole feel of this work, in which certain of the key phrases of mystical experience have become detached from their original context and yet have acquired established value, argues for a late (i.e. fifteenth-century) dating of the book. The *Theologia Deutsch* has been translated recently by Bengt Hoffman (CWS, 1980), but with a wholly unreliable introduction. A new critical edition of the text has also recently appeared: Von Hinten, *Der Franckforter* (Munich, 1982).

15 This work has been carried out again by Schröder. See Steven Ozment (1973), p. 18 n.10, for a full discussion of texts; and important articles by M. Pahnke (ZAL, 89, pp. 275–80) and K. Ruh (ibid. pp. 280–7).

16 WA, Briefe I, p. 79.

17 H. Maier, *Der mystische Spiritualismus Valentin Weigels* (Gütersloh, 1926), p. 15 (quoted in Wentzlaff-Eggebert (1947), p. 171).

18 C. Jones, G. Wainwright and E. Yarnold (eds), *The Study of Spirituality* (London, 1986), p. 410.

19 See Degenhardt, pp. 59–68, for a summary of the Wenck dispute and the influence of Eckhart on Nicholas of Cusa.

CHAPTER 5   JAN VAN RUUSBROEC

1   For the Beguine movement as a whole, see E. McDonnell, *The Beguines and Beghards in Medieval Culture* (New York, 1969) (1953), and R. W. Southern, *Western Society and the Church in the Middle Ages* (Harmondsworth, 1970), pp. 309–31. See also H. Grundmann, *Religiöse Bewegungen im Mittelalter* (Berlin, 1935; 2nd edn (Darmstadt, 1961) with new appendices).

2   The most recent critical edition of *The Seven Manners of Love* is H. W. J. Vekeman and J. J. Th. M. Tersteeg (eds), *Beatrijs van Nazareth: Van Seuen Manieren van Heileger Minnen* (Antwerp, 1971). There is a good English translation by E. Colledge in *Medieval Netherlands Religious Literature* (New York, 1965; repr. in E. Petroff, *Medieval Women's Visionary Literature* (Oxford, 1986), pp. 200–6).

3   The chief editions of Hadewijch's work are the *Strophische Gedichten* (Antwerp, 1492), the *Brieven* (Antwerp, 1947), and the *Mengelgedichten* (Antwerp, 1952), all by J. van Mierlo. See also the edition and French translation of *Mengelgedichten* by J. B. Porion, *Hadewijch d'Anvers* (Paris, 1954), with an important introduction. The complete works of Hadewijch (not including Hadewijch II) have been translated in the CWS series by Mother Columba Hart (London, 1981).

4   The whole question of the possible influence of Eckhart upon Hadewijch II (and thus, indirectly, upon Ruusbroec) is a fascinating one. It is discussed in some depth by J. B. Porion in the introduction to his work (see n. 3 above). Porion concludes that the matter is insoluble, and points to the common Beguine, Brabantine tradition.

5   The extent to which there is a Flemish school of mysticism has been the subject of much discussion, some of it a little tendencious. S. Axters, in *La Spiritualité des Pays-Bas* (Louvain and Paris, 1948; English tr. D. Attwater, *The Spirituality of the Old Low Countries*, London, 1954) argues for it, whereas Huiben ('Y a-t-il une spiritualité flamande?' in *La vie spirituelle, Supplement*, L, 1937) and Vandenbroucke (*HCS*, II, pp. 400f) argue against. It would seem on the basis of the powerful Cistercian influence in the Low Countries and the early tendency towards a love-mysticism that there is in fact a case for the existence of just such a school.

6   The role of William as propagator of the view that the faculty of love is our highest cognitive organ and the one with which we can know God must be strongly stressed. He exercised a

considerable influence on Ruusbroec, was known to the author of the *Cloud of Unknowing* (see above, p. 165) and represents a species of spirituality which was particularly congenial to the Beguine writers of the Low Countries. There is a fine recent study on him by D. Bell, *Image and Likeness* (Kalamazoo, 1984).

7 See G. Epiney-Burgard, 'L'Influence des Béguines sur Ruusbroec' in P. Mommaers and N. De Paepe (eds), *Jan van Ruusbroec; the sources, content and sequels of his mysticism*, pp. 68–85. The author concludes that their influence upon him was considerable: 'Among them we have found the account of an experience intensely lived within a perspective of return to our ideal being in God by our resemblance to him and by our participation in the flux and reflux of inner-trinitarian life. They fashioned a vocabulary before him which he refined in its technicity; they furnished him with a repertoire of images which he integrated into a trinitarian theology which is more developed and systematic to the extent that it encompasses all the stages of human life and of spiritual growth. Finally they introduced this (or established it more securely) within the twelfth-century world dominated by Cistercian and Victorine mysticism and by their Greek and Latin patristic sources' (p. 85 my own translation).

8 A certain amount of confusion surrounds the orthography and pronunciation of our mystic's name. This originally had the form RUYSBROECK (like English 'ruce' (cf. Bruce) + 'brook'), in the old orthography. This was often mispronounced in the modern period as the 'y', which simply indicates a long 'u', was taken to be part of the diphthong 'uy'. Therefore current usage is to establish the original pronunciation through the modern orthography. For details of the life of Ruusbroec, see article by A. Ampe in DS, VIII, cols 659–97 (which also contains a sophisticated analysis of his thought). See also biographical section of *Jan van Ruusbroec, 1293–1381*, ed. A. Ampe *et al.* (Brussels, 1981), and A. Wautier d'Aygallier's *Ruysbroeck l'Admirable* (Paris, 1923; English tr. F. Rothwell, *Ruysbroeck the Admirable*, London, 1925). The latter, although somewhat uncritical, is still useful.

9 The medieval sources are *De origine monasterii Viridisvallis*, Analecta Bollandiana 4 (1885), of which there is a French version in vol. VI, pp. 279–315, of the Ruusbroec translation by the Benedictines of Wisque (Brussels, 1912–38), and Willem van de Vreese (ed.), 'Die Prologe van her Gerardus' in *Het Belfort*, 10, Part 2 (1895), pp. 7–20. There is a French translation of this in Mommaers and De Paepe (eds), pp. 9–13.

10 For a discussion of the evidence, see Wautier d'Aygalliers (1925), pp. 140–3.

11 The earlier editions of J. David (Gent, 1858–1868) and the Ruusbroec Society, *Ruusbroecgenootschap* (Mechlin-Amsterdam, 1932–4; and 2nd edn, Tielt, 1944–8) are both based on the compilation of Ruusbroec's work which his own community made around the time of his death. This was in two volumes, the first of which has been lost (see, A. Ampe *et al* (eds), *Jan Van Ruusbroec 1293–1381*, p. 121). The introduction to the new definitive critical edition (*Jan van Ruusbroec: Opera Omnia*, I (Leiden/Tielt, 1981), pp. 43f) points out that earlier mss. differ significantly from this first Groenendaal edition. Unfortunately only two of volumes of the new edition have appeared to date (*Boecsken der verclaringhe*, 1981, and *Van seven sloten*, 1981, both ed. Alaerts, De Baere, Mommaers and Rolfson).

12 J. Koch has an important article on Eckhart in the Netherlands in *La mystique rhénane*, pp. 133–56 ('Meister Eckharts weiter-wirken im deutsch-niederländischen Raum im 14. und 15. Jahrhundert'). Ubbink, in his published thesis *De Receptie van Meister Eckhart in de Nederlanden gedurende de Middeleeuwen* (Leiden, 1978), studies the whole matter in great detail. He shows that three of Eckhart's sermons in particular were known: *Intravit in quoddam castellum* (DW, 2), *Beati pauperes spiritu* (DW, 52) and *Puella, surge* (DW, 84), but shows that they were not well translated or, in all probability, properly understood. Certainly none of them enjoyed the popularity of the more pragmatic *Book of Twelve Virtues* (an adaptation of Eckhart's *Talks of Instruction*) which circulated under the name of Godfried van Wevel. A certain odium attached to the name of Eckhart in the circles of the *Devotia moderna*, even though, as Ubbink shows, a number of his (anonymous) works appear to have been read. A less reliable work by M. A. Lücker, *Meister Eckhart und die devotio moderna* (Leiden, 1950), argues for a far greater interest in Eckhart in the Netherlands than appears, on the basis of Ubbink's researches, to have been the case.

13 G. Epiney-Burgard (La critique d'Eckhart par Ruusbroec et Jean de Leeuwen' in Kurt Flasch (ed.), *Von Meister Dietrich zu Meister Eckhart* (Hamburg, 1984), p. 181) takes a similar view: 'Par ce quelques examples il ressort que Ruusbroec a de la doctrine eckhartienne une connaissance partielle, car il se limite ici au seul sermon, Beati pauperes spiritu, et *partiale* car il le lit à travers la grille des articles de la Bulle'.

14   See S. Axters, 'Johannes Tauler in de Nederlanden', in Filthaut ed., *Johannes Tauler: ein deutscher Mystiker*, Essen, 1961.

15   See *The Golden Epistle*, tr. W. Shewring (London, 1980 (1930)), in which William follows a sensual/beginner, rational/advanced and spiritual/perfect division in the fourteenth, fifteenth and sixteenth chapters. The importance of this book for Ruusbroec cannot be overestimated. This scheme is used also by Beatrice of Nazareth in her autobiography and by Thomas of Cantipré in his *Vita Lutgardis* (see Axters, 1954, p. 20).

16   For my translations of Ruusbroec I have borrowed a number of ideas from James A. Wiseman's (E,M,SS) translations (E = The Spiritual Espousals; M = A Mirror of Eternal Blessedness; SS = The Sparkling Stone), from those contained in the new critical edition by Ph. Crowley and R. Rolfson (B = The Little Book of Enlightenment) and by Rolfson alone (SE = The Seven Enclosures). For B and SE I have used the new edition for the original, but for others I have used the Tielt edition of 1944–8 (T).

17   The word that Ruusbroec uses time and again is 'gebrukelik', which is an adjective derived from *gebruken* meaning 'to enjoy'. It presents real difficulties for the translator. The possibilities of an English rendering extend from 'fruitive' to 'savourous', 'blissful' and 'delightful'. None of these is entirely apposite: 'fruitive', being of Latin derivation and not familiar to all, seems rather too technical, 'savourous' is likewise a little odd, while 'blissful' and 'delightful' are both contaminated and weakened by their everyday use. The ideal translation of *gebrukelik* would be 'enjoyable', for that is its literal meaning, but unfortunately that too carries the sense of 'good fun' in English. While recognizing its infelicity, I have generally opted for 'savour', supported by 'delight', in the belief that the common use of this word to express an almost physical enjoyment well accords with Ruusbroec's spiritual idiom.

18   See in particular the article by L. Reypens in *Ons Geestelijke Erf*, 12 (1938), pp. 158–86, in which the author explores the key term *gherinen* as signifying the *motio divina*. The remote origins of this term are to be found, of course, in the biblical definition of the Holy Spirit as being the 'hand of God' (e.g. Exod. 8:15).

19   P. Henry, 'La mystique trinitaire du bienheureux Jean Ruusbroec' in *Mélanges Jules Lebreton*, II, *Recherches de sciences religieuses*, XL, no. 1–2 (1952), pp. 335ff. Quoted in Cognet, p. 281.

20 There is a major study of Gerson's response to Ruusbroec by A. Combes, *Essai sur la critique de Ruysbroeck par Gerson* (Paris, 1945–59). The matter was to resurface centuries later in the dispute between Bossuet and Fénelon.

21 Jedin (ed.) *Handbuch der Kirchengeschichte*, III/2 (Herder, 1985 (1968)), p. 476.

22 *Mystics of the Church* (Cambridge, 1975 (1925)), p. 148.

23 HCS, II, p. 439. See Jedin, III/2, pp. 520–38, and R. R. Post, *The Modern Devotion* (Leiden, 1968), for a more detailed study.

CHAPTER 6   THE ENGLISH MYSTICS

1 A standard work on the English church of this period is W. Pantin, *The English Church in the Fourteenth Century* (Cambridge, 1955). Pantin shows also that the perceived view that the papacy was the source of foreign appointments against the will of the king was ill-founded (p. 95). There is also a useful historical introduction in Chapter III of Knowles (1961), pp. 39–47.

2 Wolfgang Riehle, in *The Middle English Mystics*, tends to regard the Brethren of the Free Spirit (pp. 21,165) as being firmly lodged in fourteenth-century English life. He also believes the Friends of God to have been a presence (pp. 22,165), the *Devotio moderna* (pp. 23,165) and the Beguines (pp. 19f,165). The absence of firm documentary evidence for the presence of such continental movements in England during the fourteenth century, and the absence of an explicit concern on the part of the church authorities, such as exists for the Lollards, for example, with such movements suggests however that this is wishful thinking.

3 Richard Woods (p. 64) describes the author of the *Cloud* as a 'disciple' of Meister Eckhart, and even David Knowles (1964) believes the influence òf the Rhineland, through Tauler, to have been pervasive (p. 76f).

4 See the introduction to Künzle, *Horologium Sapientiae* (Freiburg, 1977).

5 J. Bazire and E. Colledge (eds), *The Chastizing of God's Children and the Treatise of Perfection of the Sons of God* (Oxford, 1957).

6 ibid. p. 87.

7 The critical editions are as follows: M. Doiron (ed.), ' "The Mirror of Simple Souls": a Middle English translation', AISP, 5 (1968), pp. 241–355; R. Guarnieri (ed.), *Mirouer des Simples Ames Anientes, Il Movimento del Libero Spiritu dalle Origine al Secolo*

XVI, Testi e Documenti, AISP, 4 (1965); Latin: *Speculum Simplicium Animarum*, ed. Paul Verdeyen, Corpus Christianorum, Continuatio Mediaevalis, LXIX, (1986). The translation by C. Crawford, *A Mirror for Simple Souls* (1981), is not a new one, and the edition is out of date. Edmund Colledge, Judith Grant and J. C. Marler have completed a modern English translation of the *Mirror*, which publishers are presently considering.

There is a first rate discussion of Porette in relation to Eckhart and Ruusbroec by Colledge and Marler, 'Poverty of the Will: Ruusbroec, Eckhart and "The Mirror of Simple Souls" ' in Mommaers and De Paepe (eds), *Jan van Ruusbroec: the sources, content and sequels of his mysticism* (Louvain, 1984), pp. 14–47.

8   See below, pp. 164–6.
9   For a survey of the whole English mystical and ascetical tradition, see Walsh (ed.), *Pre-Reformation English Spirituality* (London, 1965).
10 The critical edition is by J. R. R. Tolkien, EETS, 249 (1962).
11 For the works of Rolle, see H. E. Allen, *Writings ascribed to Richard Rolle, hermit of Hampole, and materials for his biography* (New York and London, 1927).
12 The standard edition of Rolle's chief work is by M. Deanesly, *Incendium Amoris* (London, 1915). The quotations are from G. C. Heseltine (tr.), *The Fire of Love* (London, 1935), pp. 59f, 64.
13 For more recent discussions of Rolle, see Knowles (1964), pp. 48–66, and E. J. Arnould, 'Richard Rolle of Hampole' in Walsh (1965), pp. 132–44.
14 This is the order as presented by Phillis Hodgson, who was responsible for the standard critical edition of the text (EETS, 218, pp. lxxviiif). It is supported also by James Walsh in his important article on the *Cloud* in DS, XI, cols 497–508
15 See Hodgson, p. lxxxiii, and Walsh (CWS, 1981), p. 2 n.4.
16 A review of this debate, including references, can be found in Knowles (1964), pp. 68–70.
17 ibid. p. 71 n.11.
18 ibid.
19 Walsh (1981), p. 9.
20 See Thompson. *The Carthusian Order in England* (London, 1930), pp. 133ff.
21 For Guigues du Pont and Hugo de Balma, see Walsh (1981), pp. 19–26.
22 A list of the early English mss. of the *Golden Epistle* is given in

the edition by J. M. Déchanet, SC 223 (Paris, 1975), pp. 112–20.

23 The Latin may be found in Migne's *Patrologia Latina*, CLXXXIV, 348, 9: 'cum modo ineffabili inexcogitabileque fieri meretur homo Dei non Deus, sed tamen quod Deus est ex natura, homo ex gratia'. The English translation is my own.

24 The quotations are from the *Cloud*, Hodgson, p. 76 (Walsh, p. 195) and p. 120 (Walsh, p. 250).

25 For the text of the translation of Dionysius's *Mystical Theology*, see Ph. Hodgson, *Deonise Hid Divinity*, EETS, 231 (1955). This includes the *Benjamin Minor*.

26 See Walsh's article in DS, XI, cols 497–508. In his introduction to the CWS translation of the *Cloud* (and in the notes), there is the suggestion that Walsh is prepared to concede more direct influence to Gallus: Walsh (1981), p. 46. Hodgson, writing much earlier, believes that the *Cloud* reflects the influence of all three of the works by Gallus on the *Mystical Theology (Den. Hid Div.*, EETS, 1958, p. xxxix).

27 The translations I have used (with occasional slight adjustments) are by Clifton Wolters, from *The Cloud of Unknowing and Other Works*, Penguin Classics (Harmondsworth, 1981 (1961, 1978), which is probably the version most widely available.

28 This image also occurs in Richard of St Victor's *Benjamin Major*, V, 2, a work which was not unknown to the author of the *Cloud* (see Hodgson, 1955, p. xxxv).

29 This image occurs also in *De Contemplatione* by Guigues du Pont. See Walsh (1981), p. 131.

30 In Chapter 68 of the *Cloud*, in fact, the author manifestly discusses the concept of 'detachment' but without knowing the word.

31 See article by D. Knowles and J. Russell-Smith in DS, 7[1], cols 525–30. Studies of Hilton include Knowles (1964), pp. 100–18; Joy Russell-Smith, 'Walter Hilton' in Walsh (1965); Helen Gardner, 'Walter Hilton and the mystical tradition in England' in *Essays and Studies*, XXII (1936), pp. 103–27; J. Milosh, *The Scale of Perfection* (Madison/Milwaukee/London, 1966).

32 Somewhat surprisingly there is as yet no authoritative edition of Hilton's work. The modern English editions available are those by Underhill (London, 1923) (slightly modernized) and Sitwell (Maryland, 1953): modernized, based on Underhill. There are also modern English translations from selected mss. by Sherley Price (1957), and Del Mastro (1979). The modern French translation by Noetinger (Tours, 1923) contains useful

notes. See also Gardner, 'The Text of the "Scale of Perfection" ', *Medium Aevum*, V (1936), pp. 11–30. For the lesser works of Hilton, see Jones (ed.), *The Minor Works of Walter Hilton* (1929), and J. E. G. Gardner (1981), pp. 51–9 (includes *A letter to a friend on hearing the song of angels*).

33 The quotations are taken from the translation by Del Mastro, 1979.

34 For Julian see introduction to Colledge and Walsh (Toronto, 1978); Knowles (1961), pp. 119–37; A. M. Reynolds in Walsh (1965), pp. 198–209 and a good recent study by Grace Jantzen (1987). There is a popularization of her work by R. Llewelyn (London, 1982). The standard text is Colledge and Walsh, and there is a Penguin translation by C. Wolters (1966).

35 Colledge and Walsh, pp. 24f.

36 ibid. p. 45.

37 The quotes in the text are from Colledge and Walsh; the indented quotations are from Wolters.

38 For Augustine Baker, see Knowles (1961), pp. 151–87.

CONCLUSION

1 B. McGinn, 'Meister Eckhart' in Szarmach (ed.), p. 248.

2 K. Clark, *Civilization* (London, 1969), p. 148.

3 It is worth noting, for instance that in his Bampton Lectures of 1899 (*Christian Mysticism*, London, 1899), W. R. Inge does not even mention the *Cloud of Unknowing*.

Select Bibliography

GENERAL WORKS

Ancelet-Hustache, Jeanne, *Maître Eckhart et la mystique rhénane*. Paris, 1956. English tr., *Meister Eckhart and the Rhineland Mystics*. London, 1957.

Bouyer, L., Leclercq, J., Vandenbroucke, F., *La spiritualité du moyen âge (Histoire de la spiritualité chrétienne, II)*. Paris, 1961. English tr., *The Spirituality of the Middle Ages*, London, 1968.

Clark, J. M., *The Great German Mystics*. Oxford, 1949.

Cognet, Louis, *Introduction aux mystiques rhéno-flamands*. Paris, 1968.

Haas, A. and Stirnimann, H. (eds). *Das einiq Ein, Studien zu Theorie und Sprache der deutschen Mystik*. Freiburg/Switzerland, 1980.

La mystique rhénane. Paris, 1963.

Ruh, Kurt, *Altdeutsche und altniederländische Mystik*. Darmstadt, 1964.

Szarmach, Paul (ed.), *An Introduction to the Medieval Mystics of Europe*. New York, 1984.

Wentzlaff-Eggebert, F. W., *Deutsche Mystik zwischen Mittelalter und Neuzeit*. Tubingen, 1947.

CHAPTER 1   THE MEDIEVAL BACKGROUND

Armstrong, A. H. (ed.), *The Cambridge History of later Greek and early Medieval Philosophy*. Cambridge, 1967.

Haren, Michael, *Medieval Thought*. London, 1985.

Jedin, Hubert (ed.), *Handbuch der Kirchengeschichte*, 7 vols. Freiburg, 1962–1979. English tr., *History of the Church*. London, 1980–1.

Knowles, David, *The Evolution of Medieval Thought*. London, 1962.

— with Obolensky, Dimitri, *The Middle Ages (The Christian Centuries, II)*. London and New York, 1969.

Lawrence, C. H., *Medieval Monasticism*. London and New York, 1984.

Leff, Gordon, *Paris and Oxford Universities in the Thirteenth and Four-teenth Centuries*. New York and London, 1968.
— *The Dissolution of the Medieval Outlook*. New York, 1976.
Louth, Andrew, *The Origins of the Christian Mystical Tradition*. Oxford, 1981.
Rashdall, H., *The Universities of Europe in the Middle Ages*, ed. F. M. Powicke and A. B. Emden, 3 vols. Oxford, 1936.

CHAPTER 2   MEISTER ECKHART

Texts

Meister Eckhart, Die deutschen und lateinischen Werke, hrsg. im Auftrage der deutschen Forschungsgemeinschaft. Stuttgart, 1936ff.
Daniels, A. (ed.), 'Eine lateinische Rechtfertigungsschrift des Meister Eckhart' in *Beiträge zur Geschichte der Philosophie des Mittelalters*, XXIII, 5 (Münster, 1923). Tr. in Colledge and McGinn (1971), and in Blakney (1941).
Laurent, M. H. (ed.), 'Autour du procès de Maître Eckhart. Les documents des Archives Vaticanes' in *Divus Thomas*, XXXIX (Piacenza, 1936), pp. 344–6. Tr. in Clark (1957), pp. 251–3.
Pelster, F. (ed.), 'Ein Gutachten aus dem Eckehart Prozess in Avignon' in *Beiträge zur Geschichte der Philosophie des Mittelalters*, Suppl. vol. III (Grabmann-Festschrift) (Münster, 1935), pp. 1099–1124.
Théry, G. (ed.), 'Édition critique des pièces relatives au procès d'Eckhart contenues dans le manuscrit 33b de la Bibliothèque de Soest', *Archives d'histoire littéraire et doctrinal du moyen âge*, I (1926), pp. 129–268.

Translations

Blakney, R., *Meister Eckhart*. New York, 1941.
Clark, J. M., *Meister Eckhart: An Introduction to the Study of his Works with an Anthology of his Sermons* Edinburgh, 1957.
Colledge, E. and McGinn, B., *Meister Eckhart: The Essential Sermons, Commentaries, Treatises and Defense*. New York, CWS, 1971.
Maurer, A., *Master Eckhart: The Parisian Questions and Prologues*. Toronto, 1974.
McGinn, B. with Tobin, F. and Borgstadt, E., *Meister Eckhart: Teacher and Preacher*. New York, CWS, 1986.
Quint, J., *Meister Eckhart, Deutsche Predigten und Traktate*. Munich, 1977 (1963). Modern German.

Walshe, M. O'C., *Meister Eckhart: Sermons and Treatises*, 3 vols. London, 1979.

Critical Studies

Beckmann, *Daten und Anmerkungen zur Biographie Meister Eckharts und zum Verlauf des gegen ihn angestrengten Inquisitionenprozesses.* Frankfurt, 1978.

Degenhardt, I., *Studien zum Wandel des Eckhartbildes*, Leiden, 1967.

De Libera, A., *Introduction à la mystique rhénane d'Albert le Grand à Maître Eckhart.* Paris, 1984.

Flasch, K. (ed.), *Von Meister Dietrich zu Meister Eckhart* (Corpus Philosophorum Teutonicorum Medii Aevii, Beiheft II). Hamburg, 1984.

Haas, A., *Meister Eckhart als normative Gestalt geistlichen Lebens.* Einsiedeln, 1979.

Koch, J., 'Kritische Studien zum Leben Meister Eckharts' in *Archivum fratrum Praedicatorum,* XXIX (1959), pp. 5–51 and XXX (1960), pp. 5–52; also in *Kleine Schriften,* I (Rome, 1973), pp. 247–347).

Lossky, V., *Théologie négative chez Maître Eckhart.* Paris, 1960.

McGinn, B., 'Eckhart's Condemnation reconsidered' in *The Thomist,* XLIV, 3 (July 1980), pp. 390–414.

Otto, R., *East meets West.* New York, 1960.

Ruh, K., *Meister Eckhart: Theologe, Prediger, Mystiker.* Munich, 1985.

Schürmann, R., *Meister Eckhart: Mystic and Philosopher.* Bloomington and London, 1978.

Smith, C., *The Way of Paradox.* London, 1987.

Woods, R., *Eckhart's Way.* Delaware, 1986; London, 1987.

Zum Brunn, E. and De Libera, A., *Maître Eckhart: Métaphysique du verbe et théologie négative.* Paris, 1984.

CHAPTER 3   JOHANNES TAULER

Texts

Corin, A. L. (ed.), *Sermons de J. Tauler et autres écrits mystiques.* Ire part, *Le Codex Vindobonensis 2744; IIe part, Le Codex Vindobonensis 2739,* 2 vols. Paris, 1924–9.

Vetter, F. (ed.), *Die Predigten Taulers, aus der Engelberger und der Freiburger Handschrift, sowie aus Schmidts Abschriften der ehemaliger Strassburger Handschriften.* Berlin, 1910.

Translations

Colledge, E. and Sr. M. Jane, *Spiritual Conferences*. St Louis and London, 1961.
Corin, A. L., *Sermons de Tauler*, 3 vols. Paris, 1927–35. French.
Hofmann, G., *Johannes Tauler: Predigten*. Freiburg, 1979. Modern German.
Shrady, M., *Johannes Tauler: Sermons*. New York (CWS), 1985.
Strakosch, E., *Signposts to Perfection: A Selection of the Sermons of John Tauler*. London, 1958.

Critical studies

Filthaut, E., *Johannes Tauler: ein deutscher Mystiker. Gedenkschrift zum 600. Todestag*. Essen, 1961.
Ozment, S., *Homo Spiritualis*, Leiden, 1969.
Weilner, I., *Johannes Taulers Bekehrungsweg*, Ratisbon, 1961.

CHAPTER 4   (a) HENRY SUSO

Texts

Bihlmeyer, K., *Heinrich Seuse: Deutsche Schriften* Stuttgart, 1907; repr. Franfurt, 1971.
Künzle, P., *Heinrich Seuses Horologium Sapientiae*, Spicilegium Friburgense, XXIII, Freiburg/Switzerland, 1977.

Translations

Ancelet-Hustache, J., *Le bienheureux Henri Suso*. Paris, 1943; repr. as *Henri Suso, oeuvres complètes*. Paris, 1977. French.
Clark, J. M., *The Life of the Servant*. London, 1952.
—— *The Little Book of Eternal Wisdom and The Little Book of Truth*. London, 1953.
Hofmann, G., *Heinrich Seuse: Deutsche Mystische Schriften*. Düsseldorf, 1986 (1966). Modern German.
Tobin, F., *Suso's Works*. New York, CWS, 1987.

Critical studies

Filthaut, E. (ed.), *Heinrich Seuse: Studien zum 600. Todestag 1366–1966*. Cologne, 1966.

CHAPTER 4 (b) THE THEOLOGIA DEUTSCH

Texts

Von Hinten, W., *Der Franckforter (Theologia Deutsch)*, Münchener Texte und Untersuchungen zur deutschen Literatur des Mittelalters. LXXVIII. Munich 1982.

Translations

Bernhard, J., *Eine Deutsche Theologie*. Munich, 1950. Modern German, based on Uhl's text of 1912.
Haas, A. *Theologia Deutsch*. Einsiedeln, 1980. Modern German.
Hofmann, B., *The Theologia Germanica of Martin Luther*. London, CWS, 1980.

Critical studies

Ozment, S., *Mysticism and Dissent: Religious Ideology and Social Protest in the Sixteenth Century*. New Haven and London, 1973.

CHAPTER 5 JAN VAN RUUSBROEC

Texts

Alaerts, J. *et al.* (eds), *Jan van Ruusbroec: Opera Omnia*. Leiden/Tielt, 1981ff.
Poukens, J. B. *et al.*, *Werken*. Malines, 1932–5.

Translations

Colledge, E., *The Spiritual Espousals*. London, 1952; New York, 1953; Westminster, Maryland, 1983.
Wiseman, J. A., *John Ruusbroec*. New York, CWS, 1985.

Critical studies

Ampe, A. *et al.*, *Jan van Ruusbroec: 1293–1381* (catalogue of the 1981 exhibition). Brussels, 1981.
Axters, S., *The Spirituality of the Low Countries*, tr. D. Attwater. London, 1954.
De Paepe, N. and Mommaers, P. (eds), *Jan van Ruusbroec: the sources,*

content and sequels of his mysticism, Mediaevalia Lovaniensia 1, 12. Louvain, 1984.

Dupré, L., *The Common Life: The Origins of Trinitarian Mysticism and its Development by Jan Ruusbroec.* New York, 1984.

Underhill, E., *Ruysbroeck.* London, 1915.

Verdeyen, P., *Ruusbroec en zijn mystiek.* Louvain, 1981.

Wautier d'Aygalliers, A., *Ruysbroeck the Admirable*, tr. F. Rothwell. London, 1925.

CHAPTER 6   THE ENGLISH MYSTICS

Texts

Colledge, E., and Walsh, J. (eds), *A Book of Showings to the Anchoress Julian of Norwich*, 2 vols. Toronto, Pontifical Institute of Medieval Studies, 1978.

Deanesly, M. (ed.), *The Incendium Amoris of Richard Rolle of Hampole.* London 1915.

Hodgson, P. (ed.), *Deonise Hid Divinity and other treatises on contemplative prayer related to the Cloud of Unknowing.* Oxford, EETS, 1955.

Hodgson, P. (ed.), *The Cloud of Unknowing and the Book of Privy Counselling.* Oxford, 1944; repr. 1958, 1973.

Translations

Colledge, E. and Walsh, J. (eds), *Julian of Norwich: Showings.* London and New York, CWS, 1978.

Del Mastro, M. L., *The Stairway of Perfection.* New York, 1979.

Gardner, J. E. G., *The Cell of Self-Knowledge* (containing *Of Angels' Song*), London, 1910.

Heseltine, G. C., *The Fire of Love.* London, 1935.

Jones, D., *The Minor Works of Walter Hilton.* London, 1929.

Sherley Price, L., *Walter Hilton: The Ladder of Perfection.* Harmondsworth, 1957.

Walsh, J. (ed.), *The Cloud of Unknowing.* London and New York, CWS, 1981.

Wolters, C., *The Cloud of Unknowing and Other Works.* Harmondsworth, 1981 (1961, 1978).

— *Richard Rolle, The Fire of Love.* Harmondsworth, 1972.

— *Revelations of Divine Love.* Harmondsworth, 1966.

Critical studies

Colledge, E., *The Medieval Mystics of England.* London, 1962.
Jantzen, G., *Julian of Norwich.* London, 1987.
Knowles, D., *The English Mystical Tradition.* London, 1961.
Riehle, W., *The Middle English Mystics.* London, 1981.
Walsh, J. (ed.), *Pre-Reformation English Spirituality.* London, 1965.

Index